LAKES HOCKEY THREE

IN THE GAME

SLOANE ST. JAMES

Editing by Dee Houpt | www.deesnoteseditingservices.com
Formatting by CC | formatbycc@gmail.com
Cover by Sloane St. James

1st Edition 2023

CONTENTS

🌶 One-Handed Reader Shortcuts

PLAYLIST

Available on Spotify

PART ONE - BEFORE

1. **Slow Down** - GRAE
2. **Numb** - Marshmello, Khalid
3. **Dangerous State of Mind** - Chri$tian Gate$
4. **Super Villain** - Stileto, Silent Child
5. **LOVE SUX** - Marisa Maino
6. **We Didn't Even Date** - Katherine Li
7. **Heavy** - Peach PRC
8. **Never Had a Chance** - Katherine Li
9. **I'm on Fire** - Chromatics
10. **Don't Care** - Katherine Li

PART TWO - PRESENT

11. **Cursive** - VIOLA, Kellin Quinn
12. **One That Got Away** - MUNA
13. **Unstoppable** - The Score
14. **You Broke Me First** - Tate McRae
15. **Yes Girl** - Bea Miller
16. **Green Light** - Lorde
17. **Remember Everything** - Zach Bryan, Kacey Musgraves
18. **Remember That Night?** - Sara Kays
19. **Therapy** - VIOLA
20. **Same Old Love** - Selena Gomez
21. **Running** - NF

22. **Overthinking** - Micky Valen, MOTHICA
23. **Stay** - Rihanna, Mikky Ekko
24. **Hate Me** - Ellie Goulding, Juice WRLD
25. **Lucy The Tease** - Allan Rayman
26. **Snap** - Rosa Linn, Luca Schreiner
27. **Give Me A Reason** - Jillian Rossi
28. **Bells** - The Unlikely Candidates
29. **Lose Somebody** - Kygo, OneRepublic
30. **Easy** - Camila Cabello
31. **Where Are You?** - Elvis Drew, Avivian
32. **Closer** - The Chainsmokers, Halsey
33. **Like You Mean It** - Steven Rodriguez
34. **Happening Again** - Katherine Li
35. **WYD Now?** - Sadie Jean
36. **Never Been In Love** - Haley Mae Campbell
37. **Moon** - Jonah Kagen
38. **Die First** - Nessa Barrett
39. **Mama Said** - Lukas Graham
40. **I Want To** - Rosenfeld
41. **Be Your Love** - Bishop Briggs
42. **I Think I'm In Love** - Kat Dahlia
43. **Beauty** - Layto
44. **Vacation** - Dirty Heads
45. **Cravin** - Stiletto, Kendyle Paige
46. **Till Forever Falls Apart** - Ashe, FINNEAS
47. **Good Morning** - Max Frost
48. **Paradise** - Bazzi
49. **Like My Father** - Jax
50. **Flesh** - Simon Curtis
51. **Like A God** - Lia Marie Johnson
52. **Animals** - Call Me Karizma
53. **Darkest Hour** - Andrea Russett
54. **Grave** - Nessa Barrett
55. **Fall Into Me** - Forest Blakk
56. **Infinity** - Jaymes Young
57. **Wagon Wheel** - Darius Rucker

MINNESOTA LAKES TEAM ROSTER

Left Wingers
#9 Lee "Sully" Sullivan (C)
#16 Jake "Jonesy" Jones
#89 Matthew Laasko
#77 Teddy Leighton

Centers
#46 Camden "Banksy" Teller
#71 Shepherd Wilder
#28 Joey Broderick
#65 Colby Imlach

Right Wingers
#33 Barrett Conway (A)
#18 Ryan Bishop
#48 Brit O'Callahan
#21 Reggie Daniels

Left Defensemen
#5 Rhys Kucera
#39 Dean Burmeister
#20 Doug Elsworth

Right Defensemen
#14 Lonan Burke
#52 Burt Paek
#3 Cory Dopson

Goaltenders
#29 Sergey Kapucik
#40 Tyler Strassburg

TROPES

Hockey romance, secret baby, accidental pregnancy, single parent, second chance romance, angst, puck bunny that got away, reunited love, light miscommunication, strong and curvy FMC, possessive/obsessive MMC, breeding kink, praise, happily ever after.

TRIGGER CONTENT WARNING

This book features pregnancy, childbirth complications, post-partum depression, bullying, slut-shaming, sexual harassment, emotional abuse and manipulation from a parent.
If you are triggered by these situations, please skip this one.

For the beta readers—
who unknowingly participated in a cruel social experiment
where I fucked with their feelings... and then laughed about it.
You earned this.

PART ONE

BEFORE

ONE

Raleigh

I love my job working for a promotional modeling consulting firm. Getting paid to party, having access to all the VIP events, and hanging out with celebrities and athletes is the greatest. I mingle, casually talk to people about a product, then the night is mine. It's a great gig; all I need to do is stay in shape and look pretty. Easy enough.

My phone reads 12:02 a.m. Perfect! Now I'm off the clock.

I'm still in shape from when I was a goalie on the varsity hockey team in Raleigh, North Carolina throughout high school. I loved playing, so much so I was hoping to play for the University of Minnesota, but I didn't make the cut.

After high school, I needed to get out of North Carolina, so I was thrilled to receive a scholarship to attend the university as a student, and that's where I've been for the last few years—Minneapolis. College student by day, promotional model by night, *puck bunny*—ew, I hate that term—on the weekends. My hockey playing days might be behind me, but I never lost passion for the sport. Or the players.

New Jersey's winger, Rahul Manzino, has already texted me for a hookup since he's in town with a trainer. But this party has been fun, and I'm not ready to leave. The Lakes hockey team is here, and they've brought in a bunch of fans.

It's such a vibe.

It's dark and seductive, the bass thumps through the floor, and the light show is top notch. Across the room is the VIP area with the team and a few other women that will probably be taken home tonight. I recognize a couple of them from other hockey events.

I squint when I look at my phone screen and then turn down the brightness before pulling up Manzino's Instagram. Even though he's one of the most attractive players on the team, I'm tempted to ditch him tonight; something's telling me to skip it. Besides, Manzino isn't my favorite player to hook up with. He's been losing his charm, almost everything that comes out of his mouth makes me cringe.

Last time we were together, he pulled the *do-you-even-know-who-I-am* card on a doorman. We met when he was a rookie and had a promising career. But he parties too much, his game is slipping, and his stats have plummeted. Last season, he tanked on the leaderboards. I scroll through the team and jersey numbers in my contacts list until I reach the right one.

> Hey, sorry to cancel last minute, not feeling well. Next time?

The little dots appear at the bottom of the screen as I wait for his response.

> #32 NJ - MANZINO
>
> I'm not in town until next season. You sure you want to do this?

Ugh, entitlement. Nothing turns me off faster. Unfortunately, it's common among hockey players. Don't get me wrong, I like to be catered to just as much, but the difference is, I have to work a lot harder for mine. He expects it.

And honestly, who doesn't love attention? The majority of humans do. Hell, even babies need it to live. Maybe that's why I crave it so much in my twenties, because I didn't get enough when I was younger. Well, not the right kind, at least. Back home, I was Raleigh, the girl with an unfortunate name and even more unfortunate upbringing.

I used to curse my figure and hated being beautiful, especially when I was younger. Men would leer at me before I could even drive. Part of the reason I loved playing goalie so much was because I could hide my body from everyone. It attracted bad attention. Unwanted attention. My looks have ruined a lot of things in my life.

However, now that I've started over somewhere new, I'm finding not all attention is bad. Like the attention from hockey players. I don't know if it's because we share common ground or knowing they are so close to something I love, but being with hockey players is the best.

We have a mutual agreement: they use me for my body and I use them for a hit of oxytocin. I'm addicted to those safe, secure feelings you get when someone hugs you. The closeness that promises everything will be okay. Those happy tingles that mimic love. It's the greatest feeling on earth.

I've slept with a lot of hockey players; their stamina is wonderful. It gives me a night of feeling whole and all the temporary, artificial love I can get my hands on. If I have to sleep with them to get those warm, fuzzy feelings, then so be it. I don't want to be a bunny, I hate it. But it's the easiest way to get a taste of what it means to be loved. Love feels good. They say it's not an addiction until you suck dick for it. *Well...*

When I look up from my phone, Conway is eyeing me again. Damn, he's really good-looking.

Normally, if I want someone new, all I need to do is hit

Follow on his Insta before he gets to town, and within twenty-four hours, I'll have a message in my DMs with the name of a hotel or bar. *It's too easy.* But unless you fuck the home team, offseason can be quiet. I'm a Lakes fan, so I prefer not to fuck them. There was one time last year when I slipped up and slept with one of the defensemen, but we were both drunk, so it wasn't memorable. It may not make much sense, but it's nice to keep some things separate. I stick with the away teams. It's easier to be noncommittal and uninvolved if they are only in town every once in a while.

I'm not naive. I know a relationship would never form between a local player and me, but it doesn't mean my heart wouldn't get addicted to the feelings that come with sex. Besides, I'd rather keep my "roster" limited. It makes me more desirable. But what's the difference between a local or away player if it's only one night during offseason?

It would be nice to hook up with a player that's on his game. Hockey is the best sport on the planet, and I appreciate the athletic ability required to excel at it. Usually, some of the other girls will stick around after work, but tonight, I'm flying solo. Oftentimes, women who enjoy athletes as I do, will travel in small packs for safety. If shit goes down, we'll help a fellow sister get out of a dangerous situation, but you don't need more than two or three girls for that. Anything else is competition.

I should probably leave or message Manzino and say *"just kidding, I'd love to take a ride on your bologna pony, thanks!"*

However, I can't pull myself away from this area. As the DJ plays a bunch of electronic mashups, attractive women weave between some of the VIP guests in the sectioned off area. It's quieter back here. There's a full bar with three bartenders. Low circular sofas are set up all around, lending themselves to more intimate gatherings among patrons.

I step up to the wall of catered food and grab a couple items. I haven't eaten all night, and my stomach is growling. I'll just hit the gym after stuffing my face. *God, this is good.*

Okay, Raleigh, food isn't love. Good feelings come from dicks, not dinner. I pop one last bacon-wrapped scallop in my mouth, letting the buttery seafood melt on my tongue. *Damn, that's delicious.*

I refocus and return my attention to the partygoers, specifically the Lakes players. Lonan's hot and single. I slept with him last year on a whim; he had a nice dick, but I could tell he wasn't into it. He was just going through the motions.

There were no fuzzy feelings that night.

My eyes drift back to Conway, he's distracted and talking to the player next to him, Brit O'Callahan. It gives me a chance to admire him from a distance. Near the back wall, I hide in the shadows to stalk my prey. He's practically a giant. I don't know his exact height, but it's up there. I'm kind of surprised he's not a goalie. He's on the older side. I'm twenty-two, but he's gotta be in his thirties.

I pull out my phone and type his name into the search bar... *let's see what we get.*

Barrett Conway. No wife or girlfriend. *Good start.* Some women don't care if a man's committed, but that's a line I don't cross. I refuse to get my love fix by destroying someone else's. I check his stats—he's solid. Has a ton of career goals. Holy shit, he's only a handful away from 200. *How have I not noticed him before?* He flies under the radar. It's always the quiet ones...

What else... he's thirty-three. I don't pass the half-your-age-plus-seven rule, but hopefully he's either bad at math or doesn't care. On my way over, I smooth out my short dress, and he catches my eye. The subtle glances from before are nothing in comparison to locking eyes with each other. A wave of energy passes between us. Goose bumps erupt down my arms. *This guy's already giving me the fuzzies and I haven't even climbed on his dick yet.*

He beams at me—*nice smile*. I'm very glad the other girls went home. He stands—holy fuck, that is a tree I would love to climb—then walks toward me. I return his grin just as another girl intercepts, record-scratching my whole plan.

She's got her hands all over him like they're old friends. *Damn it.* If I move in now, I'll look trashy and desperate.

Although, that isn't far from the truth.

Okay, new target. I'll get someone close to him. I need to save face—and quick. There's a guy nearby looking at me—that will have to do. The man is older and clean shaven, and dressed like he came from the office. I'll talk to him for a bit and then be on my way. "Hey, are you working tonight?" *Huh? How does he know that?*

"Yeah, actually, I was. How did you know?"

He smiles big. "I was watching you earlier. I'm the Chief Officer of Operations at Method Marketing, we partnered with Billboard Promotions for tonight's event. You did a great job."

"Oh! Thank you! I'm Raleigh Dunham."

"Rob Waters."

Now that I know I was being watched, I'm happy I had a successful night with some guests. "I heard we were working in tandem, but I didn't know anyone from Method was going to be on-site."

"I like to show up and make sure the campaign is running smoothly. Can I buy you a drink?"

I guess I'm networking tonight instead. "Something from Citra?"

"When in Rome..."

"I'll take a raspberry sour if they have any left." It's one of their most popular brews. I tried a sample of all the beers before tonight and made notes on each one so I was knowledgeable with potential customers and investors. The raspberry was by far my favorite.

When he comes back with a glass, we cheers and each take a sip.

"So how long have you been working for Billboard."

"Technically, I'm a contractor, but I've been with them for two years now. How long have you been with Method?"

He raises his eyebrows and blows out a breath. "Wow, I guess I'm coming up on twelve years now. You're making me feel old." He chuckles, and I laugh with him.

"Are you in school?"

"Wrapping up my degree in marketing. I go to the U of M."

"That's great, any plans for what you want to do after you graduate?"

"Hopefully be employed!" I inwardly cringe at my brilliant answer.

He grins anyway, and I appreciate it. "Well, let me give you my card." He pulls out his wallet and hands it over. "Text me whenever. I'm actually looking for an executive assistant. It wouldn't be working events like this, but it pays well and could get your foot in the door."

I run my fingers over the smooth embossed letters of the Method Marketing logo. They're a big firm in the Twin Cities. I'd miss the parties though.

"Wow, thank you so much. I'll think about it."

When I glance back at the section of hockey players, Barrett has the same girl still with him. They are sitting close enough to touch. A pang of jealousy hits me square in the chest, but I ignore it, paste on a smile, and turn back to Rob.

"Tell me more about the type of projects you work on."

Thankfully, Rob's a great conversationalist. We spend the next hour chatting about Method Marketing and current events. He's a cool guy, but not the one I had my sights set on. After an hour of watching some other girl hold Barrett's attention, I decide it's time to close out the night, say goodbye to Rob, and grab a ride home.

At least I might have found a start to my career.

TWO

Barrett

The team announced tonight I'm the new alternate captain, and I'm ready to fucking celebrate.

With *her*.

I saw her a couple weeks ago at that nightclub party. I kept close tabs on her that night and made sure she didn't go home with anyone else. I asked around, but none of the guys knew her. Lonan said he might've fucked her last season but doesn't remember for sure. She looks like a bunny, acts like a bunny, but if she is, she's not one of ours. Some women only fuck away teams. I've never seen her at Top Shelf—until tonight, that is.

I'm sitting in our corner of the hockey bar where we can get a little privacy with our team and... *fans*.

"Amy." I motion her toward me.

Our server smiles as she walks over to our seating area and leans down to hear me over the noise. "Can you tell that girl over there with the blonde hair to come over here?" I point her out.

"You're ordering women from me now, Conway?"

I smile. "Hey, have I ever asked you for more than a drink or food? I know, I'm a scumbag. I promise I'll leave a good tip if you can get her over here." I lace my fingers together to beg. "Blonde one with the brown eyes and that tight dress."

She shakes her head. "Shameless. And that's not a dress, it's underwear. I'm only doing this because I know you'll leave a good tip either way." She tolerates our bullshit well.

My eyes track Amy as she goes up to the woman I can't stop staring at. She looks at me, and I give her a wink and smile. *Works for Lonan.*

...And apparently works for me. She gets off her chair and heads in my direction. Christ, she's hot. In that painted-on dress, she looks like a fucking model. Maybe she is. She's given clearance past the roped area and stands in front of me in those fuck-me heels. "You rang?"

I do my damndest to keep my eyes fixed on hers and nowhere else. "Sorry, it's easier to call you over than to get ambushed by fans."

"That must be quite a hardship for you." She smiles, it's bright and genuine.

I hold out my palm and return the grin. Her soft hand takes my outstretched one, letting me guide her between O'Callahan and me. I check out her ass before she skims it across my dick as she squeezes in, and I take a breath through my teeth. *Goddamn.*

"Hey, Brit, how's your hamstring?" *What the fuck?* Who cares about his stupid hammy. It's old news, he's on the mend.

"Heh, it's coming along. Thanks for asking. Having a good night?"

Come on, dude. She's not even on your team.

"We'll see, won't we?" she says.

He looks down and chuckles before taking a swig of beer. She turns to face me again, and I regret wasting any time with that Kendall...Kelly...I don't even remember her name, from last weekend.

"I'm Raleigh."

12

"Barrett." I lean down to hear her, it's loud as fuck in here.

"That's fitting." A sexy smile crosses her red lips. "Barrett means bear strength... and you're roughly the size of a bear.

How tall are you?"

"Six-seven. How do you know what my name means?"

She shrugs. "I have a thing for names. Whenever I hear a new one, I look it up and see if it fits the person it belongs to. Helps me remember people. You wouldn't be easy to forget though."

Yeah, she's a bunny. It's in the bag.

"Oh, yeah? So, what does your name mean?"

"It means deer's meadow. But I was named after the city. Are you gonna buy me a drink?"

"I'd love to. You hungry?"

She's got those bedroom eyes down pat. "Are you?"

"Starving." I place our orders and get a few pizzas for the table. After Amy leaves, there's a break in conversation that my dumb ass fills.

"Soooo, do you think bears play in the deer's meadow?" Halfway through the sentence, I laugh at my own stupidity, and she joins in.

"Points for originality. You have a really nice smile, Bear."

"So do you." I'm sure she's a bunny based on the heavy flirting and the way she keeps touching my thigh, but she's also hypnotizing. Maybe I'm just a sucker for pretty blonde women. "Is there a reason you were named after the capital of

North Carolina?"

"That's where I'm from."

I wondered if she was from a southern state. She has a faint accent, but it's only recognizable with certain words.

"You're *from* Raleigh?"

"Yeah."

"No." *That's a joke, right?* "You're Raleigh from *Raleigh*?"

13

She cringes and shrugs. "Easy to remember... and one of the many reasons I went away for school. Hating my name is part of the reason I love learning about other ones."

"I don't hate your name. Raleigh is beautiful year-round."

Her eyes dance and her mouth drops open, then she nudges me. "See! That was way better than your deer's meadow thing!" She holds her hand up for a high-five and then I thread my fingers through hers.

"Okay, let's put your knowledge to the test. Our captain, Lee Sullivan?"

"That's easy. Meadow." She further explains, "So the name Lee comes from *laye*, which was a term used in the fourteenth-fifteenth century to mean meadow or clearing. So Rah-lee, Lee... meadow. But Sullivan means dark eyes. Do I get bonus points?"

"Yes, you do, good girl." I smile. She's gorgeous *and smart.* "Okay, you're right, that was too easy. Um... Lonan— what's that mean?"

"Black bird."

"Bullshit, how do you know that?" I whip out my phone and check her answer. She's right.

"When I meet someone with a new name, I look it up, remember?"

I nod in understanding. So she *knows* Lonan...

"I met him last year."

"I see." Annoying, but I can get over it. "You *met* him."

She quirks an eyebrow. "Is that a problem?"

"Not at all. Just disappointed I didn't meet you first." I don't like sharing, but I'm okay with stealing. It sounds like they are old news anyway.

"Better late than never, right?"

Before I can say anything else, our pizzas show up. Her eyes grow big looking at the food.

"Sorry sir, this one got a little done on the bottom," one of the kitchen runners apologizes to Jonesy, who shrugs and takes a slice from one of the other pizzas. After the server leaves, Sullivan lifts the corner of the pizza to reveal a crust blacker than a hockey puck. He laughs, and Banks looks irritated. He raises his hand to send it back—and probably make some unfortunate server cry. *He can be such a dick sometimes.*

"Dude, don't." I shake my head.

"What? It's burned through. You know the cheese on the top isn't supposed to be that color, right?"

"Send it down this way, I'll eat it. I like my cheese well-done," I say.

"It's not *well-done*, it's *what-have-you-done?*"

"Team Brown Cheese," Raleigh adds, reaching for a slice. We're both lying, but it's sweet she's going for it so the kitchen staff don't get chewed out. Sweet girl.

"Your funeral," Banksy responds, passing the pizza down to our end.

I put my arm around Raleigh to take it from him and place it in front of us. Satan himself cooked this fucking pie. I hold up my black slice, and she taps her equally burned one to it.

"Cheers!"

We take a bite, and I can hardly hear myself think while I get lockjaw trying to bite through this crust. It's more sound than taste. The rest of the table looks on with wrinkled noses.

"Crunchy." She nods. Neither of us can fake it anymore, and snicker at how bad it is.

"Send it back, Conway. Don't make her eat that," Sully comments.

"No! This is the best pizza I've ever had," she yells over a huge bite. "Quit trying to steal our food."

"Yeah, man. This is incredible. You're missing out."

"Five hundred dollars says you won't finish it." Banks raises an eyebrow.

I lean down to Raleigh's ear. "Wanna make five hundred bucks?"

"Fuck yeah, give me another slice, I'll double up," she whispers back.

I like this girl, she's more fun than I thought she would be, and I haven't even gotten her in my bed yet.

The pizza is... *not good*. But by the end of our meal, we're five hundred richer.

"I need a beer to wash this down," she says, reaching across the table for the pitcher.

"Here, I'll grab it." While reaching over her, I knock over O'Callahan's glass, and it spills all over Raleigh's dress.

She gasps. *Fucking hell.* Well, there goes my chance.

"Shit!"

"Cold! Cold, cold!" She takes a big inhale and chuckles and wipes the fabric with a wad of napkins while I try to contain the spill on the tabletop. Beer is dripping at our feet.

"Fuck, I'm so sorry."

"No worries. Really." I'm such an ass. "Honestly, you're doing me a favor. It's uncomfortable, and I needed an excuse to throw it out. It's way too small."

"Then I'll replace it with something you like better.

Personally, I don't mind it, but if you're uncomfortable... I know a place we could go?" I didn't plan on taking her back so soon, but I'm not going to make her sit in a sopping wet dress all night smelling like pilsner. She's likely leaving either way, might as well shoot my shot.

"Oh, you do?"

"Yeah, I'm a regular there." I smile. "Really cozy. Lots of places to lie down."

"So, what are you waiting for?"

Holy shit, is this actually working? I fed her burned pizza and spilled beer on her dress, yet she's still willing to go home with me? Being an athlete has its advantages.

We head outside and grab an Uber right before my phone dies. I tell the driver the address to my place and we talk about my job and how the team is doing. She knows *a lot* about hockey and even congratulated me on my promotion to alternate captain. It was just announced, so she must keep an eye on the team news or ESPN. I like a woman that pays attention. The car jerks, and she braces herself on the seat in front of her. Then the engine makes a weird noise.

"Fuck, not now," the driver mutters.

"Problem, bud?"

"I forgot to get gas."

Who drives for Uber with an empty tank? "No problem. I've got some cash, where's the next gas station?"

The car sputters and the engine goes quiet. *Seriously?* If it weren't for the girl next to me, I'd say that my hat trick at practice today used up any remaining good luck I had.

He pulls over and takes out his phone, scrolling through it. "The next gas station is like ten miles from the next exit." *How is that possible? We're in the city.*

"I'm really sorry, man. Shit, I can't believe this is happening."

"No, it's fine, really," Raleigh adds. "Do you have someone you can call to get you?"

"Yeah... I'm texting my brother. He said he can pick us up when he gets off work in fifteen minutes." I hear the anxiety in his voice. *Shit, this poor kid.*

"Okay, let me give you some cash." I reach into my back pocket to grab my wallet, but it's gone. My hands skim the upholstered bench. Nothing.

"I think I left my wallet at the bar." Raleigh twists her body to face me, rolling her lips together to keep from giggling. "Holy shit, what is going on tonight?"

"I have no idea."

"My phone is dead, and I've got no wallet."

She laughs harder. "My phone works. Here, call the bar and make sure someone from the team grabs it." Once we figure that out, we wait with the driver until his brother shows up. Silver lining is we get more time to learn about each other. She's great company.

"If you could go anywhere, where would you go?" she asks.

"Nowhere, I'm exactly where I'm meant to be. Well... maybe fast forward and get to my place. With you." I give her a nudge. "What about you?"

She rolls her eyes. "That's not an answer... I'd go to Hawaii."

"I'd also trade the back seat of this car for Hawaii. You go there often?"

"I've never left the lower forty-eight, but if I could go anywhere, that would be it. Sometimes I scroll the internet looking at pictures or maps of the island. It looks so different from anywhere I've ever been. Someday I want to live on the beach. Don't get me wrong, I love lakes, but the ocean is special." We catch each other's gazes for a moment, and time stands still. She blinks and looks to her lap. "You travel a lot, what's your favorite city to stay in?"

I squeeze her thigh, resting my palm over her soft skin. "Oooh, good question. Traveling with the team isn't as fun as actual vacationing. But I loved Switzerland. Though, Hawaii is pretty cool. You should definitely visit someday. And the Caribbean. And the Mediterranean. At least that's what I hear, a few of the guys spend their offseason traveling and being on the beach."

"What else do you do in your offseason?"

"Train mostly. Go out on the boat. Golf. Lately, I've been kicking around the idea to start a hockey camp." I need a project, and I've always enjoyed coaching kids. I love the charity events we do with peewee teams.

"That's really cool. How old were you when you started playing hockey?"

"I got my first skates when I was two."

"Two!?" she exclaims. "Wow, that's so young. I didn't know they made skates that small."

"Most of us started young. You know a lot about hockey. Did you play?"

"I did. I started as a squirt and continued to varsity."

My eyes pop open. "No shit? What position?"

"Goaltender."

I swallow and resist groaning. *Women goalies are so fucking hot.* "So, can you still do the splits?" *Please say yes. Please say yes.*

"Wouldn't you like to know..."

"I would give my favorite fucking stick to know."

She laughs and leans her shoulder against mine. "Yeah, I wanted to play for the U but never made it. My seasons weren't always guaranteed, as I needed financial assistance every year which was dependent on how much funding our hockey program got. It made things tricky, but I'm really thankful I was able to play through high school. Are you glad your parents started you so young? Any regrets?"

I never needed financial assistance, but my parents spent a ton of money to help me get to where I am today.

"Meh. I mean, I made it to the pros. I would never regret that or the work I've done to get here. I love hockey, but it's not everything."

She runs her fingers through her hair, almost like she's nervous.

"Wow. I don't think I've ever heard a winger say that hockey isn't everything."

"I mean, I just made C-level, I'm obviously very focused on our team, but I won't be able to play forever. I'm keeping my options open. And I'd like to use my privilege to help others do something that actually benefits the community."

"Good for you, Barrett."

Our driver is pacing outside of the car. Finally, he opens the door and motions for us to get out as the second car pulls up behind us. We get a lift from the brother to the closest gas station and wait for them to fill up the tank. *Fucking finally.*

I've got to take a piss like yesterday. "I'm going to stop in the bathroom real quick. Don't leave without me."

"Not gonna lie, after all this, it's tempting and would make a great story." She smiles.

I pinch her side and drop a kiss to her cheek. Her little shiver gives me a buzz.

After finishing in the men's room, I turn on the sink. The first one doesn't turn on. *Let me guess, they're out of soap too.* I move to the next sink and as soon as I turn the faucet knob it sprays like a fucking firehose, drenching the crotch of my pants. I throw my head back and sigh.

In an attempt to dry them off, I discover there are no paper towels left in the dispenser. *Of course.*

I give up.

At this point, the damage is done, might as well lean into it. I throw the bathroom door open and hold my hands up, hanging my head between my shoulders in shame.

As I trudge out of the bathroom, her eyes drop to my pants.

"I was accosted by a sink faucet."

She narrows her eyes. "Sure you're not just happy to see me?"

She steps toward me, and the heel on her shoe breaks.

"Ohmygod!"

I lunge to catch her so she doesn't twist an ankle coming off those ridiculous heels. I'd rather not add a trip to the hospital to this jinxed journey home.

"Unbelievable," I deadpan.

"Wait, it gets better. While you were in the bathroom, our driver left."

"Are you joking?"

She laughs. "I wish I was. When I turned around, they were gone. I've already requested another Uber." She looks down at her phone. "He's two minutes away, but you'll have to give him your address."

Raleigh is the only thing that's going right, everything else is falling apart. Including her fucking shoes.

We stand under the fluorescent lights, next to a rotating stand of maps and sunglasses.

"Thank you. This is turning out to be an interesting night."

"It's definitely unforgettable. At least I'm not the only one soaking wet now," she comments.

"All my dates say that."

"You have a lot of unforgettable nights?"

"No, that they're soaking wet." I wink.

She gives me a playful shove and glances at my pants.

"You're so full of yourself it's starting to leak out."

I grab her small hand and pull her back to my front. "This is a night I won't forget either," I mutter, and she swallows.

Her body fits nicely against mine. It's unlike any other woman I've played around with. Our breaths are in sync, and time stands still when I hold her. She has this calming effect on me, even though this night has been a total shitshow, being with her makes it feel more like a fun adventure. As much as I want to get her home, I'm actually enjoying this quiet moment under the flickering fluorescent lights of a gas station.

When her phone dings and the new car pulls up, I reluctantly let go so we can walk out together. The driver gets out of the car, waving his hands.

21

"No way, dude. I *just* got this car detailed, I can't have it smelling like piss."

I level him with a glare. "It's water. Unlock the door."

She attempts stifling the laughter, but her shoulders quake. Shaking my head, I narrow my eyes and bite my lip to keep my laughter at bay. After he releases the locks, I open the door for her. She hobbles in on one shoe and secures her seat belt. While I settle in next to her, she struggles to unfasten the ankle clasp.

"Here, give me your foot." I hold out my hand, and she angles her body to rest her calf in my palm. Fuck, she has nice legs, they're toned and athletic.

For the second time, I give my address and we sit in silence. I'm afraid to make a peep for fear of setting off some new weird chain of events that delays our arrival. To my delightful surprise, we actually make it to our destination and everything seems back on track again.

"You still want to come in?"

"After all that?" She gestures behind us. "I think I've earned it. Besides, I'm having a great time."

Her gorgeous light-brown eyes look much darker now under the shadowed awning, uplit by landscape lighting.

She's earned it, all right.

"Good. Me too." I enter in the code and place my hand on the small of her back to usher her inside.

"Okay, here we go, Bear. Hold your breath," Raleigh comments, stepping across the threshold. "We did it!" She spins around and jumps in the air, as if we summited a mountaintop by stepping through my front door.

In some ways, it does feel like that. It's been a bizarre string of bad luck. This has been the worst date I've ever been on and I'm loving every minute.

"Come here." I've been dying to get my hands on her all night. "Let's get you out of that dress."

"Or what?" She challenges me, raising one eyebrow. Oh. It's like *that*. Okay, then.

I stalk toward her until she's backed against the wall and I'm towering above her. She bites her lip and seems to shrink under my gaze. I move in to kiss her but then stop. Her eyes plead with me, and something tells me I shouldn't.

I spin her to face the wall, holding her wrists in one hand behind her back. Damn, this body, normally I go for much curvier girls, but she'd be gorgeous any size. She wiggles her fingers, trying to stroke me through my jeans.

Her touch is almost mischievous, like she's trying to incite a reaction. *She's getting one.*

"You gonna hold yourself against me or are you going to actually do something about that hard cock digging into my back?"

"You have quite the mouth on you, don't you?"

"Indeed. Want to see what else it can do?"

"Yes."

"Let me go and I'll show you"—I release her hands— "but you have to catch me first."

"Wait—" She darts across the foyer and flies up the stairs. *What the fuck?*

"Raleigh!" After all this, I'm done playing games. I want her. But why does her little cat-and-mouse trick turn me on?

"Polo!"

I smile and shake my head. *Little brat.*

I kick my shoes off and take the stairs two at a time. Her too-tight dress lies in a tiny crumpled pile at the top of the steps. *Goddamn.* Now I want to chase her. It's a new feeling for me, but the playful side of her excites me. The thought of catching her and throwing her down gets me hard.

There's no sign of Raleigh in the dark bedrooms or upstairs bath. *That leaves my office.* After pretending to peek inside, I shut the door. I know my house a lot better than she does, and I'll bet she hasn't found the hidden stairwell in the office closet. I want to find her, but first I want to have a little fun. It might be fun to trap her. Corner her like prey.

A strange primal sensation takes the driver's seat. I don't know who this girl is or what she's done to me, but her days of fucking other players is over. That ends tonight. She's my bunny now, and I'm the only one that gets to nip at her heels.

I know almost nothing about her, but one thing I'm certain of, I'm keeping this woman. She's mine.

Something about her makes me possessive. I need to claim her. Sounds cheesy as fuck, but it's as if meeting her is some monumental moment in my life. *Is that crazy?* It's a bizarre feeling of contentment, like when you slip in the last puzzle piece. Like everything in my life has been leading me to this night. I was meant to meet her. It's not love, that would be ridiculous. But... *it's not far off.* I shake my head to clear my thoughts, this shit's confusing. I don't need to figure it out tonight.

I clomp back down the main stairs and prowl up the back stairwell. It's to serve as a nanny suite private entrance. Or, apparently, when I need to ensnare a certain vixen who enjoys being caught.

As silent as I can be at six foot seven, I ever-so-gently slide the pocket door open. It feels like a whole minute passes before it's fully open. I smell her perfume; she's in here. *Looks like my luck is back.* She's facing away from me and then cracks the door to the closet and peeks out. Before she can take another move, I step forward and wrap my arms around her, pulling her back in. I love the feel of her in my arms. Naturally, she screams. I'm too turned on to laugh.

I like Raleigh—a lot. This night has been a straight-up disaster, but I've never had more fun with a woman. I'm not letting this one go. I want her at my games with my name on her back. The emotions running through me don't make sense

—*this isn't like me.* I've sobered up since leaving the bar, and the acute connection between us seems to grow by the minute. I have no proof she reciprocates these feelings, so I need to keep my shit together so I don't freak her out. I'm already freaking myself out.

Running my nose up the side of her neck, I growl against her skin. "Never run from a bear."

The gasp that leaves her mouth is so fucking sexy, it makes me feral.

"You like being chased before you get fucked, Ral?"

"I love it," she pants. *Beautiful.*

"Do you know what bears do when they capture their prey?"

She grips onto my arms, trying to push off me, but her fingers refuse to let go. She doesn't know what she wants.

"What do they do?" Her heart is pounding. *Fuck, this is hot.*

"They take them back to their den."

RALEIGH

The flirting between us has been stripped down, and now all our actions are purely instinct. Never in my wildest dreams did I think a sweet man like Barrett would capture me like this. I've always had the curiosity, but this is the first time I've gone for it. Something in my gut told me I'd be safe with him. Safe enough to be vulnerable and weak, and he wouldn't take advantage. Even if I desperately want him to...

The sexual tension bouncing between us has turned into something else. He flips me over his shoulder, and I grip the shirt on his back. I try to clamber down and get away, but his hold is firm. I can't get away from him. He ducks under the office doorway, and I assume carrying me to his bedroom.

Hopefully to be ravaged.

"Put me down!"

With one palm gripping me behind my knee, the other one comes up between my legs as he clears another doorway. *Oh my god.*

"Goddamn, you're fun to play with."

He must feel how slick my inner thighs are. I've never been so turned on before.

I bounce when he flips me onto his enormous four-poster bed. He grabs my calves and yanks me to the edge again. His teeth graze my stomach and he drops three bites in a line, spanning from under my breasts to above my pelvis. He grips the sides of my underwear and rips them off. *He actually rips them off my body.*

Then he drops to his knees and spreads my legs. As soon as his face lands between my thighs, he takes a deep breath.

He's fucking *savage.*

"Ah, Bear," I moan, grabbing a handful of his hair.

He licks up my seam, splitting me open.

"This is mine."

Warmth sweeps over me when he smiles, but when he gives me those words, it's like I can't breathe.

"Yours?" My voice is shaky. I swallow and shut my eyes. "Yeah, you taste exactly—" His tongue flattens against me and he licks again. "Like mine."

The foundation I've built around myself cracks, and an abundance of raw emotion rises to the surface. *Where is all this coming from?* I hadn't realized there was so much built up inside me until it started spilling out, and I can't patch up the holes fast enough. My brain screams at me to shut him out.

This is too close. Way too fucking close to what I can handle. It's too powerful. Too... *everything.* I fuck men to get a watered-down version of these feelings, not the real thing. It's not supposed to be like this. My heart is searching for something to attach to, but I won't let it.

26

This close connection you feel, he doesn't feel it. Bury that shit and fuck him like a bunny. Play your part and then get the hell out of here.

I try to dissociate from the swell of emotions crashing inside me, but I can't. When his mouth moves against me, it's sweet relief being blinded by pleasure. He sucks on my clit and pulls me deeper until I'm riding his face and gripping his hair. Barrett growls as he ravishes me. *Like a bear.* His trimmed beard scratches my thighs in the best way. When his fingers plunge inside me, waves of pleasure roll through my body.

"I won't stop until I wring every drop from you."

"Make me come." I don't recognize my own voice.

His hand moves faster as he adds another finger. I'm losing what little control I have.

"Let go, love. I got you." His voice is so deep, and he says it so tenderly.

Tears prick at my eyes when I come on his tongue. I hate it. Each tear multiplies as he watches me come undone. When his gaze drops, I swipe at my eyes and clear my throat.

"Condom?"

His hooded eyes narrow at me. "You okay?"

"More than okay, just in a hurry to get you inside me." I say it as unaffected as I can. *Thank god it's dark in here.*

He stretches his arm across the bed and reaches into a side drawer. He feels around, and I worry he doesn't have one. Or maybe it'd be better if it all ended now. When I hear the wrinkle of foil, I exhale. "Last one," he says, shaking the packet.

See, Raleigh? You've been picked last in a long line of other women. And tomorrow he'll go out and buy a new box so he can fuck the next twenty-four. Don't get attached to something that isn't real.

When he climbs above me, he hands over the condom to roll on. I grasp him and he groans. I want to pull all the primal

27

noises from his lips—make all of them mine. I want to be the only one to get him like this. I wish I could keep him. He's thick, rigid, and heavy. After rolling the condom down his length, I relax back into his downy comforter.

He roams his huge palms up my thighs, over my stomach and unclasps the lace covering my breasts. His hands box me in, and he sucks on my left nipple, then the right. I fist the cotton sheets beneath me; they're like lounging on a cloud.

"Fuck me, Barrett." My voice sounds hollow.

He reaches across the bed a second time and turns on the lamp. *No, no, no.*

"What are you doing?"

He sits back on his heels. "I want to see your face."

"Why?"

Sliding his cock over my clit, he spreads around my wetness. When he pushes inside, my mouth drops open. *Oh, god.* He's heaven on earth.

"*That's* why," he grunts. "You're so fucking beautiful."

I close my eyes. Heartbreak territory. *Just fuck him, pretend he's Manzino.*

That's pointless. Manzino never felt like this.

His gaze is fixed on mine, and even when I close my eyes, I can feel it. A warm hand caresses my cheek, and I resist turning into it. "Raleigh, look at me."

My eyes open and I swallow. I bite my lip until I taste copper. *I won't cry.*

He thrusts inside me. "You feel that?"

I nod. I feel more than he realizes. *More than he intends.* His eye contact is intense as he studies my face. For a second, I wonder if he's feeling the same way I am, but that would be impossible. He's Barrett Conway, and I'm the last condom in his drawer.

His thrusts are more passionate than before. I don't want to look at him anymore. It hurts.

28

"Turn off the light, Bear."

He shakes his head. "Forget it." He flips us so I'm on top.

"Let's see that split."

I nod and focus on doing a stupid split. It helps relax me.
Just have fun. Don't take it so seriously.

I force a smile at his challenge. Pushing against his chest, I adjust myself and bring one leg up to his shoulder, the other in the opposite direction, parallel to his body.

"*Fuck,* there you go."

I align myself with him and settle onto his cock, letting out a small nervous laugh that turns into a whimper.

He traces a line from my ankle, at his shoulder, to my hip.

"I knew you could do it. Very impressive."

I return to the kneeling position so I can ride him better.

How does this feel so good? So *right.* His hands reach around and grip my ass, and he lets out another growl.

"This here"—he slaps my ass and I grind against him—"makes me so fucking hard. You have an incredible body, Raleigh."

Thanks, I work really hard at it so I can get attention from players like you. Regardless, I appreciate the compliment. I lean back to give him a better view of me, and roll my hips. His jaw tics, and he's hard focused, like he's trying to deflect or something.

Now it's like a game. I like games, they're distracting.

"You going to come already?" I tease.

"I'll be honest, I'm struggling a little."

"I can see that." I chuckle. I sit up on my knees, and when he leaves my body, I shudder at the void left behind. I grab his hands and bring them up to my breasts and then slide them to my ass.

He blows out a breath. "Get on this cock, Raleigh." I shake my head. "Nuh-uh. You have to wait."

"I'm a lot of things, love. But patient isn't one of them."

"Just Raleigh." I can't have him call me that word again. "Or Ral." I bring his hand to my mouth and suck on his fingers.

"You think you're pretty cute, huh?" His other hand comes down on my ass in a loud clap, and I gasp. He pushes me off and shoves me down on all fours. *This is what I need.*

Behind me, he glides through my folds, making me moan. He drives inside and I clench down.

"Christ, Ral. You are *so* tight." Deep thrusts fill me, and I fan my fingers to brace against the headboard. "And wet. So fucking wet for me."

I grit my teeth and whine; it feels so good. I'm so close. The familiar twinge of pleasure wraps around the base of my spine. His fingers dig and the marks he leaves on me will be all that's left of him after tonight. I'll take them. As much as it's going to suck leaving, I want the memory etched on my skin.

When he leans down to whisper in my ear, I smile with anticipation. "You're mine now. Be my good bunny and take every inch." He groans and slaps my ass again.

Bunny.

The word cuts deep. I push the term out of my mind and allow the physical pleasure to capsize all the negative thoughts piling on. My legs spasm and shake as the orgasm rolls through me. He grips my hips harder as he takes me, chasing his own climax. I squeeze my eyes shut, seeing spots.

"Give me another. You can do it." *Bunny.*

I collapse on my elbows, ass still in the air.

"You have such a perfect pussy." A roar overtakes him. I hate myself. I fake a final orgasm as he finishes.

We're done here.

As an extra twist of the knife, he unloads inside me... But something isn't right. Then it clicks—*the condom!*

"Wait . . . wait," I stammer. "Did it break?"

"What?"

"The condom! Did it break?"

He slows and pulls out. "Fuck."

"Are you serious?"

I'm glad I'm on the pill as backup. But I have no idea if Barrett has an STD. These guys sleep around enough, so it's possible.

"Shit, I'm sorry, Ral. I swear I didn't feel it."

"Are you clean?" I snap, scowling. All I want to do is go home.

He pauses, probably from the sting of my question.

"Ye—yeah. I'm clean," he stutters, and disappointment fills the room as our moment together evaporates.

I exhale. *Thank god.*

"Same. And on the pill."

He breathes deep and wraps his giant arm around my waist, kissing up my spine. I despise and love how it makes me lightheaded.

I clear my throat. "We should get cleaned up."

His lips leave my flesh, and there's a suspended pause.

"Sure."

He backs up off the bed and saunters into the en-suite bathroom where he comes back with a warm towel. *Of course he does.* He couldn't be a douchebag and throw me his dirty boxers. After wiping away the evidence dripping from me, he does the same to himself and then climbs in bed behind me.

His palm presses against my stomach and then he pulls me against him again. It only makes the lump in my throat thicken. It's comfortable and easy, but I reject the silly hope that we could ever be more than a hockey player and a *puck bunny*. The sting of that word is still an open wound. Eventually his breathing slows into an even, relaxed pattern.

Our moment is over.

I slip out of his arms unnoticed and pause to make sure he stays asleep. The price of his rejection in the morning is more than I can afford. When the sun comes up, I'll be cast aside and heartbroken. Pathetic. I slink out of bed and tiptoe down the hall, pick up my dress, and shimmy it back on. I find my purse and phone by the door, then order a rideshare and walk outside barefoot, broken heels in hand. Within ten minutes, a car pulls up and I climb into the back seat of the third stranger's vehicle of the night.

Barrett Conway changed me. He killed this puck bunny, ripped her heart out, and ate it. I can't do this anymore. Tonight has made me realize how bad I want the real thing. I caught feelings within a few hours of being in his company. It's time to grow up. I'll never have a fairytale like him, but I can claim a mediocre ending—though I'll never find it while living this lifestyle.

Hockey players don't date the girls they take home from bars. They retire, go back home, and reconnect with their high school sweetheart or some B-list celebrity Instagram model. Whoever ends up with Barrett Conway is one lucky bitch. I hope they appreciate how good he is.

Tonight was incredible. But it's better to leave with a happy memory than sad goodbye.

And I'm no one's bunny.

THREE

Barrett

I can't believe she snuck out in the middle of the night! *What the fuck, Raleigh?* We had something, I know we did. At the very least I thought she would have left me a way to contact her. I open my laptop and check Facebook first. Shit, I don't even know her last name. There can't be that many Raleighs out there. I type her first name into the search bar.

Raleigh, North Carolina
City of Raleigh – Government
ComicCon Raleigh

Okay, I'm going to need some filters. I click the People tab, hoping to only see pages for actual people. All I get are hundreds of names, none of them Raleigh, but all of them residents of Raleigh. *Goddamn it.*

I look at the ceiling, as if her email address will be listed up there. Okay, what else... She played hockey in high school in Raleigh. But I don't know when she graduated—even if I did, what am I going to do? Call up the school and say I need the name of someone who graduated? They probably don't even have that information. I could ask for a last name, but I'm sure they aren't going to hand over alumni information.

Besides, there's probably a dozen different high schools in Raleigh.

She's going to college for marketing, but the University of Minnesota is huge. Pretty sure she said she has her own apartment, so it's not like she lives on campus.

Okay, fuck this, it's not working.

I'll try Instagram. When I open it up on my phone, there's endless notifications. *Jesus Christ, there's a ton of unopened DMs.* Julia manages all my social media, so I forget this account exists half the time. I open them up and scroll through, praying to see a thumbnail, name, or message that looks like it's from my girl. None are Raleigh. I return to the search bar and type in her name.

Raleigh, NC...
Raleigh-Durham Intl Airport...
Raleigh Tattoos...
Raleigh Braiding...

You've gotta be kidding me. Come on, Google, don't fail me now. I go back to my laptop and try every combination I can think of.

raleigh + minneapolis raleigh + university of minnesota raleigh + goalie + marketing raleigh + university of minnesota + marketing raleigh + raleigh, nc + high school + goalie raleigh + raleigh, nc + high school girl goalie raleigh person from raleigh, nc

Most of the things I know about her are useless info that won't be helpful in my search. Like how she memorizes the origins and meanings of names to help her remember new people. That she's never been to Hawaii, but it's the place she wants to visit most. That she can do the splits on top of me like a pro. That she's a fan of hockey with extensive knowledge of the game. How she likes to be chased before sex or the way she looks and sounds when she comes. It's exquisite.

Why is this so hard? Social media is everywhere; she must have an account on some platform. But it's her name that's causing problems, all my results are scrambled by city listings.

"Damn it, Raleigh, why did you up and leave like that?" I mutter. We had a great time! Why would she leave with no way to reach each other?

That first night we made eye contact, there was a marketing thing going on with Citra Brewing. She worked for a promotional firm. Maybe they're related. Shit, what was the name of that company? I squint my eyes and wrinkle my nose. It was something with advertising, like... banner, sign... *Billboard!*

I check to see if there are any photos from the event on their Facebook page but don't see anything. I google Billboard Promotions and am disappointed to see that their home offices are based in Colorado. Think they would give me her number? *Worth a shot.*

"Hi, I'm looking for someone who was working at an event a few weeks ago, hoping I could get their contact information. It was for Citra Brewing at the Drip nightclub in Minneapolis. Her first name is Raleigh"

The person on the phone chuckles. "I'm sorry, we don't give out any personal information of our models or promotional consultants. If you would like to lodge a complaint, you can emai—" I hang up and tap on the desk. Think, think, think. *Lonan.*

Ugh, this won't be fun, but I'll set my ego aside if it gets me another date.

> Hey, you know Raleigh from last night?

LONAN

Not really…

> She was blonde, brown eyes, super hot.

> We ate that burned pizza, I spilled beer on her

LONAN

Oh yeah, why?

> Do you have her number or insta? Or last name?

LONAN

Why would I have it?

I grumble. *Don't make me say it, man.*

> You slept with her last year.

LONAN

If I did, it only happened once. I don't keep numbers for one-night stands, and I barely even remember that. Sorry bud.

> I took her home that night, but she snuck out and I didn't get her number. If you ever see her around, will you get it for me?

LONAN

For sure.

Not to be a dick, but are you sure she was feelin it as much as you were? Maybe she snuck out because she wasn't into it.

Fuck you, Burke.

> She was into it.

36

FOUR

Barrett

"Are you coming out tonight?" Sully peeks around the corner of the locker room. We finished practice, showered, and now I'm lacing up my shoes.

I sigh. "Sure, why not." There's no excitement. I've been in a sour mood since Raleigh, but I'm still hopeful we might run into each other again. I can't figure out why she snuck out that night. We had a great time. At least, I did. Maybe it was one-sided like Lonan said. He gets around more than I do, he'd fuckin' know. I'm starting to doubt I'll find her because I've looked everywhere. The internet was no help. I checked all the bunny hangout spots with zero success.

"Sounds good. Oh, and Julia wants to see you in her office."

I groan. *Not again.*

Sully laughs. "What's the deal with her?"

"Dude, I dunno. She's so damn flirty whenever I go in there. Every time she calls these *meetings*, she has nothing important to share and it would barely qualify as an email. It's social media shit I don't care about." I scratch my scalp and scrub a hand over my face.

"Well, good luck."

"Ya..." I roll my eyes and head down the hallway to her office. Can't wait to hear what was so important this time.

"Hey, Jules, what's up?"

She looks up from her computer and her face lights up. "Aw, Jules! You gave me a special nickname, that's so cute!" *Here we go.*

"Did you need something? Otherwise, I hav'ta get back, we're running through video footage." I point my thumb over my shoulder. We already wrapped up, but she doesn't know that.

"I won't take up much of your time, I wanted to talk about your social media presence."

For fuck's sake, I don't care about social media! That's

why I have her manage everything so I don't have to!

"Don't you have like two interns that work for you, Julia? To do this kind of stuff?"

"Well, yeah but—"

"So if my social media needs work, why don't they work at it?" I don't mean to be a dick, but these conversations are getting ridiculous.

"They are, but we need a few more pictures of you. I thought we could set up a photoshoot. Maybe some that will draw some interest from women. The organization is trying to build a bigger female fan base or whatever." She throws her hand out and rolls her eyes like it's not all her idea. I can see right through her.

"Okay, like what?"

She oscillates in her chair with a big smile on her face. "Like we should do some shirtless photos. Have you picked your player initiative yet? It might attract the attention of donors. We could have profits go to any charity you're interested in."

What? No, I'm not doing that shit. This is classic Julia. "Is Sully doing it too?"

Her smile drops. "No, I haven't talked to him yet. Thought we could start with you."

I bet you did. While we're at it, let's skip the photographers and photo studio, I'll take my shirt off in your bedroom.

"My player initiative is going to be with youth hockey. I am thinking about setting up a training camp or some kind of hockey clinic, but that's not how I want to advertise, that's more Banksy's style." I push off the doorframe, needing to end this conversation before she can say anything else. "Sorry, you'll have to come up with something else."

"Dude, property is where it's at! I'm buying up houses faster than Banks can make those panties drop!" Wilder says over the group.

"Then what? You just sit on them?" Sully asks.

I'm trying to pay attention to the conversation, but my eyes keep searching the room. I didn't even want to come out tonight. I'm only here on the off chance she might walk through that door.

"I turn them into rental properties, and they make money. We can't skate forever, boys. It's good to diversify. And I'm already seeing ROIs on that shit."

"This seat taken?" a small voice says.

I scope the room one more time, then see a flash of bright-blonde hair, but when the woman turns around, it's not her. My shoulders dip back down. *Damn.*

I look down and see the petite redhead. "Nope. All yours." I scoot over.

"Thanks! I'm here with my friends, but they seem to be a little busy." She nods over at Banks and the two women fawning over him. He's the newest rookie, and is loving the attention. *Cocky little shit.*

I chuckle. "Yeah, he's like that—Hey, you don't know a Raleigh, do you?"

"Like the city?"

Exhaling, I explain for the millionth time, "Like the city, but in the form of a woman with blonde hair, who has a slight southern accent. She's about this tall..." I gesture with my hand. God, even describing Raleigh makes me feel closer to her. "Sorry, I've never met a Raleigh." *Shit.*

My eyes stay trained on the entrance of Top Shelf. If I think hard enough, maybe I can manifest her strolling into the bar. *Come on, Ral. Show up.* I wonder what she's doing at this exact moment. It's been weeks, but she's on my mind nonstop. It's torture.

"No worries. I met her a few weeks ago but we never exchanged contact info. Wasn't sure if you were running in the same...bunny circles."

She cringes. "Oof."

"What?"

"Dude, don't call us bunnies." She smiles, but I can tell the word is triggering. "You guys are bigger sluts than we are."

"Yeah, you're probably right about that. Sorry. Can I buy you a drink as an apology?"

Now I'm bummed and a jerk.

She stands. "Gonna pass. But have a good night, Conway."

"You too."

Welp. So much for that. Time to call it a night. Every time I hit a dead end, it puts a damper on my attitude. I don't even know why I come out anymore. *How does a woman up and disappear like that?*

FIVE

Raleigh

The Dust Bowl from the 1930s doesn't have shit on my vagina. It's literally been six weeks since I've had sex. Physically, it's been frustrating. My sex drive was a well-oiled machine and has been having a hell of a time going cold turkey. It's like Death Valley down there. Emotionally, the loneliness has set in and made itself at home. The withdrawal from the warm fuzzies sucks.

I'm lying on my bed, studying for my stats final, with my phone flipped upside down to avoid distractions, but it's been blowing up with messages from the girls at work trying to get me to go out. The latest one from Martha. We've worked a lot of the same gigs over

> **MARTHA**
>
> Girl! Where the fuck are you? I need my wing-woman. There are hot guys EVERYWHERE!!! How come you didn't take the Lakes Hockey gig? I thought for sure you would be here tonight. the years.

I'm done with hockey players. I'll watch the games, but

I'm over sleeping with them. After Barrett, I realized all I'm doing is torturing myself, and I can't keep doing that.

> Get an extra one for me.

MARTHA
Get him yourself! Come out with us, I'll sneak you in.

> I gotta study. Besides, I'm not feeling great.

I'm finishing my last classes, then I can graduate. I partied a little hard and didn't finish in the spring, so I'm wrapping up my last six credits this summer. They say if you want love, you must love yourself first, so here I am, nurturing my brain like I do my body.

Stepping away from the party scene has been . . . sobering, for lack of a better word. I can't believe how much time has passed. It feels like it was yesterday I was moving to Minnesota, and I'm already graduating. Well, it doesn't help that this last year has been a whirlwind of athletes and night-clubs. *What the fuck?*

It took my last one-night stand to give me that wake-up call. And now that I'm up, it's time to pay the piper. *Focus, Raleigh. Sex bad, statistics good. You need to nail my hypothesis testing for the final.*

MARTHA
Maybe you're pregnant.

Oh wait! You'd have to have sex to be pregnant...

> Ha. Enjoy your venereal disease.

She's right, there's no way I could be pregnant. The only thing that goes down there these days are vibrators and... tampons. *Wait, when was the last time I used a tampon?* I keep saying I should get one of those calendar apps, but I've never needed to. It usually just shows up and I deal with it.

Have I gotten my period since I fucked Barrett? I'm sure I had one, it was light, but it was something. *Not enough to use a tampon though.*

I shuffle back until my back hits the headboard, and tuck my knees up to my chin.

Fuck, fuck, fuck.

That's impossible. I couldn't be. I'm on the pill. And I haven't missed a day—have I? I don't remember!

Besides, the only time I'm sick is at night. I'd have to be nauseous in the morning to be pregnant, isn't that why it's called morning sickness? I'm only sick because I'm exhausted. I've been working all day and then staying up late studying. I'm running myself ragged and now I've become paranoid.

I fix my pillows, then relax a little before pulling my laptop and paper closer and opening my textbook again. Okay, *statistics*. I need to write out some example stats, the first one that comes to mind is the likelihood of there being a baby inside my uterus.

I could go to the store and pick up a couple pregnancy tests for peace of mind, and that way I'll be able to focus on my studying again and not be distracted. I can't be pregnant, I'm on the pill.

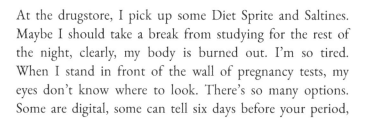

At the drugstore, I pick up some Diet Sprite and Saltines. Maybe I should take a break from studying for the rest of the night, clearly, my body is burned out. I'm so tired. When I stand in front of the wall of pregnancy tests, my eyes don't know where to look. There's so many options. Some are digital, some can tell six days before your period, another one says it gives results three ways—isn't it yes or no?

This one says triple check and has three types of pregnancy tests, but I'm sure they all require me to pee on them. I choose the three-types option because I'm curious what other ways there are. My hands shake as I place the box in my basket. I've never had to do this before.

The cashier tells me, *"Good luck"* when she hands me my receipt. I don't know if she's giving me luck for a positive or negative test, but either way, I want to punch her in the face. I'm already freaking out.

When I flip the test over, I almost vomit. The shock rolling through me has amplified all other nausea symptoms.

Positive.

Four tests.

Four positives.

I lay them out on the bathroom counter in a neat little row and swallow. What do I do now?

Running back in front of the toilet, I push the seat up in time to throw up the Diet Sprite and crackers. It burns like hell. No more carbonated beverages. Not sure if I'm barfing because of the news or the pregnancy itself—apparently the term *morning sickness* means any time of day, which is very misleading. Why don't they call it pregnancy sickness?

When I've emptied my stomach, I drop from my shaky knees and lean against the wall before grabbing a wad of toilet paper and wiping my mouth. I sit on the cold tile floor; it's freezing but seems to make the nausea lessen. I stare at the wall ahead of me. I'm pregnant. There's a *baby* inside me. *God, what have I done?* Then the tears fall.

SIX

Barrett

Took me a few weeks of research, but I've finally nailed down what I want my player initiative to be.

Growing up, I knew a couple kids better at hockey than I was. They loved playing as much as I did, but they had to drop out when their parents could no longer afford to keep them in the sport. To this day I wonder if they would be skating alongside me if money wasn't an issue. Raleigh was actually the one who made it click for me. She reminded me how important hockey scholarships are in every level of playing.

There's such a disparity in youth hockey with the haves and the have-nots. I want to create a camp that gives scholarships and discounted ice time and equipment for kids who love the game but whose parents can't manage the piling fees. By the time I was getting scouted, my family was paying almost ten thousand a year between equipment, traveling costs, ice time, and private lessons and trainers. That's absurd. A decent pair of skates alone are about a grand, and some of these kids are outgrowing them before their parents can get them paid off.

I explained it to some of the guys in the locker room.

"I love the idea, man," Lonan says. "If it weren't for growing up with the Hayeses, I wouldn't be here. My mom would never have been able to afford the cost of hockey."

"Exactly! How many other kids out there have potential to make it to the top, but they quit too young because of economic imbalances? There needs to be more equity in youth athletics. And don't even get me started on the lower income neighborhoods that have to put up with shitty facilities because there's no school funding. It's fucked up."

Sully nods. "You need any help getting set up? I'll invest in it."

"Yeah, Coach Bombay, I'll donate," Banks adds.

I laugh. "Bombay was sentenced to mandatory community service—I'm volunteering, dumbass."

"Yeah, whatever. Just let me know what you need." Everybody knows Camden "Banks" Teller comes from money, but what they don't know is that he gives a lot of it away too.

"Lakes'll get involved," Lonan adds, taping up his stick. "Auction off some jerseys at one of their little soirees or whatever."

He tosses me the roll of tape and a puck so I can do mine. "I need to bring it to the charity office and have them sign off on everything."

This feels good. I love the coaching clinics we put on with youth hockey, and every time it's my turn to coach, I have a blast. It's fun to get on the ice with the new recruits and see them improve. Some of those older kids are witty as hell and have me doubled over in laughter for half the skate. It wasn't something I thought I'd enjoy, but it fulfills something I've been missing. This is the perfect player initiative for me. I'm passionate about it and it makes sense.

Wrapping the tape around the end of my stick, I bite it off and use the puck to rub it down.

"Before you talk to charity, Julia wants to see you."

I roll my eyes. "Are you fuckin' serious?"

"We should get human resources in there with you, not on *her* behalf, for *yours*."

"Dude, I'm sayin'..." I lean my stick against my locker, wander down to her office, and knock on the door.

"B!" Her high-pitched screech pierces my eardrum.

"Hey, Julia." I made sure to use her full name.

"Wanted to ask about your player initiative. You get it squared away yet? We need to do your photo shoot." She rubs her hands together.

"I'd rather do a funny mascot one or something, it's for kids. I don't want to do the half-naked shots. That'd be fuckin' weird."

She pouts. "I think this would garner more responses. How about we discuss it over dinner?"

"Sure, I'll invite Sully. He wants to invest, he might have some ideas."

She sits back in her chair and crosses her arms. "Yeah, but this is *your* player initiative, not his."

No more beating around the bush. "This isn't a date, Julia."

She rolls her eyes and gets a big fake smile on her face. "Oh my God, B! I don't want to date you! Calm down! It's casual, why don't you meet me at Grasa at seven?"

"Six," I answer and walk away.

"Okay, six. Mister Bossy."

When I arrive at the restaurant, I'm dressed casually but Julia is not. No surprise. That dress is so low cut, it looks like she's dressed for open-heart surgery.

The restaurant is buzzing, it's a nice night and people are out on the town.

"Hi, Julia." I keep my distance from her grabby hands.

"B!" *Ugh, stop calling me B.* "Would you like a glass of wine? I got us a bottle."

"Sure, I guess." I'd rather be drunk for this.

Four glasses of wine and one steak later, I'm toast. Pretty sure I've outdrank Julia. At least I hope I have. Shit, I'm not a wine drinker. But it's made tolerating her bullshit a hell of a lot easier, that's for sure. Though the wine has only made her advances more confident.

"So"—she swirls her finger on the tablecloth—"why aren't you into me?"

Sigh.

"You're a nice girl, Julia, but honestly..." *Shit, I'm sleepy.* "...I'm interested in someone else."

"Who?"

I smile saying her name. "Raleigh."

She sits up in her chair. I've offended her. "And what does this Raleigh girl have that I don't?"

"It's nothing you *don't* have, she's just...her. We had this date, where literally everything went wrong. We were out with the team and this shitty charcoal-black pizza came to the table. She and I were the only ones that ate it, it became this funny thing. Then our Uber broke down, I forgot my wallet..." I chuckle remembering all the weird shit that went down. "God, it was bad. But no matter what happened, I had the best time with her, we had this connection that was so refreshing. I can't explain it. She was funny, smart, cool. Not like any other bunny I've met. No, she's not a bunny, that's the wrong word."

"I see."

I smile, reminiscing while playing with my fork. "And Ral

used to be a varsity goalie in high school, she was really into the sport, and she's so smart—"

"You already said smart."

Her annoyance doesn't even register with me as I push the leftover food around my plate with a fork. "She was awesome. I mean, when I was with her that night, it was like...well, nevermind. I dunno, Julia, I just wanna see her again. I *need* to."

I'm sloshed and I miss her. Shit, if I had her number, I'd be drunk texting her so hard right now. Probably best that I'm not.

"So why don't you?"

"I never got her number. It's been six weeks. She's like my Cinderella," I say, chuckling.

"You wouldn't try seeing if there was someone else you connected with?" She looks hopeful, but she's also tipsy.

"Not as long as she's around. She's somewhere. We'll run into each other again, I know it."

She slow nods. "That's really sweet, Barrett, I can respect a man on a mission. That's cool that you are dedicated to finding her." She gives a small laugh. "I appreciate you letting me down easy. Maybe I could help you find her?"

A lightbulb goes off in my head. *Shit! Why didn't I think of this earlier?*

I sit up and slam my hand on the table, far too loud. "Oh my God, of course!" I lunge forward in my chair. "You're good with social media shit! I tried searching but all my results were from Raleigh, North Carolina."

She purses her lips and offers a tight smile. Yeah, asking

for this is kind of a dick move, but if it'll help me get in contact with her, it'll be worth it. Besides, she offered. Maybe this'll finally help solidify that my feelings toward Julia are strictly platonic.

"So, her name is Raleigh, spelled like the city, but I don't have a last name. She's from Raleigh, North Carolina too. She used to be a goalie in high school. She's got light-blonde hair, brown eyes, really cute. I didn't see any tattoos or unique piercings. It would really be so helpful, Julia. If you can get me in touch, I'll owe you one."

"Yeah?"

"If you find her, I'll do whatever promo thing you want to do."

She laughs. "Wow. You want to find her that bad?"

"Yeah, it's important. Could you try?"

Her frown curves into a smile, and I relax my shoulders.

"Of course, I'll try! Anything for you, B."

This is my Hail Mary, she's gotta be able to track her down. I grin, the night doesn't seem so wasted now—*though I certainly am.*

"You'll find somebody, Jules. You're an attractive woman, you're hard-working, any guy would fall over themselves to go on a date with you."

"Not any guy..."

"You know what I mean. They will, though. Be patient. It'll happen."

She smiles and the corners of her eyes crease as she takes another sip of wine.

SEVEN

Raleigh

A small ladybug crawls along the hem of my bedroom curtains. Occasionally it loses its footing and opens its wings to find purchase and cling to the fabric. I'm not sure how long I've been watching my little friend, but it's been a nice way to pass the time. Ladybugs probably never feel shame in pregnancy. It's been about twenty-four hours since I found out I was pregnant, and I've only left my bed to pee.

I'm too embarrassed to call any of my friends or the girls from work, but I don't know what to do and could use some advice. I could call my aunt, but she'll tell my mom. My mother and I have a volatile relationship.

I was in middle school the first time one of my mom's boyfriends tried to touch me. When I told her, she yelled at him, and they broke it off. Unfortunately, she had a rotating door of boyfriends, and every once in a while, one would look at me a certain way, and it creeped me out. The older I got, the more often it would happen. Eventually, she saw *me* as the problem, not the disgusting men she let into our trailer.

It made me hate myself and my body. I felt dirty all the time. It didn't matter how many clothes I put on, they still looked. It made me hate my mother too. I told myself I'd never make the same choices she did and my life would be different from hers. Then I turned out like my mom after all —pregnant at twenty-two by a one-night stand.

As much as my mom has let me down, she's the only person I know that's been in my shoes before. I swing my legs over the side of the bed and pick my phone off my nightstand to make the dreaded call to North Carolina. It rings twice before I hear background noise.

"Mom?"

"What's up, Raleigh?" It's loud wherever she is. Probably the casino.

"Um, where are you?"

"We're in Vegas. You should see the lights here!" Her gritty, raspy voice makes my shoulders tense up. I can always tell when she's speaking with a cigarette hanging out of the corner of her mouth. That's how it was my entire childhood. A Newport sticking out one corner of her mouth, with verbal abuse spewing from the other. I can still hear it, usually paired with the sound of hollow stomps across our linoleum floor. It gives me the heebie-jeebies.

I clear my throat. Maybe I should call another time. She's been drinking. But it can't wait. This baby is growing bigger by the second. It's all I can think about, and every time I look down at my belly, I expect it to be five times bigger than it was a minute before. And if I wait for her to sober up, I might never tell her.

"I think I'm pregnant."

There's a pause, quick suck of a cigarette, and then exhale.

"What do you mean, you *think* you're pregnant?"

She's pissed, I know because she took the cigarette out of her mouth to say it.

"I was feeling sick and couldn't remember my period. I

took a test and it came back positive. I don't know what to do."

"Well, what did you expect, Ral? You open your legs for anybody with a hockey stick. Is this really any fuckin' surprise?" She chuckles.

She likes to keep tabs on my Instagram. There's a few pictures of me with players at bars and clubs. I'm almost positive she does it so she has ammunition to throw in my face, not because she actually cares to see what I've been up to. Not that it matters anyway, even before I started sleeping with hockey players, she thought I was a "hussy" because of the way my body looked. What's the difference?

"Can we not do this right now? I fucked up. I'm calling because I need advice. What should I do?"

"Welp, do you even know whose baby it is?"

I wince at her words. *I don't, but I have a pretty good idea.* I've gone without a condom with other men before, but they always pull out and I'm on the pill. The last guy I slept with was Barrett and the condom broke. And I literally *felt* him come inside me.

"Not entirely sure."

She laughs, actually laughs. I roll my eyes as an act of rebellion. She hates when I do it. Why does she have to be so mean? And she's one to talk, because it's not like I know who my dad is. The only men around were the awful boyfriends she shuffled through. That pisses me off.

"I'm sorry, did you finally remember who your baby daddy is?" I snark.

"Don't be a bitch, Raleigh, or I'll hang up. You have no idea how much I've done for you! You're a spoiled brat who thinks she's better than everyone else because you get to party with big-time hockey players, and now you're running back to me for help because you got no one else."

That hurts. I tuck my legs up on the mattress and take a

deep breath. "I'm sorry. It's just... I'm freaking out. I don't know what I'm supposed to do now."

It's quiet, and she either walked out of the noisy casino or hung up.

"Are you still there?"

"Yeah, yeah, just gimme a minute," she barks. "Okay, first, find out whose baby it is. Wait, is it really an athlete's?"

I sigh. Proving her right doesn't feel good. "Yeah."

"That's good! 'Cause babies are expensive, you're gonna need every cent you can get."

"Who's the guy?" She says it like we're trading stories, it makes me sick.

"I think it's Barrett Conway's, but I don't know for sure."

"He rich?"

How the hell would I know his salary? I haven't thought that far. Jesus. This conversation reminds me of our last big fight, the one that sent me to Minnesota. She hooked up with some rich local big-timer and bragged about all the money he made. She was obsessed with how our life would be better because of this guy. Her life improved, but mine got much worse. He was the biggest creep she ever brought home. I scratch at my neck remembering how he used to corner me in our tiny kitchen and try to put his hands up my shirt. I finally told a social worker at school, and that's when all hell broke loose between us. He ran off scared and she never forgave me for it. This is all she ever cared about. *How much money does he make?* If I have this baby, I will always put them first. *Always.*

I run my fingers through my hair again, and a few strands fall out in my hand and I shake them off. Habit.

"I don't know what he makes."

"Well, you need to tell him, like tonight, Raleigh."

"We didn't exchange numbers."

"You don't have his number? You have no way to get ahold of him?"

54

I shrug, even though she can't see me. "I was going to message him on Instagram."

She takes another puff of her cigarette. "Tell him tonight."

"I will."

"I mean it, Ral. The sooner the better. Then after you do that, get a job, Ral. A *real* one."

"I do have a real job."

She scoffs. "Yeah? Are young, unwed pregnant women in demand these days for modeling?" Shit, I didn't even consider that. "Whatever you do, you better have something with insurance so you can go to the obstetrician."

Obste-what?

"What's an obstetrician?"

The noise returns, and she laughs again. "Oh my God, I don't have time for this. Look it up. I gotta go, Jerry's won at the craps table. Do what I said, find the dad, ask for money, go to the doctor. But don't expect much from him. You're on your own now. Once you have a kid, your life is over. So better start getting your shit together." The call is disconnected.

I've *been* on my own. I set down the phone and drop my head into my hands, bawling. My only example of motherhood is *what not to do*. She's right though, I need to get a hold of Barrett. But I will not go about it the way she thinks. I refuse to be like my mom. He seems like a nice guy, I don't want to take advantage, but he deserves to know, and some child support would be helpful.

What if he wants me to get rid of it? It would be easier, but the regret would kill me. My mom told me so many times that having a baby ruined her life. If I can love this baby enough to put it first, I'll be leagues above the mother I had. I could give this child a chance. Give them *real love.* The kind I always wanted.

I grab my laptop and start googling. Obstetrician. Oh, it's an OB. Duh. *Why couldn't she have simply said that?* I also learned that pregnancy is likely the reason behind all the naps and heartburn over the last couple weeks.

I set the laptop next to me and fall onto my back, draping an arm over my face. How do I tell Barrett? He's going to flip. What do I even say? *Hey, remember me? That chick that took your last condom and then you came in me? I'm pregnant with your baby!* Fuck, I need to pace before I do this. I traverse back and forth across my bedroom. I grab my phone and look him up on Instagram.

BarrettConwayOfficial.

I click Follow and type out a message. Then delete it. The second attempt turns into my sixth attempt. Whatever, I'm not telling him over a DM that I'm pregnant. I've got to do it face-to-face. I type up one last response and click send.

Rahlee789: Hey Bear. It's Raleigh from Raleigh. Wondering if you would want to grab coffee some- time? Either way, give me a call or text. 612-555- 7332

If I am going to have anybody's kid, Bear is a good choice, I suppose. Maybe he'll be understanding and supportive? After enough time, he might even see me as more than a bunny. We could have one of those good bad dates again.

Ugh, who am I kidding? I've seen how this shit goes down in real life, celebrities get women pregnant and then hide them like a dirty little secret. I'll keep this baby for myself before that happens.

Well, step one initiated.

Onto step two. I pull up my resume and spend the next three hours working on it to make it perfect. I've got my last finals before graduation, so I don't want to send out anything until I have that diploma. Unless... I run toward the front door and grab my purse. I dig through my wallet and pull out the business card. Rob Waters. Method Marketing is a big firm. If I start right away, I could give them at least eight months of work before I give birth.

Do I have to tell them I'm pregnant? Yes, I should tell them, but what if it costs me the job? I can't risk that. This might be the best job opportunity I'll get. My stomach growls, and I zip up the wallet but keep the card out so I can put it on the fridge as a reminder. I'm going to call.

First, I need to eat. I head into the kitchen and find leftovers, but as soon as I smell them heating in the microwave, I want to throw up again. I grab a sleeve of crackers and take small nibbles until I'm able to find my appetite again. After that, it's another nap.

The next morning, I'm still tired. It's like I'm never rested anymore. Doesn't matter, I need to find a new job and get to work. First, I check my email for all the modeling gigs coming up so I can schedule as many as I can. Thankfully, most events are at night. My best chance for success is to find a full-time job so I can work during the day and then snag as many promotional gigs as I can until my body looks pregnant. This way I'll be able to save up money.

I still have a lot of money management stuff to take care of. I'll need to cancel my gym membership and narrow down those streaming services. I will need every cent, which also means no more daily Starbucks, hair appointments, waxings, restaurants, and the only clothes I'll be buying are from Target.

Sure, I've been used to all those fun little treats, but seeing myself woman up and sacrifice for my child who's not even here yet? That makes me smile. I will find a way to do this.

"Hang in there, little...seed thing." *I'll need to come up with a better nickname.* "I'm gonna do everything I can for us."

EIGHT

Raleigh

E very hour that goes by with my unanswered DM makes me more anxious. It doesn't help that I'm still hiding under the covers. My ladybug friend flew away, so I should probably leave the room too.

Shit. I don't want my kid to grow up not knowing who their dad is. I went through that, it sucked. Unfortunately, the whole Lakes organization seems hellbent on blacklisting me. I tried to contact him through the home office, and they referred me to his public relations manager. Public relations won't return my calls. I tried to go to his agent, then I ended up with public relations again. Nobody has been even the slightest bit helpful, so I'm sure at this point they think I'm some fan gone apeshit.

Finally, my phone dings with an Instagram notification and it's like a prayer being answered. *Please be Barrett.*

When I see the first few words in his DM, a smile breaks out across my face.

BCon33: Hey Raleigh, this is Barrett Conway. I don't message through my Lakes account for privacy

**reasons. I wanted to let you know I got your
message. I'm not interested.**

My smile fades.

**Rahlee789: I understand if you don't want to meet,
but we need to have a conversation at some point.
Can I at least have your number and we can talk over
the phone?**

**BCon33: If I wanted you to have my number, you'd
already have it. I'm not interested in meeting up or
talking. I need you to stop messaging me.**

I was hoping to speak with him directly before dropping
the pregnancy bomb on him. It's not like I'm asking him for
money, I just want him to know. Though, if he was willing to
help out financially, I'm in no position to turn it down.

**Rahlee789: This isn't about a hookup or seeing you
again, but we do need to talk.**

**BCon33: I really don't think there's anything left
that needs to be said. I've got a girlfriend, that
night was a one-time thing, it was a mistake. I
need to focus on my relationship right now and I
need you to stay away.**

What!?

Rahlee789: I didn't know you had a girlfriend.

That pisses me off! He said nothing about having a significant other of any kind. How many times that night did he say I was *his?* What a liar.

> **Rahlee789:** I get that I've been blowing up your DMs but it's not because I want a relationship or something, I'm pregnant. I'm sorry to tell you in this way, but you should know I'm planning on keeping the baby. We should talk either way to discuss what kind of involvement you want. Or something, I dunno... I feel like this is an in-person conversation.

> **BCon33:** Involvement? Are you fucking serious? You think you're the first bunny to pull this shit? I don't care if you're angry or jealous or whatever, but lying about being pregnant in order to drive a wedge between me and my girlfriend is pretty fucking sick.

> **Rahlee789:** Why would I lie about this? I'm pregnant, Barrett. I took 4 tests!!

> **BCon33:** Maybe you are. I mean, you fuck enough dudes, you're bound to wind up with somebody's kid, right? It's simple math. Look, I don't know how many other guys you've done this to, but it's not gonna work on me. It's not mine.

My head drops to my hands, and I dissolve into tears. Every sob makes my throat ache. He is such a prick! I can't believe I ever slept with him and felt the feelings I did for him —and now I'm having his baby.

> **Rahlee789:** I'm not trying to kid-trap you or something, I just wanted you to know.

BCon33: Bullshit. You puck sluts are all the same. Just because you're hot, doesn't make your pussy any more special than the next girl. Get over yourself, Raleigh. Even if I wasn't in a relationship, you wouldn't be worth the second fuck.

Rahlee789: You're a dick. I'm in absolute shock right now. I don't know why I ever saw anything in you.

BCon33: Lol there's only one thing I ever saw in you and it's between your legs.

Rahlee789: Fuck you.

BCon33: No thanks. Take this as a sign you should probably hang up your jersey, this is no way to find a man—or a baby daddy in your case. It's one thing to look nice for the boys, but after we've fucked you a couple times, the shine wears off and we all realize what an overused cunt you are. Just so you know, after this conversation, word is gonna get around, so if I were you, I'd stay away from the team and our families.

Rahlee789: Stop texting me.

BCon33: Congratulations on your bastard.

I angrily swipe at the tears streaming down my face. He doesn't deserve anyone crying over him. Still, at the back of my mind, I can't stop the feelings I had. He's so opposite the man I thought he was. That night I scroll through the messages over and over, reminding myself he's garbage. I didn't imagine those awful things he said. They're real.

The next day, I call his PR manager one final time. For whatever reason, I need to hear him tell me he's not interested.

"I'm calling for Barrett Conway."

"Is this Raleigh Dunham?"

"Yes..."

"He would like to pass along the message that he is not interested in speaking to you further."

"Okay, but it seems like there's some miscommunication happening. I need to speak with him for a minute. I'm not asking for his personal number, I understand you can't give that information out, but is there a private extension you could transfer me to so I could reach him?"

I want to hear him say the words. I *need* to hear his voice say he doesn't want to see me or be involved with this child.

"He has already made us aware of the situation."

"But—"

"I've already given you your answer. If you continue to attempt contact with Barrett Conway, it will be considered harassment and he'll be forced to file a restraining order. This is your final warning, if you persist, we will get our lawyers involved."

I'm stunned into silence. I don't even know what to say. Is this really happening? This has to be a nightmare. It doesn't make sense. Nobody will listen to me!

"Fuck you and Barrett Conway."

I end the call and go to throw my phone across the room, but snatch it back at the last second. I can't afford to buy a new one. And if I can't afford a phone, I certainly can't afford my own lawyer.

One thing for sure is Barrett Conway will never ever get to see his child. I will protect this baby with everything in me. This is his loss, not mine. He's the one missing out, not us. We're better off without him. It makes me sick to think I ever had any feelings toward such a fucking monster. And threatening to take legal action? This is humiliating.

Later that afternoon, I'm interrupted from my nap when my phone rings. I crack my eyes wide enough to see the word *Mom* on the screen. I'm a miserable failure. Everything I thought about Barrett was wrong. I didn't think he would react this way. He seemed like a decent human when we were together. At the very least, I thought he would be more kind.

"Hi, Mom."

"So?"

"So, what?" I know what she means, but I don't want to say it.

"Did you talk to Barrett?" I don't want to discuss it.

I close my eyes; it hurts to say it. "He doesn't want to be involved."

"Told you. Men are worthless pieces of shit."

I want to respond yes, but I can't bring myself to. My heart aches and the shame is crippling. I can't bring myself to mention the DMs. I'll never speak of those messages to anyone.

"Look, I didn't have any help raising you. Not a fucking penny. No child support, no five bucks in a birthday card, nothin'."

This has been said to me a thousand times. I sigh. "I know, Mom."

"Just sayin'... you're no different from me. I did it all by myself. And if I can do it with what little I had, then you can do it."

But I wanted to be different from her. And I will be. Mothers are supposed to love their children *first* and foremost. That's how I will love my child. I rub the lower section of my stomach.

"Thanks," I say half-heartedly.

"You're welcome, sugar. I love you. But I meant what I said about that job. You're a mom now. Time to grow up."

I shake my head. He was never meant to be more than a lesson learned, and it's a mistake I will never make again. I'm done.

The following Monday, I grab the business card off my fridge and dial the number.

"Hi, Rob. My name is Raleigh, we met at Drip during the Citra event."

"Hey, Raleigh." I hear the smile in his voice. "I was hoping you'd call..."

NINE

Raleigh

30 weeks later...

Who the fuck invented Pitocin? A man, that's who. It must have been a man. This is the worst thing to happen ever in the history of humanity. My contractions are so intense I can hardly breathe, and I keep throwing up. Is this normal? Is it supposed to be like this? They said the drug would help induce labor, but it feels like the baby is trying to blow through my stomach cavity à la the chest-burster scene from *Alien*.

"How we doing, Raleigh?" my nurse Heather checks in.

"Why isn't the epidural working?" Sweat drips from my face.

"I don't know, sweetheart. Sometimes they don't take."

I choke as two contractions meet, then grab the emesis bag and vomit. Saying these contractions are powerful is an understatement. They're unnatural.

"This is some fucking bullshit, Heather." I spit in the bag. "You know that, right?"

"It is bullshit, you're right, girl. What can I get you?"

"A better anesthesiologist would be nice, gahhhhh!" I squint and try not to focus on the pain. "But I'll settle for another...heating pad." I twist off the blue plastic emesis bag and hand it to her. "And a new one of these."

"You got it. Let me check to see where you're at."

Please say I'm dilated. Please say I can push or something. I don't know how much more pain I can take. I'm running out of energy. I always envisioned the birth of my first child would be spent with my husband by my side squeezing my hand and helping me practice my breathing exercises. Instead, it's just me. No husband. No mother. No aunt. No friend. I didn't realize I would be ostracized by my friends when I became pregnant. It's like they were afraid they'd catch it and end up with their own babies somehow. I've never felt so alone. Except for Heather. She's an angel from heaven.

"You're at a four." She sounds disappointed.

"A four! How can I only be at a four?!" I was at a four six hours ago. Tears roll down my face, and I sob. "I can't do this!"

I've been in the worst pain of my life for over twenty hours. I'm alone and scared and not sure how much longer I can hold on. *Why won't this baby come out of me?*

"Is my baby okay?" I'm panicking.

"The monitor on your stomach still has a steady heartbeat. Baby is doing fine."

Well, I'm glad they're comfortable!

"This kid is going to pay for putting me through so much agony. I'm gonna use their college fund to—aaaaaaaah!—" I take short breaths like they showed me in class. I grunt, and focus my energy. My voice comes out like it's possessed by a demon. "—buy a boat!"

My nurse gives me a small chuckle.

"It's not supposed to hurt like this, right?"

She gives me a sad smile. This can't be normal. I have a

high pain tolerance, but this shit is like nothing I've ever experienced in my life. There's not a word for it.

She holds out an emesis bag in time for me to rip it from her fingers and throw up again. My entire body is shaking. *Shit, am I going to die?* "Let me grab the doctor, are you good for a couple minutes?"

I nod and vomit again. I'm mad at my mother, I'm mad at Barrett, I'm mad at every person who has abandoned me in this pregnancy. I only like Heather, everyone else can eat stairs.

My doctor comes into the room, and I plead with her to take me out of my misery. "How we doing?"

"I'm tapping out. There has to be another way. I can't keep going."

She has me lie on my back so she can check my cervix. "Raleigh, you're not progressing. I think it's time we consider a cesarean."

"Okay." I turn my head and vomit again. I never thought this was the way my baby would come into the world, but I'm about two minutes away from asking them for a scalpel so I can do it myself. "Let's do it."

As soon as I give the nod, four more nurses enter the room, I'm unhooked from machines, and the bed is moving. I'm wheeled into the brightly lit operating room, machines are stationed in different corners. One of the machines has blankets and a little hat sitting on it. *That's for my baby.* The space is cold and sterile, but everyone present is cheery and happy to see me. Two new nurses help me sit up on the bed.

"Lean into me, hun."

I hunch forward and try my damndest to stop shaking while a *new* anesthesiologist—*thank Christ*—puts a giant needle in my back. I don't even feel it, the pain from the needle is child's play compared to what I've been dealing with. The hardest part is holding perfectly still while my body wars against the contractions.

"You're doing good, Raleigh. Almost done." They lay me back down, and for the first time in twenty-two hours, I can take a full breath. Tears of relief spill from my eyes. I truly thought I might not survive the pain.

The next thing I know, Heather is back by my side, this time wearing surgical scrubs. "Feeling better?"

"Oh my God, this is so much easier." I actually laugh.

The doctor speaks up, "Okay, Raleigh, do you feel this?" I feel nothing. *It's lovely.*

"Nope, all good."

"Excellent. We are going to perform a cesarean and get your baby out. Ready?"

"*So* ready." I smile as it dawns on me, *I'm about to meet my baby.* My sweet little boy or girl I've been carrying around for *well over* forty weeks. Heather squeezes my hand.

There's a plastic sheet blocking the view of my lower half so I can't see what they're doing. All I hear is sporadic suctioning and muffled talking between the surgeon and the techs. Every once and a while, a tool drops onto a metal tray.

The last twenty-four hours have felt like pure chaos. Foreign, guttural groans of pain coming from my throat, the constant sour taste in my mouth from vomiting, and excruciating contractions that can be described only as whatever comes after wishing for death. But here in the OR, it's peaceful. It's quiet, everyone's voice is relaxed and easy. I'm finally not in pain. Maybe I died.

"Do you think you're going to have a boy or a girl?" Heather queries, distracting my twisted train of thought.

"I'm tempted to say girl based on how stubborn they've been about staying inside my uterus, but I can't shake this feeling that it's a boy."

"You've done a phenomenal job hanging in there. You're one tough mother."

I blow out a breath of air. "That was the hardest thing I've ever done, and I still ended up here." I raise my eyes and look around. I can't gesture with my hands, they're strapped to boards like a crucifix.

"Nothing wrong with that. Some babies come out through the tunnel, yours is coming out through the sunroof. You put up one hell of a fight, Raleigh. You should be very proud of yourself. How's the nausea?"

"Still nauseous, but I don't think I'm going to throw up."

She nods. "We'll get you some meds to make you more comfortable."

Over the sheet, the doctor speaks up again, "Raleigh, you're going to feel some pressure on your stomach and some tugging, okay? That's normal."

"Okay."

Sheesh, she wasn't kidding. It feels like somebody is jumping up and down on my belly. Then it stops. Voices on the other side of the curtain seem excited and then I hear the softest cries from little lungs. "We have a baby! It's a boy!"

Oh my God, I have a son! Those tiny wails are the most incredible sound I've ever heard. *I can hear him, I can hear my baby.* I want to see him so badly.

They immediately drop the curtain and hold up the most beautiful baby boy I've ever seen. His eyes are closed, and he wiggles around with small jerky motions, the umbilical cord still attached. Tears spring to my eyes—*that's my son!*

They raise the curtain again and disappear behind it. I want to hold him.

"He's gorgeous, Raleigh!" Heather says. "They're just going to weigh and swaddle him and then you can hold your baby." It's like she read my mind. When I look over at her, she's got my phone. "I'm going to take some pictures while they get you stitched."

"Thank you!"

Heather is heaven-sent. She steps over to where they are wiping him down and snaps some photos.

"You did great!" my doctor calls out. "We're closing you up now."

I relax and tears leak from the corners of my eyes. *It's over.*

They call out his length and weight—twenty-five inches, ten pounds, four ounces!

Maybe it's a good thing I didn't try to push him out.

"Raleigh, you made the right decision!" one nurse comments.

I agree.

"Do you have a name yet?" another nurse asks.

I always said if it was a boy, I would name him Arthur. It means *bear.* Is that sick? Maybe. He can deny this child all he wants, but Arthur will always be a bear. And as much as I want to, I can't hate Barrett, he gave me my son. But what he gets of Arthur, ends with his name. Beyond that, Barrett Conway is the textbook father bear, impregnating the female and leaving her to fend for herself. Male bears don't help raise their young, which is why, despite his name, Arthur will never be his.

"Arthur."

When Heather turns around, she's carrying him all bundled up. She releases the restraints on one of my arms so I can wrap it around him. I'm able to keep my hand on him while I'm being put back together, but it's hard to see his little face while I'm strapped on my back.

"What's your last name Heather?"

"James, why?"

It's perfect.

Arthur James Dunham. I like that. Heather has been my rock today, and I will never forget her kindness. She kept me afloat and will forever be a solid part of his birth story.

"Mind if I steal that for a middle name?"

She gets all doe-eyed on me. "I'd be honored."

"Thank you for being my person today. I'm really happy you were my nurse."

"Me too. You did amazing, Raleigh."

Once surgery is over and we are brought to the recovery room, he is unwrapped and placed on my chest. For the first time, I can look down and clearly see his perfect rosy face and feel his rapid little heartbeat against mine.

"Hi, Arthur."

He opens his eyes and I burst into tears. I'm flooded with pure love. All the warm fuzzies times a million. I've never felt complete until this moment. He is the love of my life.

I don't know how much time passes while we observe each other with wide eyes. It could be a minute or an hour. I trace over his little pursed lips and stroke his round cheeks full of color. He blinks up at me when I touch his adorable little button nose. He's the most beautiful thing I've ever seen.

Heather helps unwrap him from the swaddle and lays him on my bare chest. His warm skin is softer than...I don't know. It's the softest thing I've ever felt. He snuggles into me, and this bond we've formed strengthens by the minute. It's deep and unconditional. He's the most precious thing I've ever held in my arms. I will love this child with everything I have.

"You did so great today," I whisper. "I know we just met, but I love you forever."

TEN

Raleigh

I can't do this. Motherhood is so much harder than I ever imagined. How come all these Instagram moms make it seem so easy? They all have these clean minimalist houses, their babies are clothed in designer organic cotton in neutral colors. My laundry pile of secondhand clothing is overflowing, there's seven dirty diapers stacked up on the dresser that I still haven't had the energy to get up and throw away. I don't want to walk into the kitchen because it's a mess. There are bottles piled up in the sink. I'm always exhausted. I'm still bleeding and have a wrap on my stomach from the cesarean, and now that I've sent in the deposit for daycare, my bank account is almost empty. What kind of mother am I? How do those other women do it? They have help.

They have partners and nannies and night nurses.

I have me. Every ounce of energy I have goes to Arthur, and it leaves nothing left in the tank for anything else. I'm running on fumes. I resent all these other moms that have help. With their stupid fucking smiles and bright, rested eyes. My eyes have dark circles under them. My smile is weak and forced. They all have a partner, someone to take care of them, but I'm the only one who can take care of Arthur. I'm the only person in the world this little boy has, and he's counting on me. What if I can't give him what he deserves?

It's been five weeks since I've had more than two hours of solid sleep, so I'm a zombie. He cries all the time, and so do I. I'm isolated and depressed. I love him beyond what I knew love could be, but I wonder if I made a mistake keeping him. Another family could provide for him better. Maybe he would be happier. They say it's colic, but what if he's crying because of me?

I can't think that way, though, I love my son. And even if it's selfish, I could never leave him with anyone else. They may be able to give him more material things, like new organic cotton onesies and fancy Montessori toys, but no one will ever love Arthur like I do.

No one.

I am his mother, and I'll continue to make whatever sacrifices I need to make for him. I have to try. The alternative isn't an option. My hand covers his small warm belly as he sleeps next to me in the bassinet. I can't let him be raised in the same environment I was. He deserves a clean room. *Come on, clean up one thing, Ral. Pick up one goddamn thing for him.* I start with the diapers and then the burp cloths. Then crack a window to get a fresh breeze in the room. It's a lovely day outside. Blue skies and clouds like cotton candy.

I can do this.

One thing at a time, I tidy up the bedroom. I'm already exhausted. I lie back in bed in time for him to wake up and to nurse him. I brush his tiny blonde hairs with my thumb. He's so adorable. He's worth everything.

After he finishes eating, I check my phone. While I burp him, I open the banking app again. It's not like staring at the number will make it any bigger.

I go back to work next week, and the first two weeks of daycare are covered, but it will still be close. If my breastmilk runs out I'll be in trouble, I'll need to pump a few times a day at work if I'm to keep producing. Formula is expensive. I run my fingers through my hair as my mind circles with all the worst-case scenarios I can think of. *Stop it.*

Yes, money is tight, but I'll get through it. I've only one more week of my maternity leave, so I should probably check in. Pulling out my phone, I contact my closest friend at Method Marketing: Annette in Human Resources.

> Hey! How's your day going?

ANNETTE

> Hey you! It's good. How are things?? How's the colic? Did the doctor say if there was anything you could give him? All of Rob's clients have been asking about you, they miss seeing your face.

> I'm good. He's still colicky but the doctors don't have much of a solution. Getting him to sleep for two-hour chunks though, so that's something. Tell everybody at work I say hi. I'll see them next week. Hopefully Rob isn't losing his mind too much.

ANNETTE

> I'm sorry you're only getting 6 weeks. I know you're not ready to come back, I wish it wasn't like this. If it helps, I saw some paperwork come through last week to give you a pay increase.

Is she serious?

> Really? Why? I mean, I'll take it, but I haven't even been there that long!

ANNETTE

Rob feels bad that you haven't gotten a full
maternity leave. He's been so impressed
with you. He probably wants to make sure
you come back lol

> Of course I'll be back! And thanks for letting
> me know, it made my day

ANNETTE

But you didn't hear it from me! Paperwork
will be on your desk when you come back
next week. Act surprised about the raise!

> What raise?

ANNETTE

Perfect! Now get some rest and take care
of yourself, girly!

I lock my phone and lean back in bed with a new positive outlook.

"We might have some good news coming our way, Arthur. Things are looking up, babe."

I rub his back a few more times and he finally burps. I wait with the cloth to catch any spit up, but it doesn't come. I pull him back with a big smile. "No spit up today? Good jo —" and that's when he projectiles all over my neck and hair.

My nose wrinkles. "So close, bud... So close."

I've been crying on and off all morning. I can't believe our six weeks together is up. Now I'm simply supposed to drop him off with a stranger for eight hours? Leave someone else to raise my baby? What if he thinks I've abandoned him?

Does he know I'm coming back? The parental care system in this country is fucked up.

"You okay, Raleigh?" Rob asks.

"Huh? Oh! Yeah, I'm fine, it's just allergies. I swear I'm not usually like this," I say with a forced laugh. He keeps popping up.

"It's your first day back, it's okay to be a little emotional. Do you need anything?"

"Sorry. No, no, I'm fine..." I sniffle. "Um, just a heads-up, Greenstone called, and they want to push back the ad rollout for next month because of a new product they're releasing. I told them we would need to set up another meeting with the creative directors to discuss."

"They've always got one more product. Yeah, that's fine. Works out better anyway, I want to focus on getting our new sales software launched."

"That's what I figured. I moved up those meetings, so you'll meet Jonathan on Thursday to get a status update."

"Damn, you're good. How did you know I was focused on that?"

I tap my temple.

"It's great to have you back, Raleigh. Missed you around here."

"I can tell!" I chuckle. "I still can't believe you gave me a raise while I was on maternity leave. That was really generous." When I got to my desk this morning, I signed off on a twenty percent raise.

"You've earned it. I'm really pleased with the work you've done thus far."

My stresses about money have greatly decreased since getting this job. Rob is awesome. He's appreciative whenever I do anything, and he's been incredibly under-standing of my emotions today.

As sad as I am over leaving Arthur at daycare five days a

week, it's nice knowing our life will be a little easier from now on. I'll be able to provide for him and even set a couple hundred bucks aside each month for our savings. He may not understand now, but someday, this will be so worth it for our little family.

PART TWO

PRESENT

Almost 5 years later

ELEVEN

Raleigh

"Method Marketing, Raleigh Dunham."

"Raleigh, that's a cool name. Hey! I'm Micky, I am the owner of Sugar and Ice Patisserie and Cocktail Lounge. We have our soft opening coming up next Tuesday, and I wanted to see if Method Marketing was interested in an invite to the launch? We've been reaching out to local businesses, and I'm told you're the HBIC."

I laugh. "Definitely not the head bitch in charge, but I can certainly get the right bitches to show up. We're always looking to support women-owned businesses, especially if we're neighbors. Patisserie and cocktails you say?"

"And they're delicious."

"Love the concept. What's the dress code?"

"Whatever you're comfortable in. No dress code, but if it helps, Sugar and Ice has a speakeasy vibe." I scribble down the info she gives me.

"Perfect."

After securing the event tickets for some of the Method Marketing staff, Micky and I end up on the phone chatting more about her business plan and what Method does. I lose track of time until Rob shows up at my desk. I give a small wave to acknowledge his presence and wrap up the call.

Micky continues. "Be sure to come find me at the opening. Red hair, tattoos. Ask somebody there and they'll find me. I'll set some tarts aside for you!"

She seems like a lot of fun. "Thank you so much! I'll be sure to do that. Looking forward to introducing you to some of the team next Tuesday. Congratulations again!"

I'm energized after hanging up. I spin to face my boss with a big smile on my face. Rob's had a thing for me for a while, though, not sure why. He's nice enough, but sometimes he can be intense. I try to keep a professional boundary, but he likes to push it. Sometimes I wonder if that's why he keeps giving me raises. Probably helps him sleep at night.

I can't leave, the pay is too good and we need the money. Besides, their health insurance is out of this world, and includes vision *and* dental. And two free massages every month! The benefits alone are enough to keep me. And I love my job. I especially enjoy working with women-owned startups. Give me all that independent-badass-boss energy. I'm looking forward to meeting the owner of Sugar and Ice.

"Where are we going next Tuesday?" he asks.

"I have fifteen tickets to the Sugar and Ice soft launch. A few blocks down, near Citra Brewing. Remember that dump that shut down last year? The woman on the phone, Micky, bought it and turned it into a patisserie cocktail lounge mashup. Cool, huh?"

"Oh, yeah. I overheard Patterson talking about it yesterday. Sounds great. Who are you giving tickets to?"

"Figured I'd send out an email; first come, first serve. Though, she mentioned getting an ad campaign set up, so we should reserve a few for Sales. Sounds like it's got a unique, upscale vibe, so it could be a great location for networking." *We're always looking for new places to meet with prospective clients.* "Definitely one for Emery, I think she'd be a good fit with the owner if we end up taking her on as a client."

He nods. "Are you going?"

"I was planning on it. We hit it off on the phone."

"Great, set aside one for me too, then."

"You got it, Boss."

He leans over my desk, invading my personal space.

Every time he does this, I get flustered.

"Rob." He corrects.

He's closer to my face than usual. "You got it, Rob Boss. Bob Ross. I mean, Rob. Ugh, sorry." *Fuck.* I scoot back in my chair and turn back to my computer screen, randomly clicking around to look busy. *Did I call him Bob Ross?*

"Why are you so nervous around me all the time?" He chuckles.

I don't know, you're two inches from my face! Why do you think?

"Not nervous!" I respond cheerily. "Just want to make sure everything is perfect for the..."

"The Lakes partnership?"

I point my finger at him. "Yes, actually! I have a few more questions about that."

"Raleigh, we've been over this a hundred times already."

"I know, I just want to confirm, it's only our staff and their marketing team that will be present at the banquet?"

"And their families, correct."

"We've booked the Lake Superior box and there's no tour of the arena or anything after, right?"

"No, but that's a good idea! Would you want to arrange something?"

Thanks, I'd hate to. "Sure, I'll reach out to their event coordinator while you're in your eleven o'clock." I lie.

The only thing I'm doing during his meeting is going on a date with the vending machine down the hall. I'm starving.

He'll probably offer to buy me lunch but then he expects me to eat with him too.

"Would you like your lunch in the conference room or your office today?"

"Save it for after the meeting, I'll take it in my office. Grab something for yourself. Feel free to join me if you've got time. You don't have to work so hard for me, Raleigh."

He wants me to read between the lines. But I do need to work that hard. Our life depends on it. *Arthur* depends on it.

After filtering Rob's emails and returning correspondence, I take the elevator down to pick up his lunch delivery and bring it to his office.

"Roast beef and Swiss, extra mayo." I set it down on his desk. "Oh, and I chatted with Carlos, the Lakes liaison. Unfortunately, they don't have any availability that night for tours of the arena. I'm not worried though; attendees will be more focused on the playoff game anyway. Maybe another time we can coordinate it, I bet they have more openings during the offseason when it's empty."

Even if we get that fun little tour set up, I will *not* be present. There's no way in hell I'm risking running into *him*. The only reason I'm going to the banquet at all is because Rob made it mandatory. It will be fine.

TWELVE

Raleigh

"So how long did the renovations take? This building used to be such an eyesore but it's incredible inside!"

The space looks amazing, the transformation is unreal. Sales has already given me *the look* to put this place on our shortlist for networking events. And Micky is as cool as I thought she'd be, and if I weren't so busy all the time, I'd love it if we could grab drinks.

"It was about a year altogether. It's been quite an adventure. Oh! I want to introduce you to someone." She grabs my hand, but turns her head to yell toward one of the cozy seating areas. "Birdie, get over here!"

A gorgeous glowing pregnant woman with gray eyes heads our way. *I wish I would've looked that good when I was pregnant, shit.*

"Birdie, Raleigh. Raleigh, Birdie. Raleigh works over at Method Marketing."

"Oh! Micky told me about you. You have made quite the impression on her. You'll have to come out for drinks with us sometime. Well, drinks for you, I'm due in August, so I'll be designated driver," Birdie explains.

"Congratulations! Do you know what you're having?" I ask.

"A boy, but we haven't thought about names yet."

"Boys are great. A little wild, but so much fun."

"Oh, do you have kids? I could use a mom friend—no offense, Mick." She pats Micky's arm.

"None taken, that's your mess. I'm happy to be the godmother."

"I have a four-year-old son, Arthur. I promised I would bring him home some of your desserts, Micky. Not sure how many will actually make it back though."

She chuckles. "I already put together a box for you, just give your name to the hostess before you leave tonight."

"That's so sweet, thank you!" Love this girl, she's so carefree and authentic. It's time I start living my life more like that.

Micky's gaze gets caught on something behind me and then she nods toward the entrance. "Looks like the boys are finally arriving."

"God, they are always late," Birdie mutters and then holds her arm in the air so he can spot us. "Lonan!"

Wait. Lonan? It can't be... please tell me it's not the same one. Sure, Ral, you can't swing a cat without hitting a Lonan *in this town.*

I spin around, and I swear all the blood drains from my face. It's him. Shit, I fucked this nice pregnant lady's husband way back when. Hopefully he doesn't remember me. He shouldn't, I look a lot different these days. Lonan looks totally smitten with his wife. I don't think I've ever seen him smile like that before. Good for them. Unfortunately, my outcome was nothing like theirs, no matter how much I wanted it to be.

My eyes dart behind Lonan, and there *he* is. *He's here.* All the air in my lungs is sucked out. I can't breathe.

Have you ever wanted to kill and kiss someone at the same time?

Run.

I turn back to the girls. I don't have time to find Rob. I'll text him on the way home and come up with an excuse for my exit.

"Girl, are you feeling okay?"

"Actually... um... I'm so sorry. All this talk about kids reminded me I was supposed to get back to the babysitter like twenty minutes ago. I gotta run." I clutch my purse and back up. I can't face him; I don't want to see him. Ever.

"Congrats on the soft open, this place is amazing! It was so good to meet you, Birdie."

The more I back up toward the door, the clearer his voice becomes. His laugh. I want to scream. Claw his eyes out. Something.

Micky's arm shoots up. "Don't forget your—" I'm already gone. *Sorry, girl. It's not you.*

I sneak past him in the dark vestibule, and as soon as my feet hit the bright sidewalk, I run. So much for making new friends and colleagues, he's taken that away too. There's nothing I want more than to leave hockey in my past. Something I used to love now only reminds me of him. That's not my lifestyle anymore. It ended that night. I should rue the day I met him. Fuck, I wish I could. But he gave me Arthur, and I'll never regret my son.

I thought I was past all this? Seeing him in the flesh has made my once buried bitterness unearth itself. The hurt feels as fresh as the day he sent those DMs.

"Let him go," I tell myself. "He's not worth it."

THIRTEEN

Barrett

Fucking overtime. Not just any overtime, we're on our third helping. We've been on and off the ice for over five hours. I'm ready to drop. This is the first time I've sincerely questioned if I'm too old for this shit. We barely had OT all season, but now, when it's the second round of playoffs and twenty-minute periods, we're on the third one. Ain't that how it goes?

Sully pants next to me as he comes off the ice. We're the oldest on the team. I'll be forty before I know it. Where did the time go?

Coach must know something I don't because he's still throwing me out there. *Push through the pain.* I'm exhausted and irritated. At this point, I don't even want to win to close out the round, I want to win so we can go the fuck home. We're up three to zero overall in the playoffs. If we can take this game, we'll need the break for recovery.

We're all dragging ass. Sully included, but he's still got that sparkle in his eye for the game. I never thought I'd see him retire before me, but here we are. This has been my life, what would I even do if I retired? I'm not ready to be a has been. I'd be bored out of my mind. That said, I don't know how much more my body can take. Granted, a lot is due to my current condition in OT3. O'Callahan was injured at the end of first period, so Bishop and I have been the main right wingers for most of the night. The shifts are much longer than usual. Despite my shitty attitude, I can't shake the feeling something great will happen tonight.

Dallas is playing better than usual, matching us point for point all night long. We have home advantage, so this should be over. And my gut tells me it almost is.

"Conway." Coach sends me out again.

Holding my fist up to Sully, he bumps it and hangs his head as I jump on the ice. The sweat dripping from my face is cooled as I skate out, creating a breeze. My eyes are shot, the puck seems faster than usual, but fortunately, we all are sharing the same deficit, so it evens out. A breakaway lets us crowd their goal. I keep a keen eye on my surroundings. My guys, theirs, the puck that seems to disappear and then pop up somewhere new.

Burke passes to Broderick, our center, but it's intercepted by Dallas. *Goddamn it.* Lonan pounds the ice and intercepts Dallas's pass by tipping the puck and keeping it in their end. *And grandpa is relieved he doesn't have to skate to the other side of the rink.*

I clear my head and regain focus. For the second time, we swarm the net. Broderick goes for it, their tender dives on his stomach to grab it but misses.

He. Fucking. Misses.

The now standing crowd in my peripheral explodes with noise. Holy shit. Might as well be an open net. Time stands still. Where is it? In the shuffle, my eye catches the black

between one of their defenseman's legs, and I zero in on the puck before he does, so muscle memory takes over and I steal and flip it in the net. My mind goes blank for a second wondering if that really happened or if I dreamed it.

89

When the horn sounds, I get my celly while rounding the back corner. Holy hell, we did it! *Get fucked, Dallas.*

Confetti falls from above, and we line up to do the playoff handshakes. We've got at least a week off until the next round begins, minus practices. Still, a week with zero traveling sounds divine. The adrenaline rush carries me off the ice and back into the locker room where I all but collapse on the bench. Ripping my jersey off, I lean back in my hockey breezers and close my eyes. I still feel like I need to catch my breath. Jones busts out the champagne, and after the loud pop, I crack open one eye to see white spray raining down from above. I laugh, the young pups are ready to tear it up tonight.

It's gonna be a long one.

The last thing I want to do is move my legs, but if I don't flush out this lactic acid build up, I won't be able to walk tomorrow. I jump on the bikes at a low resistance. I'm on my last legs. Literally.

After the warm-down, I strip, impatient and ready to wash the game off. I fucking smell. "Sully, Conway, Kucera!"

"Coach?" Sully answers.

"After showers, we need you upstairs."

"WAGs box?" Kucera asks.

Coach is chatting with Carlos, the org's event coordinator.

"You fuckin' wish." I slap Rhys on the chest with the back of my hand. He's so in love it's disgusting. How is this the same rookie from a year ago that refused to date or take home women?

He bites his lip. "Bet I get a nice surprise tonight…"

"Rook, we just closed out the round. We're all getting nice surprises tonight," I remind him with a smirk. Coach turns back to face us.

"Guest box, Superior on the east end. We need a quick

meet and greet. Shake a few hands, say thanks, and then you can go get your dicks sucked."

A blowjob does sound pretty great. I'll take a second release.

"What's it for?" I suspect a charity; I don't mind doing it if it's for a good cause.

"Method Marketing," Carlos, the event coordinator, shouts across the room. "They're looking at becoming a sponsor. We're trying to woo them. They're running next season's ad campaign. There's a banquet tonight for some of the directors and execs, we need a quick show-your-face snap-a-few-pictures time as a way to show our appreciation." *Thanks for what? Paying them?*

"Shouldn't they be trying to woo *us*?" Jonesy asks. *Smartest thing he's said all damn day.*

"It's a partnership. We're essentially bartering services to try them out. Look, we need this. Just give them ten minutes. Tops. We'll send in someone to pull you if it goes longer than fifteen."

I groan. I'm exhausted. The last thing I want to do is head up to the guest box and do some stupid autograph ass-kissing meet and greet with a bunch of boring executives, their snobby wives, and shithead kids. I hate pandering to these money-grubbing corporations. It's bad enough that hockey itself is so expensive and privileged that it creates a classist hierarchy among players—now we have to deal with the corporate horse-and-pony show too?

This is something I'm working on changing with Camp Conway, but when I'm forced to do this shit, it makes me feel even more defeated.

But asses in seats, right? I get it.

FOURTEEN

Barrett

This blows.

Sully, Kucera, and I head up to the club box in our post-game suits, Carlos leading the way. We would rather be anywhere else. We're dog-tired and the only energy left in us is reserved for throwing back a couple beers at Top Shelf. I should quit griping; I can spare ten minutes.

As soon as we enter through the double doors, Carlos grabs everyone's attention and thanks them for...honestly, I'm not listening. He opens a duffle bag full of Lakes swag to hand out to the directors and their families. There are tables set up throughout the massive box suite that overlooks the ice. Below, fans are still clearing out.

We make our way around the room, shaking hands, taking selfies, and signing gear while getting congratulations and slaps on the back for the overtime win.

While making small talk, I hear a familiar voice behind me.

"Arthur, can you please get your jacket? We need to leave now."

I'm in conversation with an attendee and trying to focus on what they're saying, but all I hear is that voice behind me.

My ears must be messing with me. It sounds like Raleigh.

It must be the exhaustion of the game. My mind has played tricks on me like this a million times before, and it's never her. But then I pick up on the barely there southern twang. I excuse myself and frantically scan the room for platinum blonde hair. A woman crouched on the floor gathers a handful of toy cars, but she's much curvier than Raleigh, and her hair is darker, *but that voice.*

I cross the couple of tables in front of her to get a better look. I blink a few times. Fuck me. *It's her!*

Adrenaline courses through my veins and a smile explodes on my face.

The woman I haven't been able to get out of my head for half a decade is right in front of me. And goddamn, she's even more gorgeous than I remember. My throat feels thick, and my feet move without even thinking.

She looks up at me with those light-brown eyes, and it takes my breath away.

"Raleigh?"

"Don't worry, we're leaving." I flinch. *Ouch. Nice to see you too?*

"We?"

A young boy runs up to her. "Got my coat, Mom!" He throws it in her arms. The smile on my face drops.

Shit.

I can't believe some other asshole got to her first. It's a punch to the gut, and I immediately despise whoever this kid's dad is. She should have been mine. *What the hell, Raleigh?!*

I have so many questions. The first one on my list is why she snuck out that night. No phone number, no email, nothing. It was bullshit.

She takes the jacket from him and slips each of his arms into the small coat. "Thank you, baby. Ready to go home?"

My eyes roam over her body. I can't help it, she's like straight out of my fantasy. Her being someone else's wife will not stop me from checking her out. While I admire this new sinful body of hers, my gaze snags on her hand, it's trembling.

And there's no ring.

My shoulders loosen. That's all I needed to see. This isn't game over, not by a long shot. But it's not gonna be easy. It's been over five years and she has a child—*Raleigh's a mom.*

She won't give me the time of day, but I'm not above getting to know her son to get to her. I'm going to eventually. I keep my eyes on her while I crouch down, then turn my gaze to the curious little boy and introduce myself. "Hi! I'm

Barrett. What's your name?"

They freeze, and Raleigh stands, as if she's trying to make herself bigger. He curls into Raleigh's side, clutching a stuffed koala, and she protectively tucks him behind her. His head pokes out and he studies my face. She looks like she can't decide whether to cry or kill me, but I don't know why.

Her son steps out from behind her and gives his name. "Arthur."

"It's nice to meet you, Arthur. I like your koala." He holds it out for me to see. "Did you know koala's fingerprints are almost the same as humans?"

My smile curls up on one side. "I didn't, that's really cool."

"Yeah ... Police in Australia have to make extra sure that

they don't confuse a koala bear and a bad guy'ses fingerprints when there's been a crime."

I beam at his big expressive eyes as he explains the fingerprint thing.

"Did you know koala bears are not actually bears but marsupials? They have a pouch like kangaroos," I say, trying to get on his level.

"I already know that!" He smiles and shows off an adorable dimple. His eyes sparkle in the same way Raleigh's do.

I laugh. "Well, that was my only koala fact. Guess I'll have to learn some new ones for next time." I glance up at his mom. *There will be a next time.*

My focus returns to her son. We tilt our heads at the same time and regard each other for a moment. There's something familiar about him, but I can't quite... My head straightens while I attempt to stay calm and collected. *There's no way...*

Clearing my throat, I ask, "How old are you, Arthur?"

"Four and three-quarters."

I gulp. What month did we sleep together? I'd just been named alternate captain, so... My mind calculates his age and our night together, then blood drains from my face. *It can't be.* I stand, but she won't make eye contact.

"Raleigh, look at me," I say sternly.

"Come on, baby. Say goodbye, it's time to go." She combs her fingers through her hair.

"Ral—"

"Leaving already?" a deep voice asks, stepping alongside her.

Who the fuck is this guy? My hands ball into fists.

The unease on her face transforms into a big fake smile, and she brings her hands to her sides.

"Yeah, it's way past his bedtime. He wanted to stay for the confetti drop, but we've gotta get going. Sorry we couldn't stay longer."

He moves his hand from her lower back to adjust the collar on her coat. When he's finished, he affectionately slides his hand down her arm. I want to lunge at him, but I stand here glaring, unable to take my eyes off the other man touching her. Years may have passed, but my thoughts of her never disappeared.

I tried searching for her on and off for years. I couldn't get this woman off my mind...still haven't. God, she's so different. Not only the weird, cagey attitude. She looks different too. Still drop-dead gorgeous, but more mature now. And much thicker and sexier than I remember. It suits her. *It really fucking suits her.*

I want to know what she's been up to, where she's been all this time, why the hell she walked out on me, but first I need to know more about her son. And who is this other guy? Right on cue, the asshole, who can't seem to keep his hands off her, leans down and shakes the young boy's hand. "Good seeing you again, Arthur. Be good for your mom."

Could I be mistaken, is this the child's father? Are they separated? I almost lose it when he leans forward and kisses her cheek, whispering something in her ear. Her back stiffens and she nods with a tight smile. She pulls back while I step forward, ready to knock his teeth out.

"I will!" Arthur shouts. I relax at the little voice. My body is pumping with adrenaline and testosterone, nothing would please me more than sending my knuckles through this guy's face, but her son is here. Fuck, *who is the father of this kid?*

My head is spinning.

"Raleigh, do you have a second?" I ask.

"No, I don't." She grasps the boy's small hand and walks away from me.

What the actual fuck? I don't even know what to say. I should chase after her, but I'm too stunned to move. I stare as she disappears into the hallway outside the metal doors, and when I turn around, a hand is thrust in front of me.

"Rob Waters, Chief Operations Officer at Method Marketing."

I shake it firmly. "Barrett Conway." I motion to the door Raleigh and Arthur ran out of.

"That your girlfriend back there?"

I can tell this guy's had a few drinks. And the fact he gave me his job title tells me he's got a big ego.

"Ha! I'm working on it. She's a catch. Sweet, has a good kid, she's smart...sexy." *My jaw clicks.* "I could do a lot for a woman in her position. I don't know what her problem is. Usually they're the ones chasing after us, right?" He raises his glass like a cheap toast.

Oh no, motherfucker. Don't lump me in with you.

I already know Raleigh is way too good for him. She's probably too good for me, but that won't hold me back. I nod and smirk, trying to play along. "So, how do you know her, then?" I press.

"She's my executive assistant." *Is this guy for real?*

At least I know how to find her this time. I offer a fake chuckle. "That's not an HR nightmare for you?"

He takes a sip from the highball glass of amber liquor.

"Not when you sign HR's paychecks." His grin is smarmy.

"There's benefits to being C-level, right?" *What, abuse of power?*

I clink my glass to his and bait him to see how he responds. "Bet she looks good bent over in those tight skirts when she's running around the office getting your coffee and filing memos."

He smiles and gives a slight shake of his head before taking another sip. "You have no fucking idea."

It would be so easy to coldcock him. Instead, I grit my teeth and say "It was nice to meet you" and walk away to search for Sully. He's my go-to whenever I need advice. We've played together for over a decade and know each other better than we know ourselves. He understands, more than anyone, how bad I've been searching for this girl. I interrupt his conversation with someone else and excuse us, leading him to the corner of the room.

"Come on, man. We're supposed to be mingling and kissing ass, not—"

"She was here! Raleigh. I saw her."

"No shit? Where?" His head swivels around.

"She took off as soon as she saw me." Tonight, she

certainly lived up to the meaning of *her* name. She bolted like a deer in a meadow. "She's got a kid."

"Oof." He grimaces. "That sucks, man. I'm sorry."

I shake my head. "There's no ring on her finger. But—" I lower my voice. "I think he might be mine. I mean, he could be. Pretty sure the time frame matches up, he's the right age. Shit, he even kinda looks like me! I'm freaking the fuck out, man."

His eyebrows shoot up. "What? That's a stretch. There's no way. You would have known. She would have told you, right?"

"I mean, I'd have thought, but I also thought she would have left her number that night. I dunno, I can't shake it. Something is telling me he's mine."

Sully takes a sip of his beer, and I palm the back of my neck as a thought crosses my mind: *is he mine or do I want him to be?*

He pulls the drink from his lips. "Holy shit. You're serious. What if he's not yours?" *Ignoring that.*

"Where's Carlos?" I ask, scrubbing a hand down my face.

He looks around the room and points to the corner of the bar.

"Conway..." That's a big question I'm not prepared to answer. Thankfully, he doesn't force me to. "Don't do anything crazy."

I nod and beeline it for the event coordinator.

When I get to him, he rolls his eyes at me. "Seriously? It's barely been five minutes, you promised—"

"I need the guest list from tonight."

"What? Why?"

The veins in my neck are popping out, I want to shake him.

"Carlos. I will spend the next hour here if you don't ask any questions and get me that fucking list."

"Done. I'll email it to you when I get back to my office."

"No. *Now.*"

He furrows his brows and pulls his phone from his back pocket. "*Okay...* I'll do it now."

I pull out my phone and wait for it to come through. As soon as it does, I walk away with eyes on the screen. I scan Carlos's email. There she is.

"Thanks."

Raleigh Dunham, Executive Assistant. (Chicken, +1 child meal)

Did I meet my son tonight? I break into a sweat. I might actually throw up. If that's my child...

The thought makes me livid. It seems she's done a great

job raising him, but if he's mine, then I should have known. *I should be in his life.*

He's a cute kid. He's smart. Of course he's smart, Raleigh's smart. *Even her slimy boss knows that.* Why did she fly out of here so fast? She looked disgusted with me. If anything, I should be pissed at her! She's the one that snuck out in the middle of night with no way to contact her. And may even be holding secrets from me. Big ones. If Arthur is mine and she tries to cover it up, I'll have no choice but to fight for partial custody.

She can't keep him from me, and I refuse to be a deadbeat dad. I've seen enough of that through Camp Conway, I won't be one of them. I search the email and find her work email address and tap out a message.

I have a thousand questions, and she owes me serious fucking answers.

FIFTEEN

Raleigh

hen I log into my work computer Monday morning, wedged between a million other work emails, is one with a sender that catches my eye.

Barrett Conway.

I skim through the message. This ballsy motherfucker... *Now* he wants to talk? Well, fuck that. And fuck him too. His last words to me were "*Congratulations on your bastard.*"

He's ruthless and cruel. And I'll never let someone like that near my son. I hope he doesn't see the resemblance to Arthur I do. When they're side by side, it's clear as day.

To: Raleigh.Dunham@methodmarketing.com
From: BConway@lakeshockey.com CC:
Subject: Long time

It's been a while, Ral. I've spent a lot of time trying to find you and even more time thinking about you. I believe we have some things to discuss. Give me a call. 612-555-4590 You look great, by the way.
-Barrett

"Go to hell," I mutter, checking the box next to his email.
Mark as spam.

Report phishing.
Block sender.
Delete.
Delete from trash.

SIXTEEN

Barrett

S he's ignoring me. I've sent half a dozen emails with read receipts. She read the first one. The rest have been unopened, which makes me think she put me on a block list. She wants to play games? I'll lace up my fucking skates.

She and I have unfinished business. After searching for five years, there's no way in hell I'm leaving without a fight. I'll fight her for another five with a smile on my face.

I considered emailing her boss, but it occurs to me she probably manages his inbox too.

> Hey. I need you to send an email to Rob Waters at Method Marketing. Set up a meeting this week to discuss the summer hockey camp—don't mention my name. Put something together for a possible partnership or sponsor thing. It's has to be with Rob, no one else.

SULLY

You think this is a good idea?

> I'm calling in my favor.

SULLY

K. I take it you're going to want to join in
the meeting.

Oh, I'll be there.

SULLY

Just be careful, man. It's been a long time.
A lot's changed.

Yeah... like I might be a dad.

SEVENTEEN

Barrett

"All right, everybody, line up!" I shout. "We're going to do some stick-handling exercises."

Today I'm a guest coach for one of the Title I school hockey teams in the metro. I like coaching kids. Which is why I started Camp Conway. Families and local teams can apply, we supply gear, one-on-one lessons, coaching, and discounted or free ice time at their local arenas.

Everyone should have access to hockey, but it's an expensive sport. When it costs over 2500 dollars annually—on the low end—it's no wonder the only kids playing are from the middle to upper-class families. Camp Conway helps to bridge the gap. There's so much athletic talent that goes unseen because of the economic imbalance. Think what the NHL might look like if money wasn't an issue. It'd be a lot more fucking colorful, I'll tell you that much.

Sometimes I question whether coaching was always my calling. I look forward to it, sometimes even more than games. Playing for the Lakes is the dream of every rink rat growing up in Minnesota, and I love it. But shit, I'm getting older, and sometimes, fostering the abilities of new athletes seems like better use of my time. I push away the thought, we're coming into the final round of playoffs, this could be the pinnacle of my career, it's time to stay focused.

"We're going to start with horizontal figure eights and move into triangle puck swaps!"

I have each kid gather up three pucks, two of those will be used as markers on the ice. Then I instruct them how to practice stick handling by doing figure eights around each of the other pucks.

"Remember, with accuracy, comes speed. Once you feel comfortable with staying in control of your eights, then you can worry about getting faster."

"Coach Conway, how fast can you do eights?"

I smile and line up my pucks, swiftly weaving between the two. The kids laugh and cheer. "Keep practicing and you'll be faster than me. My buddy Sully is the king of these."

They skate off into their areas and practice. I skate around and give pointers here and there.

"Nice job, Collins."

"Thanks, Coach."

"Jer, I want you to work on your reaction time, get your stick ahead of the puck faster when you're capturing. Let me see you do it again . . ."

He just needs to turn his wrist a little quicker.

"Watch my wrist, I've got a grip, but my elbow is loose." I show him how to twist his stick faster. "Now you try it."

He mirrors my movement, and the smile that grows on his face feels as good as my last hat trick.

"That was perfect! See how much faster you can gain control? Keep at it. Might feel a little awkward now, but keep practicing, and before long, you won't have to even think about it."

"Thanks, Coach. Hey . . . um . . . do you have any spots left this summer? I really wanna go, but my mom said she has to work and wouldn't be able to drop me off."

"Do you have another parent that could drop off?"

"My dad isn't—" *He doesn't need to say anymore. I understand.*

"You live in town here?"

"No, I'm out in the county."

"Where's your mom tonight?"

He points her out in the stands, and she waves.

"Have your mom meet me after practice and we'll figure something out. That shouldn't be a problem." I slap his shoulder pad.

"Thanks, Coach!"

We have a few players who need help with transit. It should be easy to work out a minor transportation problem if getting to the bus is an issue. A lot of the kids at Camp Conway come from single-parent homes. Mostly women. I can't even imagine the amount of pressure those moms are under to work full-time, maintain a home, put food on the table, raise kids, and on top of all that, get their kids involved in extracurricular activities. How the hell do they do it?

Raleigh is one of those moms. At least I think she is. Her shithead boss sure didn't seem deterred. She hasn't given me the time of day to find out if there's a man in the picture. A sick thought passes through my brain: *I hope she doesn't have a partner to help her.* It's so fucked up. I would never want her to struggle raising a child alone, but she's the only woman I've been able to think about for years. I want them both. And if that kid *is* mine, then there sure as hell better not be any other man doing my job.

After coaching, I kick my feet up on the sofa in my office and call home.

"Hey, Mom," I say over the phone.

"Hey, sweetheart, it's nice to hear from you. What are you up to today?" She's always happy to hear from me or my brother.

"Just going through some old stuff. Hey, do you have any of my baby pictures?"

She laughs. "Hundreds. Why?"

Grabbing a puck off the coffee table in front of me, I toss it in the air.

"Could you send some over? Like from when I was four or five?"

"What do you need them for?"

I catch the puck in my hand while I formulate a response. "Um... the team wants them for some social media thing."

"I see. Well, don't be surprised if they start getting letters from women wanting to know who that cute little kid is. Maybe it will help your love life."

"Nobody mails letters anymore, Mom."

"Whatever, emails and MDs."

"DMs," I correct with a chuckle and resume tossing the puck in the air.

"You know what I mean. Anyway, your uncle digitized all your photos and put them inside the cloud. I'll email you the link and password and you can look through them all."

"That's perfect, thank you."

"You bet, kiddo. Are you coming up next week? Maybe with a girl?"

"Holy shit, you don't even *try* to hide it anymore."

"I'm sorry! But you're almost forty, if you want to get settled, you need to hurry up."

I pause for a moment and consider keeping it a secret, but I can't keep my excitement buried anymore. "Do you remember me talking to you about a girl named Raleigh?"

"Of course, you've mentioned her a few times. Why?"

I bite my lip. "I ran into her the other day." I leave out that she has a son and he looks like me. She'd probably get so excited she'd have a coronary.

"Invite her!"

"Yeah, Mom. I haven't seen her in years, but the first thing I'll do is invite her to hang out with my family."

"That sounds like a great plan. I don't see any problem with it."

Of course she doesn't. I laugh. "Why don't *you* bring a date? It's time you get out there again. In fact, after you send me the info for the photo album, you should sign up for one of those online dating things."

She scoffs. "I will when you do."

I shake my head. "Yeah, okay. I'll be there next week for dinner. Is Paul going?"

"Yes, and he's bringing Daphne."

I roll my eyes. Ever since my brother got a girlfriend, she's been trying to use it to convince me to do the same. "Okay, well I gotta get going, but I'll see you next week."

"Okay, take care of yourself. Check your email!"

"I will, thanks. Love you, Mom."

Leaving the couch, I plop down at my desk and start up my laptop. While I wait for it to load, I grab a blue sports drink from the mini fridge underneath and untwist the cap with a crack and take a sip. My eyes pan to the closet Raleigh hid in all those years ago—the night Arthur was conceived.

I check my email, and as promised, she sent the info. After logging into the photo album, I search through the folders. *Damn, Uncle Ernie is one organized son of a bitch.*

Clicking on the year I turned five, I lean back in my chair while all the photos load on the screen. Scrolling through, it doesn't take long to find photos of me when I was roughly Arthur's age.

Chills break out over my entire body when I enlarge three

or four thumbnails. I laugh without humor and take another sip, shaking my head. That kid's mine. There's no way he's not. He's got my same face shape, the same white-blonde hair I had when I was younger, same exact dimple. *I'm going to be sick.*

"Jesus Christ, Raleigh. What the fuck were you thinking not telling me?" I mutter. "You really think I wouldn't find out?"

Now I'm pissed. How could she keep this from me? How could she keep this from *him*? And she's got the gall to ignore my emails? She better get ready for a hailstorm of messages. I pull up every social media site I can think of, but there's no trace of her. Except for LinkedIn. I dig through to find any other details about her life. She's kept it pretty private... Oh look, Rob Waters left her a shining recommendation back when she was a receptionist. I hate that asshole. I hate the way he looks at her. I hate the way he talks about her. And I hate that he knows my son better than I do. *Arthur.*

Hmm... What does the woman obsessed with names choose for her own child?

I type '*Arthur name meaning*' in the search bar and click enter.

The hair on the back of my neck stands on end. I push off my desk and chuck the plastic bottle across the room as hard as I can.

"Fuck!"

EIGHTEEN
Raleigh

"Raleigh, what conference room are we in?" Rob asks. I double-check my calendar. "Minnetonka."

"Great. Wanna walk?"

"Sure, just need to get this file saved and... done! Ready?"

"Yup. Can I buy you a coffee on the way down?"

Gathering my laptop and phone, I raise the to-go paper cup in my other hand. "All set."

"You never let me spoil you."

"You pay me enough to buy my own coffee." I smile. I'm compensated well for my work, my salary is twice what most executive assistants make. I also don't want to give Rob the wrong impression. He already toes the line as it is.

"I want to make sure you're comfortable here."

I laugh. "I've been here for over five years. I'd say I'm comfortable."

We walk to the elevators, and he presses the down button while we wait. "So, what's today's meeting about?" he asks.

"Lakes Hockey wants to discuss partnering on one of their player charities. Carlos, who helped with the banquet, will be there, he said he's got a few guests. Kurt from

Sales is already meeting them at the entrance, I said we could swing by and escort them to the conference room."

When the doors to the elevator open, we step inside and Rob presses the lobby button. "We want to secure this deal with them, so clearly, rubbing shoulders the other night worked in our favor. What's the charity?" he asks.

Or they're trying to let us down easy by giving us a pity project.

"They didn't say. This is simply an introductory meeting for us to get more information. I'm told they have a presentation." I pull out my phone. "Do you know what you want for lunch today? That food truck you like, Hotbox, is a couple blocks over this week. I can run down and grab something."

"You sure know what I like. Hotbox sounds great. I might join you."

"Oh, I don't mind picking it up so you can get some work done."

"Raleigh, I want to," he says, like he's doing me a favor by tagging along. "Besides, the weather is finally getting nice."

We step off the elevator and head across the campus, past the coffee kiosk, and stop at the reception area to pick up Carlos and whatever Lakes staff are joining him. I freeze when the automatic doors split and Sully and Barrett are sitting on one of the sofas. He's hunched over, arms braced on his knees, looking at the floor. Lee Sullivan nudges his forearm, and his head snaps up.

Son of a bitch. I should've known.

It's fine. *This is fine.* I can remain professional.

"Good morning!" I say with a big smile only aimed at Carlos. "What a nice surprise. I thought it was just going to be you and Lakes staff."

"We *are* Lakes staff," Barrett interjects.

My eyes dart to him for a split second and I nod. I want to ignore him but with his size, it's impossible. No wonder

Arthur's always been in the ninety-nine percentile for height. His size isn't the only thing making it hard to look away. Because Barrett in a blue suit? My God. It's not fair that he's still so handsome. He got hotter. Meanwhile, I'm rocking my fluffy summer body.

"That's true." I introduce myself, "I'm Raleigh Dunham." As if I haven't had his dick inside me. "This is Rob Waters, he's the Chief of Operations. And you've already met Kurt, our sales executive."

"Nice to see you again, Raleigh...Rob." Barrett's eyes haven't left my face once. He holds his hand out for me to shake, but I shrug and hold up my things.

"I'd shake your hand, but I have my hands full." I give a fake smile.

"You must, especially having a four-year-old and all."

I want to throw this coffee in his face. How dare he make comments like that. This is such a bullshit meeting. I've left him alone like he asked, so why's he so hellbent on trying to talk to me again? If he's trying to come back into our lives to get close to my son, he better be prepared for all twelve rounds.

Rob thrusts his hand out to take Barrett's hanging one. "Hell of a game the other day. Our team loved the box and swag, that was a nice touch. Though, I think your overtime goal was the highlight of the night for them." I try to take a deep breath, but it doesn't take long before I'm back in his eyeline.

"Wish I could say the same." His gaze could be felt from a mile away. It still affects me, *but what's that thing they say about love and hate?*

When we're done with the stupid, needless introductions, I lead the way to the conference room. "Can I get coffee for anyone?"

"No, we're good, Raleigh. Thanks," Sullivan answers. I wonder how much he knows about Barrett and me.

"Great."

I let Rob do all the schmoozing on the way to the room. When we get there, I use my back to hold the door open, then nod to the long table in the room. "Choose a seat wherever you're comfortable." I hope the smile on my face doesn't appear as stiff as it feels.

When Barrett ducks under the frame, he holds the door open over my head. "Go sit down, Raleigh."

I walk to a chair without acknowledging his courtesy.

Rob sits at the head of the table, facing the projector screen. I sit on the side a couple seats down. Sullivan sits across from me with Carol, Peter, and Carlos. I expect Barrett to follow, but no, he sits on my side of the table. Twelve other chairs to pick from and he chooses the one right next to mine.

His cologne brings me right back to that night, feeling dejected and heartsick. My throat aches as my emotions spiral. Despite having an incredible night together, it led to one of the darkest years of my life. It shouldn't bother me anymore, it was so long ago. I've left it all behind me and I'm no longer a naive twenty-two-year-old. I swallow, and open my laptop.

"I emailed you multiple times, though only one read receipt," he whispers.

"Interesting. Maybe they went into my spam folder," I mumble.

I open my Notes app and begin taking minutes. As long as I keep typing, nobody will see how much my hands are shaking.

They actually have a legit presentation. This ought to be entertaining. It's a relief I don't need to chime in much. I do everything I can to ignore the man next to me, but every single time he moves or speaks, it derails my thoughts. Typing up his dictated words is painful, and it's impossible to retain anything he's saying.

I hate hearing him speak. I hate his ideas. I hate his voice. He seems unaffected. It wasn't his world that got flipped upside down. It was mine.

After what feels like forever, the meeting wraps up and I hustle to gather my things.

"Oh, I wanted to ask, would you mind if Sully and I got a tour of the campus? It's quite impressive," Barrett asks.

"Why, thank you." Rob checks his watch and looks at me.

I shake my head. "We've got meetings all afternoon, unfortunately. Maybe another time."

"Raleigh could give the tour," Kurt suggests. *Goddamn it, Kurt. Read the room.*

I look at Rob, hoping he'll save me. He's hesitant but then says. "I can have Sondra cover your updates. Why don't you give the tour and then we can head out for lunch together."

"Oh, um, I really don't—"

"She'd be happy to!" Kurt says, giving me a stare. Fucking Sales, they'll kiss anyone's ass. *He* should be the one giving the tour, not me.

"Of course I would." I glower at him, pissed that I'm being volun*told* to do something I don't want to. "Let me drop off my things at my desk and I can meet you back here in five."

I can't believe this is happening. I hurry back to my desk and set down my laptop and toss my coffee in the trash. Coffee is the last thing I need. I've already got the shakes from nerves and anger and probably some weird post-traumatic stress response.

Before going back down, I step into the bathroom and touch up my makeup. Every ounce of youthfulness I had was sucked out of my tits after Arthur was born, and my eyes look tired. I haven't been sleeping well since seeing him at Sugar and Ice. I want him to know I'm every bit the woman I was before. Just because there's a few more pounds these days, he hasn't broken me.

I straighten my outfit in the elevator and pluck a piece of fuzz off my pencil skirt. *It's only a tour.* You've done these a hundred times.

When I head back to the conference room, only Sully and Barrett are left, and they seem deep in conversation, but I interrupt their hushed voices.

"Ready?"

"Yes." They follow me out of the room, and I transform into *tour-guide Raleigh.*

"You've already seen the reception area." I gesture to the right and continue walking. "I can show you the atrium and then we can walk by some of our top campaigns near the waterwall."

I turn around to only Barrett is left. In the background behind him, it's easy to spot the equally tall Lee Sullivan as he exits through the reception area.

"Where'd he go?"

"Looks like this is going to be a private tour."

NINETEEN
Barrett

She narrows her eyes at me. "This is unnecessary." It's intended as a warning, but everything that comes out of her sounds sweet.

I glance over her shoulder and gesture with a nod. "Let's go."

It's hard to resist dropping my gaze to her ass when she turns around. Her piece of shit boss was already checking her out the whole way to the conference room. I'm every bit as guilty, but considering we may share a child, I'm entitled to a little leering. Raleigh with curves is something else. God, she makes me want to fall to my fucking knees. Motherhood looks good on her. She's even more stunning than I remember.

"Are we going to—"

"This is the atrium; it features a sixty-square-foot living wall. It's made up of pothos, philodendron, dracaena, and anthurium plants. There are also a few ferns hiding in there. This was part of the architect's vision when the campus was built." She points to the corner. "It signifies our growth and constant evolution."

She knows a lot about the building, but all I care about is if Arthur is mine.

"Who—"

"Whatever question you're about to ask, it better be regarding the tour."

"—is the architect?"

"John Lange."

We stare at each other in silence. I puff out a breath of air, annoyed but amused at her quick reply. She turns on her heel, and I follow down a quiet hallway until I spot a closed-off room behind a partition wall. Then I grab her elbow, pull her inside the hidden chamber, and shut the door—halting the bullshit tour.

Once I flip the light switch, I notice how small the space is. A small table with four chairs takes up most of the room with a whiteboard and projector mounted to the far wall. It's private and quiet with no windows. Perfect.

"You can't—"

"Is he mine?"

She shoves my hand off her elbow, and I step closer. Again, she tries to distance herself but backs into the table. Her hands drop to her sides, and she lifts her chin in defiance. She's trapped, *just how she likes.*

"What are you talking about?"

I shake my head and smile. "Now's not the time to be cute. Arthur—Is. He. Mine?"

Craning her neck to make eye contact, those warm-brown eyes appear cold and callous... There's fear behind them, but she's trying to hide any sign of weakness.

"Is he?" I ask again.

Her eyes narrow. "No, he's *mine!*"

"Who's his father?"

"Are you serious?" She shoves at me again, but I'm too big for her to budge.

"You need to tell me if he's my son."

She gawks at me and then narrows her eyes. "I don't owe

117

you shit. You weren't the only guy I slept with. I'm a puck slut, remember?"

My nostrils flare. The disparaging term irritates me.

"Yeah? The condom break with any of them?" I grit out.

She's silent. *Come on, sweetheart. I'll wait.*

"What do you want from me?" *What do I want?* I want answers!

"When's his birthday?"

More silence. It's not doing her any favors. I almost laugh. Those thick pursed lips are telling me everything I need to know.

"Answer me, Raleigh."

"May twentieth."

That's within the window I already calculated. "Holy fuck." I run my hands through my hair and spin in a circle before standing in front of her again, this time begging. "You have to let me see him."

She grabs me, digging her claws into my biceps. There's a fire in her eyes like I've never seen before. She pushes me into the door and shoves her pointed finger into my chest. *Shit, she's strong.* If I knew she wasn't hurting inside, this would be such a turn-on.

"First of all, fuck you for even having the *audacity* to request something like that after everything you put me through. Am I even allowed to be this close to you? And where's your girlfriend?"

I flinch and screw up my face.

"What the hell are you talking about?" Her chest is almost touching mine. She steps back, so I use the opportunity to advance. "I have been looking for you for years—"

"That's a bold-faced lie! I contacted you after I found out I was pregnant, and what did you say?"

I search her eyes, there's zero memory of this. I would have fucking remembered someone telling me they were pregnant.

"I have no idea! Because you never told me!"

"You called me a liar, you insulted me, called me a whore, and threatened me with a restraining order. And, just so you know, I never wanted money. All I wanted was for you to know he existed. This is *your* loss, not mine. *You* missed out —"

"A restraining order?!" *Why the hell would I do that?* Any Lakes player could back me up on this. They know I never got over her. She's known as *Runaway Raleigh* by the team, they constantly give me shit about her being my one who got away.

This time I'm the one stabbing my chest with my index finger. "I wanted to see you again. Why didn't you leave your number, huh? This could have all been solved if you hadn't slipped out in the middle of the night!"

"I did! I left it with your agent, your public relations team, your social media staff, I reached out to every avenue I could think of. I'll never forget the things you told me, your messages said plenty about the type of person you are."

"I never got any messages. I swear to God, Ral. Give me names. I don't know what happened back then, but whatever you think happened, you're wrong. And I'm not leaving today without your number."

She scoffs. "Why do you even care? Why now? You have some amends you need to make for your own self-enlightenment? Well, fuck if I'm going to help you achieve that. You can rot for all I care."

Holy shit. Who is this person?

I give a suspended blink and shake off her verbal slap in the face. "I haven't been able to get you out of my head since that night."

"Yeah, me neither," she spits. "Nobody *fucks* me like you do."

Ouch.

I lift my chin and look down at her through hooded lids. "What's that supposed to mean?"

"You know what it means. I'll never trust a word you say. A broken heart and a battered reputation are a small price to pay when you're not the one footing the bill."

"I broke your heart?"

A serious miscommunication went down. We're not on the same page. We're not even in the same goddamn book.

"Forget what you did to me, you broke *his* heart!"

"Please." I fold my hands together. "Please, let me meet him again. You have no idea how hard the last week has been on me."

She scowls. "Oh, have the last few days been hard for you? Try the last few years."

"Raleigh, I swear I didn't know. Let me fix it!"

"You can't fix it! You can never make up for those years. You did this to yourself. You don't get to try and swoop in when it's convenient for you. That's not how children work." My mouth is gaping. I don't know what to say.

"You're right. Fuck, you're absolutely right. I am *sorry* for whatever hell you've been through over the years. I can't imagine. But I can't let you go again—"

"You don't get to say that!"

"Okay, okay." I raise my eyebrows and hold up my hands. "Listen, I'll follow whatever rules you want. Just don't shut me out. What do I need to do?"

"Nothing. Just keep living your life and stay out of ours."

Not happening. It feels like I'm in some confusing dream. She's talking nonsense. There's been a huge error, but I can't figure out where it began.

"I can't do that. Give me your number."

She shakes her head and looks off to the side. "The irony."

"I'm not the only one to blame here. Let's not forget, you

120

walked away from me! And from now on, I need direct communication with you—because whether you want to admit it or not, that's my son."

"He will *never* be yours. There's no paternity test."

"Fuck a paternity test, all I needed to do was look at him! You already gave me his birthdate. Do you really think you can keep me away from him, Ral?"

The transformation she makes after that statement is downright frightening. Her eyes widen, and somehow, that small five-foot-whatever form is suddenly full of menacing intimidation. She nearly growls as she says, "Are you threatening me for custody? You will not take my son away from me. That boy is my world, and I am an excellent mother. I've been the sole—"

"Jesus Christ!" She's irate, tears are welling in her eyes, and I've turned her into this. "I would never *take* him from you. All I'm asking for is a chance to know him."

What have I done? I've broken this woman and have missed out on years I'll never get back. I can't figure out what the hell happened, but I'm not wasting any time finding out. I check my watch. Shit, I'm supposed to be lacing up my skates now.

"I want to continue this conversation, but I've got a game tonight and need to get to the arena. Give me your phone."

She stares at me with distrust, and I speak as calmly as I can. "I'm not going to steal custody from you, Raleigh. I can see you're an excellent mother, you're doing an amazing job."

I don't know what makes her do it, but she unlocks her phone and holds it out to me. A photo of Arthur is the wallpaper behind her apps. He's curled up in a blanket with that same stuffed koala bear he had at the arena.

After adding my phone number into her phone, I text myself to make sure I have hers. Before handing it back to her, I skim her other text conversations to see if there's any that seem to be a romantic interest. No heart emojis on any of the contact names is a good sign.

"Is there a boyfriend I should know about?"

She crosses her arms over her chest. "I don't see how that's any of your business."

"It is if he's around my son."

She shakes her head and presses a finger into her sternum. "I've told you, he's *my* son. I've been raising him. He only has one parent, and I'm very careful about who I let around him."

I give her phone back.

"Good, then you won't mind making sure Rob doesn't go near him." She tucks the device into her hand. "You may hate me now, but I'll wear you down. I'm going to take you out again and we're going to do this right."

"I don't date hockey players anymore."

"Do you fuck them?"

"Go to hell."

I ignore her answer. We'll get there eventually. I'm not done with her.

"I'm going to call you every day. I want you to answer. If you block my number, I will come back here and find you." She looks away from me with a trembling lip, and I tilt her chin up to look at me. "Never run from a bear." Her lips part. "I never ran. You did."

Our game tonight is heated. All I can think about is Raleigh and Arthur. I'm seeing red. My son has gone his whole life without a father. I haven't been there.

I didn't know.

How could something like this happen?

And what's with the restraining order she mentioned?

When I hit the ice, I check Colorado's forward into the boards and bomb across the blue line. Sully passes to me, then I fake a return and pull the puck back to deke out their winger. Changing directions, I get the opening I need and shoot the puck into the net. The crowd goes nuts, but all I can think about is her. She and Arthur should be in the WAGs box tonight with Birdie and Micky and the other wives.

"Atta boy, bud! You're on fire tonight!" Burke says.

I nod and head to the bench. I'm envious of Lonan. Sure, he went through his own time of being separated from Birdie, and it was longer than five years, but he has her now. *Does he even realize how lucky he is?* His wife is pregnant and he's here to experience it. He doesn't have to face the pain of realizing he's abandoned his family. He got to find out with her when she took the test, got to watch her belly grow, he gets all the doctor's appointments and ultrasounds. He'll be there for the birth. For the first word, first steps, first birthdays.

I sit on the bench, and Sully climbs in after me. I grab my water bottle, and we stare out at the game. He's probably the only guy on the team that can pick up on my mood. "You good?"

"Fine."

"You need to compartmentalize that shit. We're in game four."

I point toward the jumbotron. "I'm putting points on the board, aren't I?"

"Your head is somewhere else." *No shit.*

After three more shifts, second intermission comes around and I grab my phone when I get back to the locker room. I tap her name. It rings four times before she answers.

"Hello?"

"Hey. It's me." As if she doesn't know, I'm the one who programmed my name in her phone. As soon as I hear her voice, the fury from the game fades and I exhale.

123

"What do you need, Barrett?"

"Just wanted to check in on you after today. How was the rest of your afternoon?"

"Fine…"

"What about Arthur?"

"He's good too—wait, what time is it? Aren't you playing tonight?"

"Yeah, we're in the second intermission."

"And you're calling me? Shouldn't you be focusing on the game or looking at plays or something?"

"Probably. But I told you, I'm going to call every day.

And I wanted to talk to you before you went to bed." She starts to say something but stops.

"Goodbye, Barrett."

"Goodnight, Raleigh."

The sound of her voice calms the storm raging inside me.

A smile grows on my face, and I'm ready for the third period.

She answered my call. I hang up and turn around to see Sullivan standing there with flared nostrils—*he's pissed.*

"Who shit in your protein shake?"

"Are you fucking serious? What is this obsession you have with that woman? You've spent years looking for her in every bar we go into, you've barely fucked anybody since her, and now this—calling her during intermission? This isn't healthy, man. You're turning into a monomaniac, you think she's gonna be charmed by that shit?"

"She's hesitant, but I'm winning her over."

"See? You're not even fucking listening to what I'm saying! You're losing your mind. You should have been going over plays with me, we're in the playoffs! This should be your top priority! This is it, Conway, it's what we work all year for!"

I snap. "It's not enough for me!" I take a deep breath. "Okay?"

"What's that supposed to mean?!"

My arm is twitchy. I roar and throw a punch into the dead air. "I need more in my life. I'm tired of missing out on shit like starting a family or meeting somebody. The last however many years have been planned around the NHL season, and it's been a hell of an experience, but there's a lot of shit we sacrifice for it. I'm sick of the constant traveling, the practices and games, the press boxes, the bars, and the fans—and I know you know what I'm talking about, you hate that shit too. Playing hockey was my dream growing up, and I'll always love this sport, but will I love it as much as my child? My wife? I missed out on five years, Sul! Five! Not just with her, with my kid! I owe it to them to show up now."

I can't simply waltz back into their lives, I have to earn my spot. Prove I'm willing to put them first.

Getting Raleigh to take me back might be the hardest but most impor-tant thing I'll ever do. We still have futures after this career is over, life doesn't end when we stop playing hockey. And they are my future.

"So, fuck off about telling me what my priority should be, you have no idea what I'm going through."

Coach yells, "Tunnel!" and the guys start lining up for our last period. Sully stares at me in a daze, but follows me out.

Banksy leans in and whispers, "If you guys get a divorce, will we still be a family? Do I get two birthday parties?" Fuck him too.

After our win today, I should be more excited than I am. I love this team, but there's a heavy weight on my chest that won't leave until I have them.

Silver lining? Whether she likes it or not, Raleigh and I will be connected to each other for the rest of our lives.

TWENTY

Barrett

T his is the worst fucking rabbit hole. Raleigh has spoken with me a couple more times over the phone and has asked about some messages on Instagram she received. I had no idea what she was talking about. I disliked social media, all this shit is over my head. I've been through my DMs twice today trying to find them, but there's nothing.

After my morning workout, I knock on the social media office door and step inside.

"Hey, Peter, I need help with my Instagram. Gotta sec?"

He looks up from his laptop and gives me a smile. "Sure, what's up?"

"There's this woman I'm talking to—"

"Dude, if this is about some leaked nudes or something, we need to include—"

"No! No, nothing like that." *How many dicks does he look at daily to make him assume this was about nudes?* He relaxes in his chair. "Okay, cool. So what's the problem?"

"There's messages that I supposedly sent years ago. But I never check or do anything with my DMs. Julia managed—" *Holy shit.*

"Who's Julia?"

Why the fuck didn't I connect the dots earlier? After I walked her to her car that night at the restaurant, she came onto me and tried to kiss me. Aggressively. I brought it up with the team managers the next day. I figured she'd get a slap on the wrist and wouldn't be allowed to call me into her office anymore, but that wasn't the case. She continued her little tirade for the next few months before they finally let her go. *Was this her revenge?* I didn't realize she would get fired over it. Would she retaliate this severely?

He blinks at me, waiting for an answer. I don't have time to explain, and I don't want to either.

"How do I find out if there's someone blocked on my account? Not just my Instagram, but all my socials."

He raises his eyebrows. The kid looks at me like I've told him I prefer using the Pony Express to Twitter.

"Sorry, man. I know you're probably in the middle of some stuff, but can you help me out? It's urgent."

He holds out his palm, and I hand over my phone.

"You need a phone upgrade," he says, tapping around the screen. "Damn, this thing's slow."

"I'll look into it."

"Instagram, you have a Rahlee789 blocked." Chills shoot up my spine.

"Unblock her."

He nods and moves to the next app. "Facebook, Raleigh Dunham?"

"Unblock." *Holy fuck.*

"Snapchat, RaleighNotNC."

"Unblock." I shake my head; I didn't even know I had a Snapchat account.

"Twitter—"

"Unblock."

"Nothing blocked on LinkedIn... Do you use Pinterest or TikTok?"

"Do I look like I use Pinterest or TikTok?"

He chuckles and hands my phone back. "Fair enough."

"Thanks," I say over my shoulder as I leave his office.

"Sure thing, Conway. Let me know when you're ready for that upgrade!" Pretty sure he's internally cackling at my expense.

As I walk through the Lakes offices back to the locker room, I dig through each social media app, searching for DMs sent to or received from Raleigh. There's no sign of anything, but I'm sure any evidence was deleted long ago.

When I get back to the locker room, I grab my bag and head out. They might be deleted on my end, but maybe she still has them. Fishing my phone from my pocket, I tap her name from my Favorites menu. "What do you want, Barrett?"

I look forward to the day when she answers my calls with a smile, rather than all the warmth of a pissed-off DMV clerk.

I push through the heavy doors to get back to my car. "I need to see you. I can't find any DMs on my end. Are they still on your phone?"

The line is silent while I wait for her reply.

"Probably."

"Can I stop by to see them tonight?"

"Why?"

Why?! Because this whole misunderstanding seems to stem from those messages! "Because I just left the social media office and found that you were blocked on all of my social media accounts—that's something I never did."

"I can't tonight."

She still won't let me near him.

"Well, can I swing by during your lunch?"

She sighs and it feels like forever until she speaks.

"I guess so. But you're going to have to get here soon, I can only give you fifteen minutes. My afternoon is busy."

My truck is already in view, I jog to it, throwing my bag in the back seat.

"I'm on my way."

"Meet me at the front entrance."

I get lucky with parking and pull right up to the sidewalk. My eyes found her the second I pulled onto the street. She looks hot as fuck. The houndstooth skirt she's wearing clings to her hips, and the taut black tee stretched over her tits is a personal punishment.

It's unusually warm out for April and I've never been more thankful. I want to dig my fingers into those wide hips and never let go. She is focused on her phone, but when she looks up and sees me, her chest rises on a sharp inhale and then she tucks a strand of hair behind her ear. *Hard not to smile at that.*

I hop out of my truck and round the front to get to her. "You look very nice today."

Her eyes are the only place I let my gaze wander even though they are dying to check out the rest of her.

"Thank you," she chimes. "I need to grab some food for Rob. Mind if we walk?"

"What time do you have to be back?"

"His meeting gets done at one."

"I thought you could only give me fifteen minutes? Sounds like you don't need to be back for another forty five?"

"I need half an hour to go through his emails that came through this morning," she explains.

"Let me take you to lunch. *Please.* You and I both know if you bat your eyes at him twice, he'll forget his own name, much less what his inbox looks like."

A hint of a smile pulls at the corners of her lips.

"I can't blame him," I add, hoping to coax out the rest of her grin. A blush deepens her cheeks and she bites her bottom lip. I lick mine in response. Fuck, I want to kiss her. I have always regretted not kissing her that first night.

I grab her hand and start walking. "Come on, let's get you fed."

"I'll let you buy me a coffee. That's it." She gently retrieves her hand, causing disappointment to pool in my stomach. I slow my pace to follow her lead across the street to a café on the corner.

I'll take what I can get. For now.

We enter the café and find a place in line. It smells like fresh bread and oregano. I'm always hungry, especially around her. "What's good here?"

"Rob likes the mortadella."

"I don't care what Rob likes. What do *you* like?"

She clears her throat. "They have a brisket Reuben that's pretty good. And a Mediterranean salad that I get sometimes."

We get to the front of the line, and I gesture for her to order her coffee.

"A small vanilla latte with hazelnut."

"And a mortadella, two brisket Reubens and two Mediterranean salads." I add. "Mortadella to go, everything else for here."

She pinches the bridge of her nose. "Barrett," she chastises. I like the way she drops the T at the end of my name. I've noticed her accent is more pronounced when she's irritated..

I swipe my card and pay, throwing a couple bucks in the tip jar.

"Let's find a seat." I don't feel bad about placing my hand on her lower back. I'm using every chance I get to touch her. We find a quiet table near the corner and I pull my baseball cap lower. I want us to enjoy a private conversation in the cozy atmosphere. The tinted windows make it seem later in the day. Walls are covered in mismatched wood boards and about a hundred Edison bulbs hang in clusters from the ceiling. It's almost romantic.

"They give me a company card to pay for his lunches, you know."

"I know." I nod. "But you can tell Rob I'm the one that bought his lunch today."

She shakes her head. "This some kind of pissing contest?"

"It's no contest."

She rolls her pretty eyes. My fingers itch to touch her.

"Can I see the messages now?"

I didn't notice the amused smile on her lips until it disappeared with my last words. She unlocks her phone and taps the screen a few times and scrolls, it appears she's scrolling through *a lot* of messages before handing over the open DMs from *me*.

BCon33.

That's not my username.

I look up from the screen and meet her eyes momentarily.

"My username is BarrettConwayOfficial."

"Yeah, that's from your personal account, BCon33."

"I don't have a *personal* account. I can't even handle my own Instagram, much less juggle an additional one."

She narrows her eyes and tilts her face away. "So you...?"

I shake my head. "Someone set up an impostor account.

"This wasn't me."

Whoever did this, will pay dearly.

She clutches her stomach and turns her head to gaze out the large café windows. My focus drops back down to the phone as my fingers scroll through the phony messages. It's chilling to think of someone else speaking to her using my identity.

When I get to the responses, I freeze. The more I scroll, the worse it gets. I can't believe what I'm seeing.

With wide eyes, I read, "*Take this as a sign you should prob-*

ably hang up your jersey, this is no way to find a man_ or a baby daddy, in your case. It's one thing to look nice for the boys, but after we've fucked you a couple of—I can't say the rest. Hostility like I've never known rages inside me.

I swallow down the hurt I feel for her. The anger I feel for us. *All this time. She tried so hard.*

"Raleigh." I clear my throat, the emotion climbing higher. I can't believe she went through this. And not only that, but she thought these vicious words were mine. No wonder she hates me. I don't blame her. *They're unforgivable.* "I didn't send these. This is not..." I shake my head. "I would *never* speak to you this way, Raleigh." I'd never speak to anyone this way.

Thinking of a young, newly pregnant Raleigh reading these messages and thinking they were the thoughts of her child's father, crushes me. I scroll back up and screenshot each one.

She timidly runs her fingers through her hair.

"Are there any more?" I ask, texting the screenshots to myself.

"No... That's it."

I force myself look at them one last time.

"These messages are disgusting."

I understand her reaction to me now. Her anger may be old, but mine is fresh and new. *I'm on the warpath.*

"They are," Raleigh agrees, taking a sip of her latte. I slide her phone back across the table.

"What were you saying about the restraining order thing?"

"After these messages, there was this small niggling doubt in my mind. The things you said were so...cruel. I don't know why, but I needed to *hear* you say you wanted nothing to do with us. I called your agent and the organization, and every time, I would get referred to your PR." *Julia.* "Anyway, eventually this woman answered and told me that if I continued to attempt contact, that you were going to file an order of protection against me. I was twenty-two at the time, I believed her without thinking twice. I was pregnant and broke, it scared me. That was the last time I tried to contact you." Her eyes fall to the table, and it destroys me.

I restrain myself from pulling her into my arms. My hand envelopes hers, but I crave more. Touching Raleigh feels as natural as holding a hockey stick. Her skin is warm and soft against my calloused fingers.

"There are no words big enough to apologize or make up for this, but I am so sorry."

Her throat bobs and she nods with glossy eyes. "I don't know what you want me to say." She winces and frowns while shrugging. It's clear she's fighting her emotions. "We had our shot."

She's shutting down on me, and it pisses me off she's giving up so fast. I still feel so much for her.

"Why did you walk out that night? Why didn't you leave your number?"

"Why didn't you try to find me?"

With a forearm resting on the table, I spring forward. "I did! The very next day, I searched for you. On and off over the years I would look for you. Do you have any idea how difficult it is to find someone named Raleigh when you have no last name?"

She stares at me for a while, and I can see the hurt there. "Do you want me to forgive you? Is that it? I've accepted what happened and moved on." *She's killing me.* "It's not worth the effort, we weren't meant to be."

"Bullshit. If we weren't meant to be, you wouldn't have come into my life again. *We* are worth it. *Our son is worth it.*"

She flinches at my words, and I take a deep breath, trying to calm down. I'm devastated at what we lost and that I have to build trust with her and with Arthur when it should have been there all along. It feels like I'm losing her all over again.

"I'm going to see what I can do about these." I wiggle my phone. "But as far as you and me…"

Our eyes meet and we study each other. I struggle to find the right words to say. I *want* to say I've never stopped thinking about her, that she's a terrific mom, and more gorgeous than I remember. That I'll never leave again and won't stop until both of them are mine. *That I want her more than I've wanted anything. I want my name on her back. On her driver's license. On her lips.* But those things will scare her away.

She's delicate and fragile, and the damage we have to repair will take time. I've obsessed over her for so long. But for every second I've spent thinking about her, she's spent those seconds hating me. It's not going to happen overnight.

"Order number one-thirty-two, Barrett!"

I tap the table for a second, not wanting to leave this bubble. "Be right back."

When I return from grabbing our lunch, she's looking at the messages.

"What are you doing?"

"Sorry, it's been a while since I've read them. I sorta forgot."

"You should forget. It doesn't matter. None of those things are true and they were written by someone who envied how much I wanted you."

"What do you mean?"

I sigh. "The person who set up that account pretending to be me, I think it's the woman who managed my social media, it would have been the same woman that you spoke to in PR. I hated Instagram, Facebook, Twitter, and all the other apps I was supposed to be tracking. There were so many rules on what we could and couldn't post, I didn't want to deal with it.

So I let her manage everything. She had a thing for me, I never reciprocated.

"One night we had dinner together, it was supposed to be a work thing. I told her it wasn't a date, but when I got to the restaurant, it was clear she thought otherwise. I rejected anything happening between her and me and explained I was hung up on you. I was drunk, and went on and on about you and this connection we shared. She seemed understanding and even offered to help track you down—I was all for it. I told her everything I knew about you."

Raleigh unwraps her sandwich. "So that's how she knew I played hockey..." She takes a bite and I'm reminded how sexy she looks when she eats. *And my dick twitches thinking about her doing the splits on me again.*

"Can you still do the splits?" I wink at her, trying to lighten the mood.

She tilts her head to the side, unamused. I drop it. *Way to be, dumbass.*

I mumble a half-assed apology and continue. "After dinner, I walked her to her car. She came onto me, I told her no and took an Uber home. Because of the incident, I brought it up to the Lakes organization. She was reprimanded and eventually let go. I'm an idiot for never making the connection there." My teeth sink into my sandwich. *Damn.* "I don't have much of an appetite at the moment, but this is alarmingly good."

A small smile graces her face, and it feels like a huge win. "Right?"

"I mean, it's not as good as our first pizza together, but it's a close second."

She raises her eyebrows, as if she thought I could forget anything about that night, as if I haven't replayed it a thousand times in my head. Warmth fills her cheeks. "God, that pizza was bad."

I smile; it doesn't seem like that night was so long ago. But the last five years might as well have been a lifetime.

Well, Arthur's lifetime.

"I fucked up, Ral. I never should've had her in charge of that shit. There was never any girlfriend. If I'd known, I would have replied to your first DM and asked for your number—another thing I should have done earlier. I have so many regrets."

She takes a bite of her sandwich and chews while listening to what I have to say.

I can't believe we're here sitting at the same table together. She's right here. "You know, every time I went to a bar, I looked for you, hoping you'd walk through the door. Not sure if that counts for anything..."

She swallows. "I didn't go out much after our night together. It messed with my head. And then Arthur happened."

What messed with her head? And I want to know everything about Arthur.

"Can I ask more about that?"

She blots her full lips with a napkin. Her long lashes, honey-cinnamon eyes, and plush lips make me fucking weak. I can't stop staring. *Why didn't I kiss her when I had the chance? How does she kiss? How long do I have to wait to find out?*

"No. Not yet."

That's all I get before one of the other customers recognizes me. I'm friendly and take a quick picture, but in that small amount of time, another person notices. All I hear is the ring of her *no*. And she's shut down. *Goddamn it.*

It's an on-and-off flow of autographs and requests for selfies for the rest of our short lunch together. I'm struggling to keep my patience with fans, but it's something we're trained to do. Unfortunately, there's no time to go in depth and ask her the things I want. Even if there were, it's not like she'd answer them. I need to get her alone. The more I try to learn, the less she gives me, and before I'm ready, it's time for me to walk her back to work.

I carry her box of leftovers from the café and hold every door, sparing no opportunity to show her I care.

"Can we have dinner some time?"

She sucks in a breath and holds it while gazing up at me. Her eyes ping-pong between mine. When she finally exhales, she shakes her head. "That's a big ask. I'd have to get a babysitter, plus I don't know if I'm ready for anything one-on-one. And"—she looks back toward the café—"that was tough for me, even without the interruptions."

Distancing herself from me won't work, she'll soon find I can be stubborn as fuck when it comes to getting what I want.

And I want Raleigh and Arthur.

"That's fine, you don't need a babysitter. I could come to you or you could come to me. Just the three of us at home. No fans."

She combs her hair with her fingers, I'm already learning her subtle nervous habits. I like that she's contemplating the suggestion. "I dunno… what are we supposed to tell him?" *She said* we.

"I can be an old friend. He doesn't have to know." I want him to know, I want to tell him I'm his dad and apologize for not being there, but I'll agree to any terms that allow me to get my foot in the door. The wheels in her head are turning.

"Can I think about it? He's not used to me bringing around strange men. I don't want to confuse him."

I'm glad he's not used to it. The relief she gives me with that statement…

"Of course you can."

"Okay…um, I've got to get back." She throws her thumb over her shoulder, and I hand her the leftovers and Rob's sandwich. She lifts the box. "Thanks for lunch."

"Anytime. I'm still gonna call you tonight."

She nods and bites her lip, spinning around and walking back inside.

As soon as Raleigh is out of my sight, I'm texting my lawyer.

> Here's the screenshots you asked for.

After I heard there were messages, I contacted Gary to see if any action could be taken after the fact. He said it was possible, but first he needed to see that they actually existed. *As if this was some lie Raleigh came up with.* I get that he's trying to protect me, but I'm the one who sought her out, not the other way around.

> Is there any way to see if Julia sent these?

GARY

These are helpful. Thanks. If we can get access from the Lakes servers, we can see if they were sent from the offices.

God, these are brutal.

> They're fucked up.

GARY

Has anyone else on the team ever mentioned weird stuff with their accounts? I'm guessing most of them actually use their social media, though.

> I'm already kicking my own ass, I don't need you to do it for me.

GARY

Just throwing it out there. Anyway, if this happens to be the result of a disgruntled Lakes employee, we will be likely dealing with the whole org, especially employee negligence and falsifying your identity.

> I don't have a problem with the Lakes, I'm not going to put my contract in jeopardy by putting them in the line of fire, they had nothing to do with this. Julia took action all on her own.

GARY

These messages are awfully personal. We may want to look into submitting an HRO against her.

> Not yet. I don't want her to catch wind of what's going on and try to come after Raleigh or Arthur. I don't trust her. But when we do, be sure she pays for every day I missed out on with my family.

GARY

Sure you don't want a paternity test?

TWENTY-ONE

Barrett

K ucera gets another goal. The fans are losing their minds. He's doing really well for his second season.

"Shift change!"

I jump back on the ice with my line and get into position for the drop.

Sully narrows his eyes at me, and I know what he's thinking: *stay focused.*

I'm agitated, but fuck, I have every right to be. I've never had something big enough to take my head out of the game, but finding out you have a son you didn't know about, qualifies. We're up by three points in the third period. I make my passes, and my stick handling is right where it needs to be. I'm skating my ass off, and sweat is sluicing out of me. Yeah, I'm a little on edge.

At puck drop, I crowd Colorado's winger, Grutzmacher, he's chirping some bullshit at me, trying to rile me up, but I ignore him and focus on our play. As soon as the puck hits the ice, their center snags it. We chase it down, as Burke and Kucera do a fine job defending our goal, but I end up in a puck battle with Grutzmacher, and my back against the boards. My patience is thin with anyone standing in the way of what I want. This puck included. I'm able to snake it out and pass to Sully who takes off in a breakaway, but as I push off to follow, Grutz slashes the back of my knee with his stick and pain shoots up my leg.

I don't even wait for the call when I spin around and give him a shove. He shoves me back, and I drop gloves. The refs blow their whistles, stopping the play. *That's* when they decide to call? Not when Grutz gets the back of my knee? If this ref had one more fucking eye, he'd be a cyclops. Grabbing the back of Grutz's neck, I take a swing at him. He grabs my jersey at my shoulder and throws a punch, but I've got at least eight inches on this dumb motherfucker. He's fighting in the wrong weight class.

I knock his helmet off and clock him in the jaw before they pull me off and escort me to the sin bin. *Fuck that guy.*

In the penalty box, fans slap the plexiglass behind me, but there's so much adrenaline in my system, the pounding is muted and dull. I'm torn between watching the game and hanging my head in embarrassment. Two minutes of being disconnected from my team because I couldn't keep my cool. Our med, Jenny, motions to Coach to pull me off the ice. The back of my knee is numb where he got me, and she'll need to check it before I'm back on.

Honestly, I don't even care if they pull me for the rest of the game.

"Hey, Ral."

"Hi, Barrett."

"How was your day?"

She sighs. "It was fine."

My back is starting to hurt from carrying all these damn conversations. This afternoon feels like forever ago.

"Do anything fun over your lunch break?"

"Nothing worth noting." I hear the hint of a smile in her voice—it's almost flirty—and my eyes pop open. *That's something.*

"How was Arthur's day?"

"He had a good day too."

She said too—which means her day was better than "fine."
We had lunch this afternoon and she had a good day.

Am I grasping at straws? Fuck yeah, I am.

"Did he tell you anything about it?" I want to know what he says when he comes home from school or daycare or wherever he goes when Raleigh's at work.

"He said he learned a new song about the days of the week and was really excited."

"How does it go?" Wish I could hear him sing it.

"I dunno, it's like all the days of the week sung to the tune of *The Addams Family* theme song." The smile in her voice reemerges, and my fist shoots into the air. *She's talking to me.*

"Seriously?" I laugh.

"It's catchy as hell. He got it stuck in my head." It sounds like she's putting away dishes. "It'll definitely help me remember them all."

She's gradually dropping some of her defenses, giving me more than bare minimum. The smile on my face is ear to ear.

More progress.

TWENTY-TWO

Raleigh

He sent me lunch. *Again.*

> I can't eat like this everyday. I've gained enough weight after having Arthur.

BARRETT

Good, I like you curvy.

> Shut up

BARRETT

Never

> You are going to ruin Reubens for me.

BARRETT

Well, I wouldn't want to to do that. What other food do you like?

> I'm not telling you.

BARRETT

You'll tell me when you get sick of the Reubens.

Have you thought about dinner yet?

I sigh. I have thought about it. He's been adamantly denying everything, he's not this good an actor. I can't imagine not knowing my own son. Maybe it wouldn't hurt to let him come over for dinner. I grew up without a father and it sucked. If his dad wants to make an effort, I shouldn't stand in his way, but I'm terrified of him letting Arthur down.

Let me talk to him. If he says yes, then okay. But nothing out in public. You can eat with us, but it's a casual, weeknight dinner. Don't get too excited. Nothing fancy.

BARRETT

I don't care about the food, I just want to see him. Does Wednesday night work?

As long as you don't mind fish finger dogs.

BARRETT

HOW DID YOU KNOW!?!? They're my favorite!!!

I roll my eyes and try not to laugh.

Oh, I'm sure.

We usually eat around 5-5:30. I'll text you and let you know.

BARRETT

Thank you for this.

It's up to Arthur.

After getting Arthur strapped into his booster seat, I walk to the driver's door and get in.

"How was your day today, kiddo?"

I peek at him in the rearview mirror.

"It was good, we got to paint with marshmallows today!"

"Fun! Did you eat any of the marshmallows after there was paint on them?"

"No! I licked the paint off first."

I take a deep breath. He'll be shitting rainbows all week. *This kid.* "Yeah, and how did that taste?"

"Gross."

"I bet. Hey, what do you think about having a friend over for dinner tomorrow?"

"Who?"

"His name is Barrett. You met him when we went to the hockey game. Right before we left."

He scrunches up his nose. "The giant with the hair on his face?"

I laugh. "Yeah, the giant with the beard." *I hate that I still remember how his trimmed facial hair felt between my thighs.*

"Sure! He's nice. And he knew koalas are marsupials."

"Well, yeah, but *everybody* knows that..."

He holds up his finger. "This is true. Can we have cereal for dinner?"

"Tonight or when he comes over?"

"Both! Cereal is a top food." I swear he could eat it for every meal and never get sick of it.

"You can have a small bowl while I make dinner, but you have to promise to eat some real food afterward."

"I will!"

I throw out one last chance to turn this thing around. "If you don't want him to come, you can tell me, Arthur."

"No, I want him to have dinner with us. It will be like a party."

"A three-person party?" I ask, looking in the rearview mirror again.

"Yeah! We can get balloons!"

"I don't think we have any balloons."

"We do! They're in the birthday box!"

Stupid birthday box.

"Okay, *one* balloon. But that's it. The rest we need to save for your birthday party."

"A red one!"

TWENTY-THREE

Raleigh

This night is bringing on more anxiety than I anticipated. My pacing is going to wear a hole in the floor. And I'm not the only one. Arthur keeps bouncing off the walls with this idea we're having a *party*. I'd rather spend an entire Saturday at Chuck E. Cheese's child rat casino than have this "party."

"Arthur, be careful with that balloon or it might pop before Barrett gets here."

He slows his running, but barely.

I look around at the house and check that it's clean and picked up. It is, except for whatever toys Arthur's taken out since we got home. Our house is a lot smaller than what Barrett is used to, but it's a nice size for the two of us. I bought it for the backyard anyway. It butts up to a large park with a nice walking path that leads to a playground. It's convenient and saves me having to buy a swing set.

I'm chopping up the cabbage for coleslaw when Arthur announces, in the loudest volume ever, that a black truck is in the driveway.

"The giant is here! And holy fart feathers—he has presents! I told you it was a party!"

"Don't say fart feathers!" I call from the kitchen.

I can't have him bringing presents and setting this standard that Arthur's going to receive gifts every time he comes around. Okay, fine, I'm getting ahead of myself. Who knows if he will even want to have future visits after tonight. This dinner is a trial run.

"Let's call him by his name, Arthur. His name is Barrett. Not '*the giant*,' okay? He might not like that."

Arthur throws the front door open. "Barrett! We're having a party!"

He laughs on the other side of the door, and I try to suppress the butterflies.

"Awesome! Can I come?" His, well, *giant* feet thud over the threshold and I wash my hands.

"Yeah! Are those presents for me?"

I wipe my hands on a towel as I walk out of the kitchen.

"Arthur, let's be polite and not ask for gifts." Barrett's smile is radiant. *Why did I think this would be okay?*

"Hi, Barrett."

Crouching at Arthur's level, he hands over the bags to him. "Yeah, buddy, these are for you." He looks up at me again. "I hope that's okay."

My cheeks burn for no reason. None. Certainly not from how hand-some he is.

"Kind of wish you would have cleared them with me first." I have no idea what's in those bags, it could be anything.

He nods and brings his attention to my son again. "So, you and I are new friends, but I actually knew your mom a long time ago. *Annnnnd*, I didn't realize you had four whole birthdays that went by, so I got you something small for all the ones I missed."

Damn him. Why does he have to do sweet things like that?

"Holy fart feathers! This is a birthday party!"

I pinch the bridge of my nose. "Dude, what did I say

about fart feathers?"

"Don't say it."

"Yup. Let's work on that."

"Sorry. Can I open them now?" Arthur looks up at me, eyes pleading.

"If Barrett says it's okay. But open them in the kitchen so I can finish working on the coleslaw."

Arthur grabs up the bags and rushes to the table.

"Can I help?" Barrett rises back to his full height and smiles. *Heaven help me.*

"Sure. I'll let you do the hard part, putting the frozen fish in the air fryer."

I go back to chopping and tell him where to look in the freezer. "I used to make it fresh and roll the fish in bread-crumbs, but Arthur says these taste better, so"—I shrug—"you're stuck with frozen tonight."

He smiles as he pulls the bag out of the freezer. Mother-fucker looks happy to just be in our presence. It's so weird.

"Which one should I open first?!" Arthur asks Barrett.

"Whichever one you want."

"The red one! Red's my favorite color."

"Mine too."

Of course they have the same favorite color.

He tears into the bag, tissue paper flying. "It's a piece of paper. What does this say?" Arthur holds it up.

"Those are tickets to my hockey game... if you want to go and your mom says it's okay." Then he murmurs to me, "I put you and Arthur on the list for the box, but I understand if that's a lot right now. So you've got the seats if that would be more comfortable."

The *box?* Is he fucking serious? I pull back from slicing up produce. "Are you talking about the WAGs box?" He side-eyes me but doesn't answer. *What the fuck?* That's for wives and girlfriends.

"A camera!" Arthur shouts, digging into the green bag and pulling out his gift.

"What?" I lower my voice back down. "I know you're new to this, but you can't give a four-year-old a digital camera."

"Relax." He chuckles. "It's made for kids, it's fine." *I wasn't aware they made digital cameras for kids.*

"It's so you can take some family pictures with you and your mom." *And dad, I'm sure.* "But you have to send me a copy so I can put it in a picture frame at my house."

Why does the thought of him keeping a photo of Arthur and me fill my stomach with that scared-excited feeling?

"Cool! I want to try it!"

"We'll probably have to charge it first. Here, let me take a look." Arthur hands him the box, and Barrett nods to the other gifts. "Open another one."

"Okay!" More rustling of tissue paper. I still can't believe he showed up with four presents. He probably thought this was the last time I'd let him near Arthur.

Am I a mean mom for wishing he didn't bring gifts?

"More paper! But this one has a koala on it. Barrett, it's a koala! Read it!"

Barrett laughs. "Those are zoo passes so you can go see the koalas with your mom whenever you want."

"Mom, we can go to the zoo!"

Arthur must be on cloud nine. "That was very thoughtful. Thank you."

He leans against the countertop while I slice. "You're welcome."

"Okay, I'm opening the last one! It's a bear!"

Barrett clears his throat and then looks over at Arthur. "I know you like koala bears, but since koalas aren't really bears, I thought I would get you a teddy bear. Because your name means bear."

The knife falls to the cutting board, and I fan out my fingers on the counter.

He looks down at me while talking to Arthur. "Did you know your mom used to call me *Bear*?"

I purse my lips. *This was never supposed to happen.* He's pushing these probationary privileges—big time. If he says a word to Arthur about his connection to him, I'll turn this knife on him without thinking twice.

Arthur laughs, unaware his mother is about to unravel at the seams. "No, that's silly! Why did she call you Bear?"

I swallow and pick my knife up to return to chopping. His gaze burns through me, but I don't look.

"Because my name means bear too."

Taking out a bowl, I throw all the chopped cabbage and carrots inside.

"Come on, little man. Let's get this camera set up while your mom finishes cooking." Arthur runs out of the room.

As Barrett passes behind me, he leans down to my ear and whispers, "Did you really think I wouldn't notice?" I open my mouth to speak, but he's already gone. *Shit.*

As I finish cooking, I listen to them play together in the living room. I was half hoping Barrett would be uncomfortable around him, but it's the opposite. I eavesdrop on their conversation while finishing the dressing for the coleslaw.

"Wanna play garbage man?" Arthur asks.

"Sure, how do we play?"

"I'm the garbage man and I go around to clean up the garbage."

"Cool. Can I be a garbage man too?"

"No, you have to be the garbage." I snort.

"Perfect. I'm great at being garbage. But I'm a lot of garbage. Do you think you can lift 240 pounds of trash?"

"Yeah! Look at my muscles!"

"Wow," Barrett answers, surely admiring Arthur's baby

muscles. There's a pause and then Barrett says, "Uh oh, we might need to ask your mom for some tape."

"Why?"

"Because you're ripped."

"Huh?"

I giggle to myself, amused at how the joke landed so flat.

"It was a joke, you know because *ripped* means you have big muscles."

More silence.

"We'll work on the jokes next time."

Thankfully, he can't see the smile on my face. I wish I could stop it, but it's involuntary. Listening to my son play and be silly is impossible to ignore. As hard as it is to admit, it's kind of incredible. They've formed this little bond before dinner's even finished cooking. He pays attention to Arthur and talks *to* him rather than *at* him. He asks him about his interests and ideas, not canned questions about what he's learning in school. And he really listens to him. He seems genuinely invested in spending this time with my son. I can't deny he's making an effort.

I pull the fries out of the oven, but as I plate everything,

I'm hit with a wave of self-consciousness about the menu. Arthur loves tonight's meal, but I'm guessing Barrett Conway isn't accustomed to eating '*fish finger dogs*' which are essentially frozen fish sticks on squished hot dog buns with slaw and aioli—a.k.a. garlic and mayonnaise.

Whatever, this is our life now. He wants a piece of us? Have at it. What you see is what you get. Our chicken is dinosaur shaped, sandwiches come with the crust cut off, and every pancake has mouse ears. It's *glamorous.*

"Dinner's ready."

"Nice!" they exclaim in unison.

Arthur squeals as he rides on Barrett's back into the kitchen. When I see my son grinning like that, it's impossible not to smile. Barrett pauses his piggyback ride and bites his lip while very obviously checking me out. I respond with an eye roll and turn around so he can't see the irrepressible blush. *Why does he still affect me like this?* It's only because he's physically attractive and it's been too long since I've had an orgasm.

"Arthur, don't forget to wash your hands."

He runs off to the bathroom, and Barrett washes up in the kitchen sink while I set the plates on the table. It's strange having the table set for three people. We don't usually have guests eating dinner with us.

"This looks really good, Ral."

I put my napkin on my lap. "You don't have to say that."

"Say what?"

"Oh yeah, Bear, fish finger dogs are the height of elegance." I bounce my eyebrows once.

My child comes tearing into the kitchen and pulls out the chair next to Barrett.

"How about you let me worry about what I like and don't like?" He takes a huge bite and smiles. "...I like when you call me Bear and I like fish finger dogs."

"I *love* fish finger dogs!" Arthur says, digging in.

"Derishush!"

"See?" Barrett says. "Better than the Reuben."

That's a load of shit, but I appreciate his attempt. I smile around a bite and pick up a french fry. "You guys are ridiculous."

He groans out loud after taking a bite. Then Arthur joins in, and they're making total buffoons of themselves. It becomes more and more exaggerated, and Arthur's never giggled so much at dinner. I eventually lose it and have to cover my face from laughter. Tonight is more enjoyable than I expected. I'm trying to let my guard down, but it's hard.

I always said I wouldn't stand in the way of Arthur and his dad if he wanted to build a relationship with his father. I wish my dad had made even a fraction of the effort Barrett has tonight. But he still needs to show me he's up for the job if he wants to be a part of Arthur's life. Parenthood is hard, and I've always done it alone. I don't know if I'd even know *how* to co-parent with another person.

I look over the two of them; they're so similar. It's strange to see them together like this. It feels like two worlds, my past and my present, colliding. Though, deep down, I know Barrett and Arthur have been connected since conception— half of Arthur is Barrett whether I like it or not. My mind wants to believe that this scene could be the future, but envisioning that is out of the question. Barrett could leave tonight and never return. This could be the end for us. But, damn, it's hard to ignore how good he is with Arthur... And Arthur seems to enjoy him too.

The worst thing I could do is get him attached and then have Barrett bolt on us. That would wreck him. I know how bad it hurts because it wrecked me. I hope he understands what's at stake by him coming around. This isn't some "try it for a while and see if I like it" situation, he's either ready or he's not. And he needs to decide after tonight. And if he's not, then he needs to leave us alone. I can't have the inconsistency of someone coming in and out of his life.

Unfortunately, I can already see Arthur is getting attached to Barrett, so I hope he sticks around for his sake. He's my baby, I never want to see him hurt. However, when I look at Barrett, his eyes tell me he's hurting too. I suspect he's becoming equally attached. It defrosts my cold heart.

Only a little.

"Mind if I grab another one?" Barrett asks. That was fast. I sort of stare at him for a while, *what's your plan with us*?

"Raleigh?"

"Um, yeah, there's plenty more on the stove."

TWENTY-FOUR

Barrett

I t's rare I describe a house as cute, but Raleigh's little bungalow is adorable. Walking up through the front gate and seeing the warm-yellow siding with flower boxes in the windows reminded me of her softer nature. She can act tough and be defensive, but this house is filled with sunshine, and that's all I need to know about how she and Arthur live.

I will never get over missing Arthur's first years. My mind often wanders into how our lives might have been different had we stayed in contact. Would we have stayed together? Would I still be playing? What did she look like pregnant with my son? Would we have more kids? It's surreal to see Raleigh so immersed in mom-life. She's got it all, from the finger-painted artwork on the fridge, down to the fish stick cuisine... We really gotta work on his finger painting though. NASA wouldn't approve of their rockets looking like giant intergalactic penises.

I'm jealous of her life. I know it's not as easy as she makes it seem, it's not all rainbows and space dicks, but it's filled with love. She's changed a lot. I wish I could have been here to see the transformation. Raleigh has done an amazing job raising our son without me, I only wish she hadn't had to.

And God, Arthur's a great kid. He's curious and smart. He's respectful and funny. His laugh is contagious—it's the sound of pure joy. And I love how much we look alike. We have blonde hair, he's got a dimple like mine, his nose and smile are mine, but those eyes are all Raleigh.

I've coached mites, so I know he's tall for his age. Has he ever been on skates before? Does he have the same hockey talent as Raleigh and me? He'd make one hell of a goalie with my height and his mom's skills. Or maybe sports won't be his strength, maybe he'll be into science or books or art. Either way, I hope she lets me stick around to find out. I need her to let me in so I can prove I'm not going anywhere.

After the meal, Arthur gets set up with a television show, and I clean up the toys we were playing with before dinner. When I head back toward the kitchen, I resist leaning against the doorframe and ogling the domestic porn of Raleigh at the sink doing dishes.

I sidle up next to her. "Can I help?"

"Sure," she says, handing me a wet plate.

I take one of the towels from the wall hook and begin drying.

"Bet you didn't think I could eat six fish finger dogs, huh?" I nudge her with my hip.

She chuckles. "I did not."

"You're a good cook."

She hands me another plate. "Sorry we don't have a dishwasher, you're probably not used to doing dishes." *There she goes again.*

"Are you always this defensive?"

"I'm not defensive."

"You're making a lot of judgments about me. And a lot of assumptions about what I'm thinking. If you want to know

156

something, ask me. I'll tell you anything. But stop trying to read my mind...*because you suck at it.*"

She scrubs a bowl and then drops it back into the sudsy water and turns to me. "You're right. We've led very different lives over the years, and I'm feeling a little insecure. The version of me you used to know doesn't exist anymore."

I scoff. "That's bullshit."

"What?" She blinks at me.

"I said *that's bullshit*. You have new facets, but the woman I met back then is still a part of you. You're more well-rounded now." I finish drying a glass and set it aside.

"That's for sure," she quips. I'm not a fan of this negative self-talk she's picked up.

Snatching the sponge from her hand, I hold it out of reach. "What do you mean by that?"

"Nothing...I've changed a lot."

"We both have. Five years is a long time, and you had to grow up quickly. You were only twenty-two back then... I can barely remember being twenty-two."

She hums in agreement. "Sometimes it feels like forever ago, other times it feels like yesterday. Can I have my sponge back?"

I drop it in the water for her to fish out, and she slaps my stomach, leaving a wet handprint. I like it. "For me, it feels like forever ago." *Especially when I look at Arthur.* I've missed so much of his life, all of it. I want to apologize to him, to tell him I'm sorry I wasn't here for him and his mom, but I can't. There won't be another day that goes by without me being a part of his life, but Raleigh has to give me the green light before he can know he has a dad. Respecting her wishes is something she needs from me, and I'll give her whatever she requests. I'm prepared to give her everything.

She may not think she's the same Raleigh, but she's in there, and I'll help her see it. Sliding the towel over each fork, I glimpse her body. She's the whole package, and I want her more than ever before. I've been pining for her for years, she's a craving, and now that I'm next to her again—close enough to smell her perfume—it's torture to not pull her into my arms. My attraction to her has only intensified.

Absence makes the heart grow obsessive, or whatever.

She finishes the last dish and wipes down the countertop. She's very tidy, but the house still looks lived in. It's comfortable and reminds me of the home I grew up in.

"Well...thanks for coming to dinner." She's kicking me out. "Arthur, it's time to say goodbye to Barrett. We need to get you ready for bed."

"Can Barrett read me my story?"

She looks at him with soft eyes. "I think Barrett needs to be getting home."

"If it's okay with your mom, I'd be happy to," I petition. I need this. "Can I?"

She looks between the two of us but lands on him. "Okay —but *one* story. None of that sneaky stuff because he's new, Arthur. You know the rules."

She cuts her eyes to me. "He's a trickster, watch yourself."

Arthur hops off the couch and runs down the hallway, and I follow Raleigh behind him.

"Can I see your bedtime routine?" I'm hoping someday I can be a part of it, so I want to observe.

She eyes me up and down. "Sure."

"Okay, Arthur, let's show him how we get ready for bed."

He darts into the hallway. "First, we brush our teeth!"

Raleigh stands next to him in what seems to be the one and only bathroom. They stand side by side and brush their teeth together. It's precious.

He calls out each part he's brushing as he goes. "Sides... back... front... top... bottom... tongue... spit."

She spits her frothy toothpaste out right after he does. "Clean chompers?"

"Clean chompers!" He bites his teeth together in a huge smile.

"Now what?" I ask.

"Bathroom, privacy please," he says, herding us out of the room.

We stand out in the hall while he hums a song as he goes to the bathroom. After a flush, the sink turns on and he continues the off-tune melody that sounds made up.

He swings the door open and holds up finger guns. "Time for pajama-rama-ding-dongs!"

Holy shit, this is even more entertaining than I thought it'd be. With his chin held high, his little feet march off toward one of the bedrooms.

He opens a drawer and pulls out a matching shirt and shorts covered in fire trucks and dalmatians.

"Does he need any help?"

"Nope, he's able to dress himself."

He swaps the play clothes for pajamas and then leaps into bed, burrowing under the covers with his koala.

"Hey, Barrett, why are koalas so sleepy?"

Shit, I studied this. I've been brushing up on my koala knowledge in case he quizzed me.

"Wait, I know this... um, something about all the eucalyptus they eat. Am I right?"

He blinks at me. "They're tired from being so cute all day."

I chuckle. "That's a koala-ty joke."

His eyes grow big and he laughs like it's the funniest thing he's ever heard. Which only makes me laugh more.

"Mom, did you hear Barrett's joke?"

"I did, he's a funny guy, huh?"

"You are a koala-ty guy!" He's almost five and this is the

first time his father's ever read him a bedtime story. I'm definitely *not* a koala-ty dad.

Raleigh holds out three books for him to choose from. He picks one about a mouse and a yellow blanket. I read him the story, loving every second. When he laughs at my various character voices, it makes me feel on top of the world. I can't believe she gets to do this every night. I wish I could too.

When I'm finished, I close the book. "And they all lived happily ever after."

He furrows his brow and sits up. "That's not in the story."

"No, I freestyled that part."

"What's ever after?"

"It's another way of saying forever. After the mother mouse fixed his blanket, they were happy forever—happily ever after."

He thinks on it for a second.

"That's nice."

I nod. "Thanks for letting me read you a story and have dinner with you and your mom tonight."

"You're welcome. Thank you for my presents."

"You bet. Sleep tight, Arthur." I stand and hold my fist out to him, then he bumps his knuckles against it.

I step back and lean against the doorway, letting Raleigh crouch down to say good night. I'm grateful to witness this sweet, private moment between them. Appreciating her more than ever before.

She rises to her feet and flips off the light.

"I hope you are happily ever after, Barrett," he calls.

My lips curl up into a smile. "I hope you are happily ever after too, bud. Good night."

"Good night." He waves.

"Open, cracked, or shut, kiddo?" Raleigh asks.

"Shut."

"You got it. Sweet dreams, I love you," she says.

"Love you too."

Raleigh and I retreat into the hall, and she clicks his door shut.

She straightens the throw pillows on the sofa when we enter the living room. I sit down and pat the spot next to me.

Before she sends me away, I need her to see this.

"There's something I want to show you."

"What?"

I pull my phone out and open the text thread from Sully.

This is why he's my best friend. He read through all our old texts and found examples of me *not getting over her,* in case it would help. Thoughtful son of a bitch. He knows how bad I need this.

> SULLY
>
> Kayla's asking about you.

> Not interested. Ral or bust.

> SULLY
>
> Dude, you gottttttta get over that chick.

> I can't.

I swipe to the next frame.

> thought I saw Raleigh leaving the arena, chased her to the parking lot, yelled out her name, she turned around...it was Fred's daughter.

> SULLY
>
> You're losing your fucking mind.

> I know.

Another one.

SULLY

Lots of pretty girls here tonight…

> Any blonde-haired ones with golden skin and southern accents?

SULLY

Wtf? Did you just say "golden skin"?

> You know what I mean.

SULLY

Lol no I don't. And no. Sorry bud.

She laughs and flips through the various screenshots. Her eyes meet mine and she's still smiling. Fuck, having that happiness aimed at me almost knocks me over.

SULLY

You over Raleigh yet?

> Nope.

SULLY

Just checking

She hands it back, and I pull up the video he sent. The guys are shout-singing "Wagon Wheel" in the locker room. As soon as it gets to the part about hoping for Raleigh, the camera pans over to me and all the boys sing louder, pointing in my direction. I learned to despise that song. Every time it came on, it was the same old shit, and annoyed the hell out of me, but it might actually be the thing to save my ass now. In the video, I look away but nod and raise my hand. I want her to see that even *then* she had me under her spell. Everybody knew about it, so much so that my infatuation with her became a locker room joke.

"This is from a year and a half ago."

She laughs and replays the video. I roll my eyes. "Okay, we don't need to watch it more than once."

She spins away from me on the sofa, phone still clutched in her hand. "Yeah we do—Camden Teller drops his towel in the last frame."

I grab her side and steal my phone back, stuffing it in my pocket.

"Oh, she's got the jokes tonight!"

"My jokes are pretty *koala-ty*," she mocks.

Her smile drives me wild. She's loosening up.

"I know this makes me look a little obsessed, but it's the only evidence that proves I never stopped looking." She purses her lips and nods. *Now or never.* "And I still have feelings for you."

Her eyes snap to mine, and she winces. "It was one night, Bear." *Uff.*

"You really don't feel anything anymore?" My eyes search hers for a sign.

She shrugs. "I spent a lot of time hating you. It's hard to forget, even if the hatred was misplaced."

Feels like I'm taking a puck to the side. "Do you feel *any* attraction toward me?"

"I mean... yeah, but—"

Thank God. I stand and fold my arms across my chest. "But what?"

She rises off the couch and plays with her hair while she paces. "Of course I'm attracted to you. I mean, look at you." She turns on her heel and gestures at me. *I can work with this.* "*You* haven't changed at all. But *I have*,

I don't resemble my old self at all. It's not like it used to be."

I drop my hands. That's such shit.

"You look better than I remember."

"Well, *I remember* every compliment you said about my body that night. And every single one of those things is no longer true. I'm not the same person you were attracted to then."

I toss my chin up. "Show me."

"What?"

I grab her hand and pull her toward the hallway. "Which one of these is yours?"

"Barrett, no!" she whisper-scolds, trying not to wake our son.

I make a guess on the door at the end and feel around for a light switch. When I find it, the lamps on each nightstand illuminate the bedroom in a soft glow. After pulling her inside and toeing the door shut, I engage the lock on the knob.

I take a moment to survey the space. This is hers. The ceiling is vaulted, and crisp-white walls make the dusty-blue upholstered headboard on her bed the main focus of the room. I cross the wood floor to the walk-in closet and open the door, thankful to see a full-length mirror on the backside.

Perfect.

I swing it open and sit on the floor in front of it, pulling her down with me. I place her between my open legs.

My gaze meets her in the mirror's reflection. "Show me what's different."

She looks pissed. "This is stupid."

"I'm really fucking tired of the way you talk about yourself."

"Fine, but you asked for it. Everything is different! My stomach, my thighs, my boobs, everything!"

"Show me." *Risky.* She flinches at the rigor in my voice. I'm over this attitude. I know her body is differ-ent, but what she views as unfavorable, I see as mouth-watering.

"No."

I shake my head. "Well, one thing hasn't changed, you're still a fucking brat. I want you to see what I do. Take it off, or I promise you your punishment will be far worse than stripping for me."

She begins to stand. "I'm not—"

I pull her back down and drop my voice to a lower octave. "Stop."

She bites her tongue and pauses. Her chest rises and falls, either out of anger or passion. Probably both. I patiently wait for her to concede. Then she plants her hands on the floorboards on either side and narrows her eyes. When her shoulders start to relax, I move my hands to her front, unbuttoning her jeans.

"Lift."

Her pupils dilate and she raises her ass for me to peel the jeans off. I get hard at the sight. I can't believe this is my Raleigh. This woman was made for me.

She's a fucking showstopper.

I loop my fingers into the sides of her panties. "Again."

"You're going to be disappointed," she says, lifting again. That pisses me off. I wrap my arm around her stomach and rip off her underwear with the other hand, like I did our first night together. Her gasp is the same as before, and those big eyes are spitting daggers at me.

"Arms," I instruct. She holds them up and lets me pull the

T-shirt over her head.

"*Fuck*," I mumble.

I unclasp her bra and slide it off one arm at a time as her breaths come faster. She tucks her knees up to her chin and crosses her ankles to hide herself. *That won't do.*

"Why am I the only one that's naked?"

With Raleigh sitting between my thighs, her back pressed to my chest, I wrap my arm around her neck, putting her in a firm headlock as we stare at each other in the mirror. Her hands reach up to pull at my forearm and bicep. I'm not cutting off her airway, but it's enough to remind her I could if I wanted to.

"Because this is about you, not me. And if I was naked, I'd already have you stretched around my cock."

Her throat bobs and her pulse pounds against my arm.

"We're going to start at your pretty face and work our way down."

She tugs at my arms again.

"First, your hair." She's kept the length, but it has more curl to it now. No longer the stick straight blowout from before. She's traded the platinum-blonde for a darker, wheat colored version that looks more natural. "You don't style it the same, but it still wraps perfectly around my fist like silk." I sift her hair through my fingers and wind it around my palm. Her breath quickens. "You play with it when you're nervous, don't you?" She gulps.

"Your light-brown, cinnamon eyes...and how dark they get when you see something you want." The honey flecks in them turn to molasses. Once I say it, her piercing stare turns into seductive bedroom eyes. I have to take a second to collect myself. Her beauty is obliterating me.

I put tension on my grip as I withdraw my hand from her hair. The lips I've always wanted to kiss, part slightly, and I go there next, rubbing my thumb over her pout. "I have thought about these lips endlessly over the years. Next to not getting your number, my biggest regret was not kissing you..." Everything in me wants to cover her mouth with mine. I'm desperate to know how she tastes.

"Bear..."

A grunt leaves my throat. *I love when she calls me that.*
Does she realize what it does to me?

"I'm not done."

Dropping my hand, I sweep the thick curtain of hair to one side and trace her shoulder blades. "Here...and here..."

How pretty this back would look bent over my lap. My hands travel up over her shoulder to her collarbone. She takes a deep breath.

I glance at her face once more before pushing her legs down by her knees.

"Drop your hands."

It takes her a second, but she drops her arms from mine and rests them on her lap, leaving her breasts exposed. I suck in a breath before groaning. She's stunning.

"Fuck, Raleigh... and here." I run my fingers over her peaked nipples, and she pushes her chest into my hand. She wriggles, but I constrict my headlock on her. I cover her breast with my hand and knead the soft flesh. A small squeak leaves her lips, but she bites down to prevent any more from escaping.

"That's okay, love. Keep making those sounds. I want to hear all of them." I tug her nipples, and she arches her back slightly. Her teeth trap her bottom lip, but she surrenders and releases a raspy exhale. Her sluggish blinks give in and she closes her lids. "Eyes open." When our gazes meet again, they're dark and heated. *How long has it been since another man has made her come?*

"Tell me what you like about what you see so far."

"I...I like my arms."

I smile and lean down to kiss behind her ear. "Good girl," I whisper. "What else?"

Her eyes bounce between mine in the mirror.

"I like my nipples."

"Me too."

I graze my hand from her breast down to her stomach and hips.

"This is perfect. Fuck, I love these new curves. Can you feel how hard you make me?" My erection is pressed to her back, there's no way she hasn't noticed.

167

"What else?" I skate my hand up and down her soft stomach, and she leans into me. *It feels fantastic.*

"My sides," she mumbles on an exhale. *Hell yeah.* "You're doing so good."

"I like this part of my stomach where Arthur used to sit. High in my belly." Her fingertips brush her upper abdomen. "His little feet would kick my ribs right here. It hurt then, but I miss it now."

God, baby, I could make that happen for you again. And this time, I promise to be here to feel the kicks myself.

I stroke my thumb over that spot. "I wish I could have seen you pregnant with our son." My eyes drop down her stomach, and I see the light horizontal scar low on her belly. *Is that...*

"You had a c-section?" She nods.

"I will never forgive myself for missing that." *Ever.*

"Spread your legs."

She juts out her chin.

"Ral, open your fucking legs." Her thighs part but not enough.

"Wider," I growl.

I blow out a breath of air and have to momentarily look away to keep it together. I've seen a lot of pussies, but none compare to hers. My mouth salivates when I return my eyes to her reflection. She tries to turn her head away from the mirror, but my bicep holds her in place. I keep her locked in the crook of my arm, and she pulls at me. Once she realizes it's futile, she drops her hands but keeps her eyes fixated off to the side.

"Fucking hell, Raleigh. How are you so beautiful?"

"That's enou—"

"Look at yourself. What do you like?"

She brings her gaze forward and holds eye contact with herself in the mirror. "I don't like this game."

"Look at your body."

I hook my free arm under one of her knees and yank it to the side. *Good God.* I groan at the image in front of me. Even in the low light, I can see how slick she is. I kiss the back of her neck.

"Tell me what you like about yourself. How are you struggling with this? It's *so* easy."

"It's not easy! I dunno. My knees?" She fidgets, and I tighten the headlock again.

"Wanna know what I like?"

Her eyes snap to mine and she stares at me in the reflection. We look damn good together.

"Your hips." I slip my hand under and grab a handful. "This ass."

I take her hand and slide it between her thighs. "Right here..."

I place my fingers over hers and rub them over her clit. "You have the prettiest pussy I have ever seen." She shudders, and I want to bite her shoulder so bad.

She sighs. "Bear?"

"Yeah, love?"

I apply pressure to her fingers, and she whimpers for me.

"Don't stop."

I give myself a minute to observe her desperation and draw out the anticipation. Her chest rises and falls. She's so needy, and *I love it.* When I can't stand it anymore and I'm convinced she won't fight me, I release her from the headlock. My fingers weave with hers, and I guide her hands behind my neck, out of the way. Her breasts swell, and she interlocks her fingers, holding onto me, granting free rein of her body.

My heart is pounding out of my chest.

I've wanted her like this for as long as I've known her. Everything in me is screaming to flip her over and punish her. If she can't say anything nice about her body, I'll fuck her till she can say nothing at all.

169

"When was the last time you were touched?"

"Too long."

I move both hands between her open thighs and strum the pad of my thumb over her nub. She rewards me with another moan.

"Yeah. More of that," I urge. I've replayed our night together nonstop, but this time I get a new storyline. These are new memories for us to make together.

Feeling her writhe against my cock and watching it in the mirror is some sick torture. I want to eat her, fuck her, and make her sob my name over and over until she can't breathe.

I push down my own desires and focus on her.

"Look at this clit. Do you still like it when I—" She gasps and looks down to watch me touching her. Her pupils dilate and her breath hitches.

"Oh my god," she mewls. *There we go.*

"I love the noises you make, I love your scent." I drag my finger around the edge to gather the wetness and bring it to my mouth, savoring her. It's pure bliss. My lips brush the shell of her ear. "You still taste like mine."

Her back hardens and eyes glisten. "Don't say—"

"You've always been mine, Raleigh."

I'm not holding back my feelings for her. I fucked up our first night when I kept my thoughts to myself, and that silence cost me years I'll never get back. She looks up at the ceiling, as if gravity will absorb the brimming tears. She clears her throat and faces forward again, but this time her gaze seems to look right through me.

"Just make me come."

I refrain from questioning how she can so easily shut down her emotions. It's more important to put the pleasure back on her face. That's all she's going to give me tonight anyway. I sink a finger inside, and she squeezes my neck.

170

Her mouth drops open, then I add another until I get the moan I want from her. *That's the one.*

"Goddamn, Ral. Still so fucking wet and tight. I've missed you so much." I pump my fingers in and out. "Think how pretty you'd look taking my cock like this. Does it feel good?"

"Mmhmmmmm."

"That's my sweet girl. Come on my fingers, baby."

I wrap an arm around her stomach and lift her up slightly so I can hook my feet inside her ankles and spread her wider.

Blood thunders through my veins, and my vision blurs.

"Oh, fuck yeah, look at you."

I thrust faster and her limbs tremble. Her symphony of sexy cries fills the space.

"Oh my god, *Bear.* It feels so good."

"I love it when you say my name like that." She's so small in my arms. My palm grinds against her clit, and she's nearly gushing around the fingers fucking her hot cunt. Her hands drop to my thighs, and she pushes herself up, bracing her shaking body and giving me a better view. *Jesus Christ.*

"You're breathtaking, love."

"Wait, wait. I'm..."

"Let go, Raleigh. I've got you."

Her abdomen flexes under my arm as her body clenches my hand so hard it nearly pushes me out of her. My dick has never been so jealous than when she begins to come. Her eyes grow big, and her mouth drops open on a silent scream, and her pussy clutches me harder with each pulse. *Unreal.*

"Right there!" I growl. "Look how gorgeous you are, coming on my fingers." She moans louder in response— I've hit my mark. "Look at your eyes, your mouth, your breasts, this delicious pink pussy."

I smile at her beauty as she falls apart. "Fucking unbelievable. Do you get it now? Do you see why I've never gotten over you? Why I'll *never* get over you?"

She's still climaxing. She needed this more than I realized. Which means she hasn't had it in a while, *at least not this good*.

"Bear!" she says, almost in a panic.

"That's what I see every time I look at you. *Every fucking time, Ral.* You make me crazy."

She groans, still coming, struggling to breathe through it. I tap her G-spot in a quick rhythm, and her eyes roll back a little.

"Good girl, keep coming for me. You're doing so well. That's it, be my greedy girl."

When she collapses, I usher her onto my lap, then cradle her spent body in my arms. As soon as I pull my fingers out, her thighs press together.

"Don't close your legs." I want to see every spasm while I taste her. "You're done hiding from me."

I suck my fingers, licking them clean, and then all the vulnerability and openness she had with me slides off her face, replaced by glowering eyes and a tense jaw.

"No, we are done. This was a mistake." She shakes her head and stands up, covering her exposed body with her hands.

Whoa, what the fuck?

My head cranks back, and my brows furrow.

"Come here," I murmur, holding out my hand.

She scoffs and starts pulling her clothes back on. "Did you not hear me? I mean it. You had your fun, but playtime is over. This is *my* life. *Our life.* You can't just show up with presents and orgasms and expect to be a part of everything. It doesn't work that way!"

"What are you talking about?"

"This'll affect Arthur too, and I won't let you hurt him the way you hurt me. We are finished, Barrett." Fuck that.

I will never be finished with her.

My laugh has her fuming, and she turns her back to me. I

step behind her, wrapping her hair around my palm and pulling. She gasps, forced to look up at me with blazing eyes.

I lock my lips on hers, upside down.

Our kiss is searing. This is the kiss I've dreamed about. Her lips are soft and plush and she tastes like everything I imagined. Electricity shoots up my spine. After a beat, she reluctantly opens for me, and I lap at her mouth, leaving traces of her taste on her tongue. She rests her hand over mine and kisses me back—and fuck if I don't fall for her right then and there. I compel myself to pull back, but not without first nipping at her bottom lip.

"We're not done, love. This is just the beginning."

TWENTY-FIVE

Raleigh

BARRETT

Let me take you out on a date.

> That's not an easy task. I'd need a
> babysitter, it's a whole thing.

BARRETT

We can bring Arthur with us. I have no
problem paying for a sitter, but if you're not
comfortable, let's take him along.

> You can't bring a kid on a date.

BARRETT

I can do whatever I want.

> Oh yeah? What are you going to do to
> include him?

BARRETT

Easy. We could go to the zoo— we've got
passes—or bowling, there's a couple G-
rated animated movies at the theater.

We could hang out at my place down by
the lake, I've got a decent beach.

Or we could go for a hike, a bike ride, check out a new playground, have a picnic.

There's mini golf, the arcade, the children's museum, the children's bookstore.

Go to the amusement park or visit the aquarium.

We could watch planes fly over us at Fort Snelling. Take him to a fun restaurant.

I could buy him some skates and we could go to the arena, probably get Fred to give him a ride on the Zamboni if he's around.

Jesus, did you think all that up just now?

BARRETT

Yeah. Well... actually I was hoping someday I could take him out for a boys day. So I've been bouncing ideas around.

I see. I don't know if I'm ready for that yet.

BARRETT

I know, I wasn't going to say anything until I knew you felt comfortable with me spending one-on-one time with him.

Thanks, I appreciate that.

BARRETT

But I won't be as patient with you.

I'm already being sucked back into Barrett's orbit. I haven't felt that heady vibration of feelings and attraction in years. I forgot what it was like to feel wanted in that way. It's been so long. I'm addicted, I need more. And that orgasm, *holy shit*. I don't even remember the last time I had one so powerful.

TWENTY-SIX
Raleigh

Arthur is humming in the back seat while I drive us to the zoo to use his passes from Barrett. He's only had a couple interactions with him, but he's done phenomenal. Though, I'm unsure if I am ready for him to become somebody who shows up regularly in Arthur's life.

Am I being naive and putting Arthur in jeopardy of having his heart broken? What if parenthood becomes too much for Barrett and he decides he can't handle it? Sure, we have good days, but Arthur is still young. He comes with mood swings and whining, some days are really fucking hard.

Barrett hasn't seen that side.

The twenty-minute drive to the zoo is the perfect environment for my anxiety to build. I'm guilty of overthinking things when I get stressed out, and nothing has brought on more stress than Barrett showing up. I'm torn at how I feel about his return. Those gifts were sweet, but they don't make up for his absence. Why the fuck couldn't he have checked his own Instagram? This literally could have all been avoided if he read his goddamn DMs. I'm not blameless, I should have exchanged contact info with him earlier. I should have said goodbye.

It's not his fault, and yes, a lot of my anger is misdirected, but after writing him off for so long, it's hard to switch gears and welcome him into our lives with open arms. There's so much making up to do. It's going to be a lot of work, from all three of us. Do I let him try? He's clearly putting in the effort. He has stayed true to his word by calling and texting every day.

Arthur wants a dad; he's mentioned it before. If I was simply looking to give him a father, I'm sure I could find someone, but any man who's expressed an attraction hasn't felt right. It always appears like they're interested in me, and my child is simply part of my baggage. Arthur deserves a good role model, one who's present and invested, not just along for the ride. There's also the matter of co-parenting. I don't know if I'm ready for that. We have all these set routines.

Fuck, I'm getting way ahead of myself.

I turn the radio up, trying to drown out my thoughts. Why am I already entertaining these ideas? Probably because it seems like we're on the precipice of some next step with Barrett. If he's interested in being a dad, then I should allow him to prove himself. I'd want him to give me a chance if the situation were reversed, right? Whatever, I would have checked my own fucking messages instead of getting someone else to do it for me. Ugh, I could go around in circles with this all fucking day. If I'm looking to place blame, it should be on that PR woman. Not Barrett.

I park the car. "We're here!"

Arthur unbuckles his booster seat. Hopefully it's not too nuts today. I grab our backpack lunch and walk around the car to open his door.

"Take my hand." His little fist clutches mine, and I'm suddenly very appreciative for this gift, it's a special day for me to have with Arthur. The zoo is expensive, we haven't visited many times. Which sucks, especially since my child is such an animal lover. I open my wallet and pull out the zoo membership cards.

"Can we see the koalas first?"

"There's a lot of terrific animals here, so let's start at the beginning and work our way through as we go. We don't want to miss anything, right? But we can spend extra time checking out the koalas when we get there."

He nods and tugs me toward the entrance. We walk through the big automatic doors, then I hand the membership card over to be scanned. We're ushered through and given a map, which Arthur takes control of. I'll let him lead the way.

We turn the corner into a dark room that's swallowed up by an enormous glowing aquarium that reaches the ceiling.

"Whoa!" he says, running over to the massive glass wall. He spins around for a second to make sure I'm behind him. "Mom, look! A hammerhead!"

I stand behind him and watch the huge shark swim above us. "Wow. It's big." Yeesh.

"It's huge!"

With gaping eyes, he stands in wonderment of the sharks and tropical fish. It's magical. A sea turtle stops right in front of him, and they regard each other. Arthur is entranced. I pull out my phone and snap a photo of his silhouette observing the creature on the other side. It's a priceless moment.

We watch the fish for a while longer, and when we step away, I pull up the photo and text it to Barrett.

> Thank you for the passes. He's loving it.

BARRETT

> Great photo. I'm glad he likes it.

> He likes you a lot.

BARRETT

Yeah? I like him a lot too. How's his mom feel about me?

Coming on a little strong...

BARRETT

Do you want me to stop?

I want to type back no, because being the object of his affection feels amazing. But, it's also a little *sudden*. And scary.

I don't know.

BARRETT

Let me know when you do.

At lunchtime, we find a shaded spot outside and I pull sandwiches and snacks out of our backpack.

"Do you want your chips now or save them?"

"Now, please."

"Here you go." I hand them over along with the water bottle I brought for him.

We bite into our sandwiches and munch on chips while we watch the caribou graze in the meadow. "They have fuzzy antlers." I nod in agreement.

"Hey, I want to ask you something."

"Yeah?"

"What did you think of Barrett?" I stuff my hand back into my small bag of chips, trying to act casual as I ask him the important question.

"I like him. He brings me presents."

I roll my eyes and chuckle. "Okay, but let's pretend he didn't bring you presents, would you still like him then?"

"Yes. He's cool and funny and nice. He's good at playing with cars. He gives good horsey rides."

Yeah, I've gotten those horsey rides too.

"Would you want to hang out with him again sometime? You can say no."

"Yeah! Can he come over for dinner tonight? Would that be a good idea, Mom?"

"I think he's busy tonight with a hockey game. But maybe we can set something up for another day."

"We can go to the hockey game! I have tickets, remember? Barrett gave them to me!"

"Yeah, but that makes for a long day, kiddo. Hockey games can go late, way past your bedtime." I hate saying no to such an excited face.

"I promise I'll sleep in tomorrow and won't wake you up!"

I purse my lips and wince. I really don't think it's a good idea. "I'll think about it."

"That means no." He pouts.

"No, it means *I'll think about it.*"

He's right, I always say no whenever I say I'll think about it. Now I'm the asshole. I should actually consider it. If we go, we're not sitting in the box, that's for sure. I'm not subjecting him or myself to the awkwardness of those introductions.

Hard pass.

> I'm not ready for you and Arthur to have one-on-one time, but I'm working on warming up to the idea. For now, I'd like to keep his interactions with the three of us together.

Sometimes I forget we're still getting to know each other. I'm nervous, yet everytime we're together, his presence calms me. There's something about our connection that runs deeper, and it's not just Arthur, it's always been like this with him. That's what made the rejection from the past hurt so much, but he seems awfully determined to heal our old wounds.

BARRETT

U understand. What about us?

I type from the heart, trying to be as honest as he is with me.

I'm conflicted. You still give me those same feelings which really pisses me off because I don't want to have them. Things would be easier if I could stay mad at you. Then everything could go back to normal.

BARRETT

I never want to relive that version of us, I fucking hated it. That wasn't normal. We're what's missing from each other's lives. When I came over for dinner? That's our normal. Eating together, playing with our son, kissing, making you come night after night. We can have that, Ral, it's ours if we want it. We just need to take it.

It's not fair for him to say those things. He's playing underhanded.

You're shaking up my life.

BARRETT

That's how I felt the night I met you.

I'm wiling to work at it, are you?

TWENTY-SEVEN

Raleigh

It's almost dinner time and he's still sleeping. The zoo wore him out. I need to decide whether we will go to this stupid hockey game tonight... He's probably going to be up anyway since I let him sleep so late, we have the tickets, he wants to go, it's the playoffs, there's not many more chances until next season. I'm the only one standing in our way.

Ever since Barrett's text about letting ourselves have it, all I've been able to think about is how often I stand in my own way. *Like the game tonight.* I'm constantly playing it safe and never going outside my comfort zone. I've lost touch with the wild side I used to have.

Sitting on the edge of his bed, I rub his back. His eyes blink open and he looks like a cherub with his sleepy rosy cheeks.

"You still wanna go to that game?"

"Yeah!" His eyes light up.

"If we go, you have to go straight to bed as soon as we get home."

The way his face lights up has already made it worth it. "I'll fall asleep in the car before we even get home!"

"And I want top-tier behavior while we're there. No running up and down the aisles, if you're bored, that's fine, just let me know and we can find something else to do."

"Okay!" He jumps to his feet.

I sigh. "All right, let's get you dressed in some blue and green clothes."

"Why?"

I internally cringe. I haven't taken him to enough sporting events. "That's what you do when you go to games, you dress up in your team's colors. Our team is the Lakes, and they wear blue and green when they play on the ice."

"Mom, I have a green shirt *and* a blue shirt. Which one do I wear?"

"Whichever one you want. And put on a sweatshirt too. It can get cold in the seats. I'll bring your hat and mittens."

"What are you going to wear?"

I have a Brickhauer jersey, he doesn't even play for the Lakes anymore. I have no idea if it even fits.

"I don't know yet."

My anxiety kicks into overdrive when we get to the arena and I pull out our tickets.

These are glass seats.

My silly brain thought that our seats would be somewhere in the middle of the stands. Arthur is losing his goddamn mind. This will warp his expectations for every future sporting event. I didn't anticipate being seen by Barrett and I'm feeling very exposed with no other fans to hide behind. But my inner hockey fan could never let me give up front row playoff tickets. These are once in a lifetime seats.

When the arena darkens, spotlights swirl over the crowd.

Arthur gawks at the light show. Then the goal horn blares, and he jumps, slapping his mittened hands over his ears. The crowd claps and cheers around us.

"It's loud sometimes!" I shout over the noise. Reaching into my pockets, I pull out the earplugs I brought for him and put them in his ears. The players step out on the ice for warmups, and the roar of the fans grows louder. They skate their half of the blue line, some slow, some racing around, pounding the ice. I sit back a little farther in my seat.

Off to the side is the new, younger, and *hotter* generation of women to hook up with players, and it kinda brings me back. My life was empty then. Now, here I am with my four-year-old, I'm no longer able to fit into single-digit dress sizes, and the early signs of wrinkles have developed at the corner of my eyes. Those days were fun, but I'm happier now. My nights aren't nearly as wild, but they are secure and filled with cuddles from my little man. Even on the nights when I stare at the ceiling and let the loneliness consume me, I know my life is far better now than it was when there was a hockey player sharing my bed.

I'm thankful Arthur can't read yet, because the signs being held up... *Yikes, these are some thirsty bitches.* I point out the players. I show Arthur how they each have different numbers on their jersey.

"Which one is Barrett?"

"Thirty-three."

"He's a winger!"

I smile and pull his pom-pom hat down further. "How did you get so smart?"

"It comes naturally."

I laugh. "And so modest."

The players stretch on the ice and adjust their skates.

They skate in circles and flip pucks into the net.

"Why does that guy look different?"

184

"That's the goalie, he stays in the net to make sure the other team doesn't get any pucks past him."

"They look funny."

"They have a lot of pads on so they don't get hurt when the pucks fly toward them. Did you know I used to play hockey when I was younger? I was the goalie on my team."

He gawks at me. "You looked like *that*?"

"Well, I definitely wasn't as tall as Strassburg, but I had quick reflexes."

"Is that why you have a jersey?"

I look down at the jersey I put on over my hooded sweatshirt. I used to wear it as a dress back in the day. *Not anymore.* "I've always liked hockey, but I'm only a fan now. I don't play anymore."

"Are you as quick as that goalie?"

"Nope, that goalie is much faster than I ever was."

"Can I play hockey?"

I swallow. "If that's something you want to try, we can get you signed up for lessons."

His arm shoots out. "Look! Thirty-three!"

My eyes follow his finger to Barrett. He's coming around at a fast clip, but he's mostly facing the other direction while skating backward. I hold my breath until he moves away from us again. I try to focus on different players, but I can't take my eyes off Barrett. Neither can Arthur.

"Hey, he has an A on his jersey!"

"Yup, that stands for alternate captain."

"Or Arthur!"

He makes me laugh again. *"Or Arthur."* I smile.

"Barrett is fast."

He sure is. Why are all hockey players so attractive? *They aren't, you're trying to make excuses for your attraction to* that *one.* I give up, he's fucking hot. There. I said it. And Barrett Conway on skates only fuels my staring. He's so focused and coordinated and aggressive. And tall. Jesus. Thank God for all the ice to keep my internal temperature in check.

I enjoy watching hockey, but it's usually done through a television screen these days. I forgot what it's like to be so close to the action. So close I have to look up to see his face. I didn't text him to tell him we were coming. He's bound to see us at some point, but I'm not going to bang on the glass and be a distraction.

After the national anthem and the puck drop, the game gets an energized start. It's amazing how enthralled Arthur is already. I suppose there's hockey in his blood, so it only makes sense.

"They're super speedy!"

I nod and try to track the puck—old habits and all that. A puck battle breaks out ten feet down the glass from us and everyone jumps to their feet. Glass seats give the advantage of seeing the true speed of the players. They're impossibly fast.

Once they get a breakaway, Sully and Banks push it toward the goal, Lonan sneaks around the side, and when they deke the puck back to him, he snaps it in. Everyone jumps to their feet screaming, including my four-year-old. I'm not sure he even knows what happened. The horn blares and the Lakes take the first point.

"Every time a team gets a goal, they blow the horn!" I yell.

"I know, Mom!" *Well, look who's the expert now.* "This is so much fun! Barrett is awesome!" I roll my lips together and nod.

We finish the period and then I take him to the bathroom during intermission.

"Can we get something to eat?"

I don't want to pay nine dollars for a pretzel, that's why I stopped for fast food on the way in.

"Let's see if we can wait a little longer, the lines are really long."

I hope he forgets about it. He can't be that hungry, he ate all his meal, plus half of mine.

He asks about the Zamboni and the peewee hockey players that play before the second period begins. The Zamboni is definitely a hit, might have to take Barrett up on that offer to give Arthur a ride sometime.

After the game starts up again, things get a little more tense. A fight breaks out nearby with Kucera and another player. I cover Arthur's eyes, and he tries to peel my fingers off his face. *Not happening, kid.*

"Mom! I can't see! I can't see!" He tugs at my arms, but I keep him shielded.

"I don't want you to see. You can watch the fights when you're older."

As it breaks up, I remove my hand, and he glares at me. I have to resist laughing at how perturbed he looks. We return our eyes to the game and cheer when it's appropriate. We sing the hockey anthem and jump around when the songs tell us to. I'm glad we came out tonight, it's a great ending to our mother-son day.

Most of the team is down on our end. Barrett is right there. Arthur is jumping up and down, pointing him out. Then number thirty-three checks another player against the boards in front of us, and that's when it happens. He does a double-take and smiles before pushing off the glass and skating after the puck again.

"He saw us!"

"He sure did."

Yeah, Barrett, we're here. We came to watch you play. Don't let it go to your head. I'd been anxious about him seeing us all night, but now it doesn't seem like a big deal.

Maybe it's the look he gave us.

The Lakes get another goal, but so does the other team. With only a few minutes left in the second period, someone wearing a Lakes polo and khakis shows up in front of us with nachos and hot dogs, a couple of drinks, and a branded Lakes bag.

Barrett.

"He thought you could use some snacks." We all know who *he* is.

"Thank you so much!" I say. It's sweet. Arthur is thrilled and thanks the staff member before they jog back up the steps. While he digs into his salty chips and cheese, I peek inside the bag. Two jerseys, one adult and one youth size, both with the number thirty-three and CONWAY printed on the back. Barrett is going to spoil this kid rotten. He's a giver, in every meaning of the word. I will need to lay down some ground rules about the presents though.

"What's in there?" he asks, peeking over the rim of the bag.

"There's a jersey for each of us. That was very nice of Barrett, we'll have to tell him thank you."

"Can I wear mine now?" I pull it out, and he squeals about it being the same one that Barrett has. After wiping his fingers free of cheese sauce, I pull the jersey over his head and roll up the sleeves. My lips press together as I resist nagging Arthur about keeping it clean. There's no way we're walking out of here without a ketchup stain, so why ruin the fun. I'm trying to live in the moment. I take off my old jersey and pull the new one over my head. Both of us donning his name and number on our backs.

Arthur is having the time of his life. Poor kid, I shouldn't have waited for tickets from Barrett to bring him to a hockey game. He clearly loves it. Granted, it's hard not to with seats as great as these. After the nachos and hot dog, which I'm still shocked he ate the entirety of, his eyes soften and grow heavy. I'm stunned it took this long for him to get sleepy.

By third period, he's leaning against me and dozing off. I

wrap my arm around him and smile as he sleeps during one of the most intense parts of the game. Barrett scores a goal, afterward skating by our seats and giving a small wave. That smile of his is a weapon when it's pointed in my direction. My heart flips. That last one puts us up by two and wraps up the game.

After they shake hands, they head back through the tunnel. A couple minutes later, my phone vibrates in my pocket, and the excitement of getting a text message from him has started.

BARRETT

How did Arthur like it?

> He loved it, thank you for the tickets, I didn't realize they were glass seats. And thank you for the snacks and gear. You didn't have to do that.

BARRETT

Yeah I did. My name is the only one I want to see on your back.

> Ohhhh, it's a possessive thing.

BARRETT

Hell yeah it is.

Can you wait for me? I can have someone bring you back.

> I have to get him to the car, I parked in the east ramp and he's already passed out. Raincheck?

The arena is packed, I don't even bother trying to stand in line holding my sleeping child. My arms will be asleep after the first fifteen minutes. He's big for his age. I sit back and stroke his hair as he slumbers through the noise.

When it finally slows enough to see the doors through the

crowd, I loop the Lakes bag over my arm and gingerly transfer my sweet, tired child into my arms without waking him. He sighs and settles his head on my shoulder. I make it up the stairs and stand in the throng of fans as we shuffle toward the exit.

"Raleigh!" I can't tell where it's coming from, until I look to the left and see Barrett standing at an emergency exit, holding the door open with a security guard that waves us into a long industrial concrete hallway. Inside, I'm left standing face-to-face with the hottest man I've ever seen. Freshly showered and in that fucking blue suit that steals my breath away. The lock engages on the heavy metal door and the ambient noise of the crowd is snuffed out.

He holds his arms out to take Arthur, and I hand him over, giving my numbing arms a chance to relax.

"What are we doing?"

"I'm making sure you and Arthur get to the car safely. East ramp is a trek, this is faster." He rubs small circles on Arthur's back as we stroll, revealing his nurturing side, which is so fucking attractive after watching him slam two-hundred plus pound hockey players into the boards less than an hour ago. My ovaries feel like they might explode.

"Thanks, I appreciate the shortcut."

He glances down at me. "I'm digging that jersey."

I chuckle and look down. "Oh, yeah?"

"Yeah... the name Conway suits you."

My heart feels like it's in my throat. With burning cheeks, I try to come up with a witty retort, but I'm too distracted. The nervous laugh that comes out instead couldn't make me more obvious that his remarks affect me the way they do.

We saunter down the echoing hallway, taking twists and turns through the maze of passageways until we reach a stairwell. He holds the door open for me, Arthur heavy and limp in his arms. Barrett makes carrying him look so effortless.

"I'm parked over there." I point to the side of the concrete parking ramp, and Barrett nods.

When we reach the car, I get him buckled into his seat and his head lolls to the side, and sure enough, there's ketchup on the collar of his new jersey.

"Thanks for helping me get him to the car. As you can see, his first hockey game was a big success." Technically his first game was the night of the banquet, but he didn't really watch it, so this feels like his first official game.

"Anytime, Ral. Thanks for coming tonight, seeing you in the stands was..." A smile spreads across his face and his eyes sparkle. "It was awesome."

"You played a great game, we loved watching you get the last goal. Congratulations on being tied up three in three this round. Are you nervous?"

"Nah." He's playing it cool. "You might be my good luck charm. I don't suppose you'd let me fly you and Arthur out to the final game?"

I shake my head. "Definitely not."

"Might be fun..." He bites his lip, and those blue eyes bore into mine. It gives me butterflies.

"Sorry, best I can do is put it on the TV at home."

"Watching it on TV isn't nearly as good as the real thing though. Box seats are pretty cushy."

I roll my eyes. "Good night, Barrett." Grabbing the driver's side door handle to climb inside, he holds it shut.

"Hey."

It catches me off guard and I startle, but before I can say anything, his hand is on my hip, pressing me against the car.

"Barrett, what if he—"

"Sees his dad kissing his mom?"

My chest pounds and I can't breathe. "Please, don't."

He stares at my lips, and I think he's about to lock his mouth on mine, when he leans over and places a peck on my cheek instead. He tucks a few loose strands of hair behind my ear. Does he hear my heartbeat? It's deafening in my ears.

"I'm still calling you every day. I want to see you when I get back from Seattle."

I keep my eyes fixated toward the ground and give a tight nod. "Okay."

"Okay... Give Mini Bear a fist bump for me."

TWENTY-EIGHT
Barrett

The plane ride to Seattle is energized, but we all feel the underlying pressure of this being the last game in the third round. We need this win to go to number four. If we don't win, we're done for the season. Jonesy cracks his jokes as usual, trying to keep things light. I slide my headphones over my ears and recline in my seat with my eyes closed, visualizing our plays. Over the last couple days, Sully and I have been spending every second going over game tapes and finding our weak spots as well as Seattle's.

No matter how much I focus on the game and how much footage I watch, Raleigh and Arthur are never far from my thoughts. I want to win the playoffs and get our chance at the Stanley Cup, but if I could use the offseason to build something with them, that would be incredible. I want them all to myself this summer. For now, though, I need to make hockey a priority too. Before I go into full hockey mode, I shoot off a text.

> Thinking about you

RALEIGH

Funny. I was just thinking about you too.

> I'll be home Friday night. What are you guys doing on Saturday?

RALEIGH

I don't think we have plans.

> Good. I'm going to need some Raleigh and Arthur time when I get back. Maybe we could go to a park.

RALEIGH

His favorite is Trillium Park.

> It's a date. I'll call you later. xo

Now that I have that set up, I can give my focus to our final game this round. Seattle has been playing well this year.

And now they've got home ice advantage.

After a night at the hotel, we get on the bus and head to the arena. Game night has everyone on edge, but nobody talks about it. We all have each other's back while on the opponent's territory and we are leaning on one another.

You could cut the tension in the locker room with a knife.

"Hey, would everybody just fucking breathe?" I say to the boys.

Jen leads us in some meditation before the game while we envision what we need to do. By the end, we're a little less jumpy and more focused. When we hit the ice, my heart is pumping. *This is it.*

Warm-ups go well, Strass is blocking shots like a champ. I'm feeling good about tonight. I try to get the guys to shake off some of the noise. Tune out the crowd, focus on our plays, our strategy, pull up those weak areas and show our strengths like never before. We kicked their ass at our house, now we gotta do it at theirs.

"How ya feeling?" I ask Sully. We practically share a brain on the ice, yet I can't imagine where his head's at. He's retiring, and these playoffs have been fucking with his psyche pretty hard. This could be his last hockey game. That's some heavy shit.

"Ready."

"You're a hell of a captain." I remind him.

He shakes his head. "Don't even start with that."

"Alright, you're a shit leader and you skate like old people fuck."

He holds his glove out, and I bump mine against it.

"Always could count on you for a pep talk."

After another quick speech in the locker room and the national anthem, we come back out to center ice for the drop. Banks lowers into position and the stands grow quiet as the crowd's anticipation builds. I drop down and prepare for his pass. When the rubber hits the ice, it's on.

We capture the first round and it's the fucking start we need. I snag and pass to Sully, then he passes to Banks before it's snagged by Seattle. They're as tense as we are. We combat their advances on Strass for my entire shift.

O'Callahan jumps on the ice, flying past me as I return to the bench. I'll have a better sense of how they're defending after a few shifts. They're playing well. Sully enters the box soon after me and hunches over. We're a couple of old bastards. Next is Banks. He leans in.

"I'm gonna go deep, I can steal from their D-men. Their left is weaker."

I nod, we knew this going into the game tonight based on the footage of their previous games. "I'll get in the slot for a blind pass."

"Conway!" Coach shouts, and I swap out with O'Cal.

My skates pound ice to get into position. Lonan checks their guy into the boards and dekes it back to me on the side. The opening I had is closing fast, I send it out, but my pass is missed by Bishop. *Fucking hell.* I need to get my line out here, but the puck is in our zone, so we can't do a shift change. Kucera intercepts like a fucking bulldog and sends it out. *That's what I'm talking about.* As our puck moves up, we finally get to swap the line, and Sully and Banks get on the ice with me. Coach calls me in, but I ignore it. We need this set up.

We go for a dump and chase. Even though Sully and I are the older guys, we are still some of the toughest skaters on the ice. It works, and their defensemen are spinning around to race us to the net. It's a split second, but it's enough to get possession. Sully gets ahead and I pass to him, Kucera blocks for him, and he makes the first attempt on goal, sailing it into the five hole.

"Fuck yeah, Sully!" The horn sounds and he looks up to the scoreboard, taking a deep satisfied breath before he drops his chin. I can see on his face this is going to be an emotional game for him. We skate off the ice to get a fresh line and I ask the zebras to give me the puck, in case it's his last goal. I don't want to think that way, but it's a possibility.

At the next drop, they get a breakaway and make a goal on us. Well, that was fun while it lasted, all forty seconds. The first two periods are more of the same. By the third, we're fucking beat. It's been neck and neck, with zero new goals made. A few bullshit calls keep us under their thumb.

I'm thinking we will go into overtime.

During the intermissions, we've discussed how they're playing, but every time we think they're going to zig, they zag. It's frustrating as hell. Banksy looks like he's ready to kill somebody. He better pull it together, the last thing we need is to give them a power play. It's time to close it out. I don't want another twenty minutes of this shit.

"Come on, boys, let's push!" I shout to the line, running it up the boards. We've got five minutes left in the game.

My name gets called and I get back out there for whatever

number shift this is of the night. Lonan does a stellar deke to Sully, and I get into position, my third attempt on goal is blocked. *Goddamn it.* Kucera sends it around the net, but the pass to Banks is intercepted.

We chase down the puck, but their rookie is carrying well and we're struggling to gain possession. Banks gets in front of it, ready to capture and flip, but their D-man hooks his handle with his skate. We wait for the refs to call but it's radio silence. What in the actual fuck is happening with these calls tonight? Coach is screaming from the bench.

"You pregnant, stripes? You've missed the last two fucking periods!" I shout. We're getting railed by these refs.

Another shift change and we get a second to cool off and regain our focus.

"That's bullshit. We need another official," Coach shouts from behind me.

"Shake it off, bud," I say to Banks when he slides next to me. He doesn't say anything, he's stewing. I can't blame him.

When our line is back up, the first thing Banksy does is gun it for their defenseman and drop gloves. *Shit.* The rest of us grab a buddy player from the opposite side, as much as we all want to gang up on their guy Harris for his hooking, we need to keep it clean.

"Don't go too far, man."

Again, we wait for the refs to step in, but they are doing fuck all to break it up.

"Banks!" Sully shouts, he's a little closer than I am. We drop our guys and go to pull Banks off the guy. If the refs aren't gonna do their job, then we'll do it for them. Half a second before we get to him, he knocks the guy's helmet off and gets him right in the fucking teeth. Blood sprays onto the ice.

"Goddamn it!"

We yank him back, but it's an automatic penalty. We're fucked. I swear to Christ that was a setup.

Banks goes into the sin bin and we fight for our fucking lives on a power play. We dig deep but it's not enough, with three minutes left, they get one on goal. The horn sounds and the Seattle fans lose their minds. Brush it off, brush it off. A lot can happen in the time left.

The next three minutes are hell on earth. We give it everything we have; I see it in the face of every guy on the ice. When the final buzzer sounds, we're lifeless and defeated. It's over. Round four is gone. I look at Sully and throw my arms around him. He looks rough. We played well tonight, but we went up against a solid team and some refs that need to be fined. I'm sure the Lakes will file for disciplinary action.

The team has the decency to give Sully a send-off. As the announcers give a synopsis of his career, I'm the one getting emotional. Fuck, I can't believe the next game I play will be without him. We've been playing together a long ass time. I've been so busy thinking about how he will feel after his last game I didn't take the time to prepare for not playing alongside him. He's been my closest friend for years. The only one who understands the job and has been with me since my rookie days.

We go through the line, shaking hands, and Sully gets more hugs than handshakes from the opposing team. Lee Sullivan has gained a ton of respect during his career. He's a powerful player, but an even more powerful leader. Every hockey stick clacks on the ice. He waves to the stands, thanks the fans, especially the ones that followed us here. Shortly after, they announce the retirement of number nine for the Lakes team.

"A true class act," an announcer comments. He is. Normally when a player skates his last game, his family is in the box. But we've been Sully's family. There's no woman or kids in the box waiting to give him a hug when he comes off the ice. It's us. Hockey has always been his focus, it's his life. That dedication made him a hell of a captain. He's a man of few words, so he hasn't mentioned what his plans are. I think it's because he doesn't have any.

If Raleigh pushes me away, is this what my future looks like too? Playing my last game with no one in the stands for me to go home to? I don't want it to be that way. There's more to life than hockey. What comes after this stage in our lives is important too.

Sully and I aren't that old, but we're pushing forty. And while having an exceptional career in the NHL is the dream, it's not everything. There's likely another forty years left to live after retirement. I don't want to spend them alone. There has to be more to life than hockey, somebody to share it with. If there's no other love besides this sport in your life, then where does that leave you when it's time to hang up your number?

TWENTY-NINE

Raleigh

"Wow, Mom. You look really pretty."

I turn and cock my head to the side. "I look like I always do."

"No, you look extra pretty today. It's different than how you normally are."

I double-check my reflection in the mirror. I don't look *that* different, but maybe I spent a little longer on my hair today, and I tried out a new mascara. I adjust the light wrap sweater, and twist to check my backside—at least my ass looks great.

"I always look pretty." I nudge his shoulder with my hip. "Are you ready to go?"

"Yup! I have my picture right here." He holds out the drawing he made.

"Where's your shoes?"

"I dunno."

What is it with kids and fucking shoes? It's like they repel each other.

My bag has enough snacks to feed an army, and a couple toys to keep him busy, if it comes to that. *The Boy Scouts ain't got nothin' on me.*

After a quick bathroom check and finding his shoes, I load Arthur into the car and head out for a casual day at the park.

The weather is perfect for May, sunny with a cool breeze.

"Do you think he's sad about his hockey game?" Arthur asks, from the back seat.

"Yeah, he's probably a little sad. But I know he's excited to see you."

"I hope he likes my picture. I used all the Lakes colors."

"He'll love it. You are very artistic, kiddo."

When we pull up, he's already pacing the sidewalk. I run my tongue along my teeth to make sure none of my lipstick accidentally rubbed off. Arthur unbuckles himself, and I get out of the car to open his door. I have to jump out and grab it before he slams it into the car parked next to mine. He's already bounding out and running up to Barrett, waving around his hand-drawn picture like a flag.

Barrett scoops him up, it looks so natural, and takes the paper from his hand.

"What's this?"

"It's to cheer you up. Because you didn't win the trophy."

His eyes rove over the drawing of Barrett and Arthur on hockey skates. His eyes become glassy, it might not be noticeable to most, but I see it. The first time I got one of Arthur's drawings of the two of us as a family, I felt the same way.

Barrett clears his throat. "Wow, buddy, this is the best drawing I've ever seen. Can I keep it?"

"Yeah, I made it for you! Does it make you not sad?"

I stealthily pull my phone from my pocket and snap a photo of them.

"It definitely makes me not sad!" He laughs a little. "It makes me very happy! Thank you, bud. This is the coolest."

He sets Arthur down and holds out his hand in a fist bump. Observing him interact with another man is fascinating, their relationship is different from ours. It's a side of

Arthur I don't get to see. It's funny and a little heart wrenching to see him imitate Barrett.

His gaze reaches mine and then wanders to my feet. I tuck a lock of hair behind my ear, feeling extra exposed under his scrutiny. He made it clear he's still attracted to me when he came to dinner almost two weeks ago, but it's still a struggle to not be self-conscious now that we have all this added sexual tension between us. Those giant arms envelop me in a hug, and I inhale his scent. It's clean and woodsy.

"Hey, beautiful," he whispers. His words bring me back to that night, but I hold my composure.

"Hi, Barrett." I hoist my tote bag on my shoulder.

My brain is short-circuiting, unable to stop thinking about everything *else* he said in front of that mirror. The more I try to come up with something, the more my mind recalls the image of him putting me in a headlock and finger-fucking me into oblivion. I can feel the blush rising to my cheeks.

Arthur runs ahead and finds a stick, tapping it on the side-walk as we make our way toward the playground. When it comes into view, he takes off in a dead sprint for the swings.

"That send-off for Sully was a tearjerker," I say. If we don't start talking about something soon, I will need a new pair of underwear.

"Oof, yeah. You should have seen the locker room, we bawled like babies."

I look up at Barrett, I'm not short, but our height difference is still startling sometimes. "How's he doing?"

"He's good, trying to figure out what to do with his time.

He golfs, but I've been telling him he needs some new hobbies. Or a girl."

"I always assumed he was married."

He's such a quiet guy, never seemed into the parties, though I remember seeing him around. Sully's old enough to have settled down, but I suppose Barrett is too.

"No, he and I are the old bachelors on the team. Makes me feel old. I mean, look at Kucera, he was practically Arthur's age when I started my NHL career and he's already engaged to Micky."

I smile at the mention of my new friend. "I really like her, we're going out for drinks this weekend."

"Who?" He shakes his head. "Wait, you know Micky?"

Oh, that's right. He doesn't even know I met a couple of his teammates' partners...

"Uh, yeah. She called up Method and gave us some tickets to her soft opening for Sugar and Ice. We chatted on the phone for a while and then we met in person at the event."

His arm shoots out to stop our stroll and he scrutinizes me. "I was at the launch, why didn't I see you?"

My nose scrunches and I grimace remembering my behavior that night. Toeing a divot in the grass, I sheepishly answer. "Because I saw you first?"

When I glance back at him, he rubs the back of his neck and stares at me, his feet moving again. "Thank God for that stupid meet and greet at the arena, otherwise I don't know when our lives would have crossed again. I don't like thinking about it. Were there any other times you *saw me first?*"

I shake my head, and he seems relieved.

"Part of me thought you must have moved back to North Carolina to be near your family or something. I couldn't understand how we never ran into each other again."

Yeah, right. I'd never subject Arthur to my mother or the men she lets into her life. I feel guilty he has no grandparents, but having none is better than having my mother.

"No, I haven't been back there for a long time."

"Do your parents come up and visit?"

"It's just my mom. And no, she doesn't." There's an awkward lull in conversation.

"I don't want you to take this the wrong way... but what kind of support system do you have?"

I press my lips together in a stiff smile. It's understandable why he'd think I would take that as a threat. A couple weeks ago, I was looking for any sign of him insinuating I was an unfit mother. Our entire history is basically one giant miscommunication, mostly due to outside influence. *This* is our fresh start. Even if it does mean we're doing everything backward.

It's obvious we are attracted to each other. We're sexually compatible, Arthur's proof of that. *So was the other night.*

But sometime soon, we need to discuss what is happening between us. Is he trying to be involved with Arthur's life? Is the intention for us to be a family?

Oh God, what if he's feeling obligated because of some deep moral compass bullshit? My stomach drops. I mean, it makes sense. That's not what I'm looking for, we aren't some pity project. We are fine on our own. I only want him to be involved in Arthur's life because he *wants* to, not out of some familial duty.

"Raleigh?"

"We don't need a support system, you know."

He pushes his tongue into his cheek and shakes his head. When we find an open park bench, we take a seat to talk and watch Arthur drag a new stick he found through the sand, drawing out what appears to be a treasure map on the playground. I can feel Barrett's eyes on me, but he must be giving me a moment to collect my words.

"Tell me."

"Tell you what?"

"Whatever the fuck it is that's got you stuck in your thoughts again."

I ask the question that's been bouncing around in my head nonstop for the last minute. "Do you think you're morally obligated to be involved in our lives?"

He pauses for a while. "Yes and no. I want to make sure you and Arthur are taken care of, you've done an incredible job, but it sucks to find out you've been doing it alone for so long. It's unfair to you... That said, it's not why I'm here. I'm here because... fuck, I don't even know how to explain it."

"Try." I purse my lips.

He inhales deeply and releases his breath. "Do you not feel this?" He gestures between us. "This... pull—or whatever you want to call it."

I blink at him. *That is not what I thought he would say.*

He groans. "Okay, look, this isn't going to make sense, but I'm going to explain it the best I can, and hopefully you'll get the idea and I won't scare you off. That night—that *first* night —it was hot... God, I loved chasing you down," he recalls, smiling as if he's replaying everything in his head. "I loved how playful you were."

He's right, it was crazy hot foreplay.

"...But as soon as I slid inside you, it was like a switch flipped in my brain. Like, that was it. My vision was perfectly clear and you were all I wanted. My heart was at peace. My soul was on fire. Life seemed brighter and more optimistic. It felt like we were... I don't know, like we had already known each other and I knew it would always feel like that when we were together. I knew you were someone important I didn't want to let go of. I'd never felt anything like that before you and I've not felt anything like it since. Well, until I found you again."

This isn't happening. I can hear the sincerity in his voice.

"And then you left," he reminds me. I feel terrible, but I need to explain where my head was that night.

"You called me a bunny."

He jerks his head back. "What?"

"That night, you called me a bunny. During sex."

Arthur runs up to us, panting, before Barrett can respond.

"Mom, do we have anything to drink?"

I reach into my bag and pull out a pouch of apple juice. I puncture a hole with the straw and hand it back to him.

Barrett looks at me like he just watched his dog get run over.

"Having fun out there?" I ask with a smile.

He nods, still sipping juice from the straw.

"Don't forget to come up for air." He stops sucking and takes a deep breath before handing the drink back.

"Thanks, Mom!" he yells, hauling ass back to the jungle gym.

"Fuck, I'm so sorry."

I nod. "I *do* know what you mean, I felt it that night too. But when *that* came out of your mouth... it put me in my place. I was simply another bunny to you, and I realized those feelings I had were one-sided. That's why I left. I didn't want to be kicked out in the morning, the rejection would've hurt too much. Figured it would be better to leave on my own terms." I shrug. "I should have called you out on your shit and made you apologize to me right then."

It hurts knowing we both messed up something that could've had a different ending.

He shakes his head and drops it into his hands. "I had no intention of being done with you. Shit, I was prepared to put you in the WAGs box the next day." He chuckles, but the smile doesn't reach his eyes.

"I don't know why I called you that, it was stupid. I remember thinking that you had slept with other players, but I didn't want to share you with anyone. I wanted you to only be a bunny for me, and wanted to be the player to lock you down. The last one you ever slept with. At the time, I didn't realize how offensive it sounded... it was probably extra insulting, considering you played hockey. Fuck, Raleigh. I'm sorry."

I sigh out the sadness, and this time, I don't breathe it

back in again. It feels good to get all the hurtful memories out in the open. Now that it's off my chest, our situation seems less complicated. Maybe we could start over.

"It's good to clear the air...and for what it's worth, you were the last hockey player I slept with... So, now what?" I ask, looking up at him.

He brings his hand up to the back of my neck and pulls me toward him, pressing his lips to my hair.

"I finish what I started and lock you down."

He scoots closer and we watch Arthur in silence, occasionally laughing at his silly antics. Arthur pretends his stick is a cane and hobbles around like an old man.

"He can't get hurt. I need you to realize what you're signing up for. Please don't make promises you can't keep."

He tilts my chin up to face him, and the seriousness in his eyes is something I won't soon forget. "I'm keeping this one."

Containing the smile that's trying to spread across my lips isn't easy. "Just like that?"

"Unless you have a time machine..."

It would've been nice to go back and right our wrongs, the mess would have been a lot smaller to clean up back then. "And Arthur?"

"I'll follow your lead. I'm ready whenever you are." He leans forward, forearms on his knees, and looks back at me. "How are you feeling about it all?"

After blowing out a breath, I tell him the truth. "It's a lot... I'm scared."

His head hangs between his shoulders and he nods, gazing back up at Arthur. "I understand... but there's nothing you could say to make me not want this with you. I'm not giving up."

"So your plan is to wear me down?" I joke.

"If I have to." There's no humor in his voice.

"You realize you're coming on a bit strong, right?"

"I'm being transparent. Last time, I avoided telling you how I felt because I didn't want to come on *too strong*. That didn't work in either of our favors, so this time I'm laying it all out. You will never have to wonder how I'm feeling because I'm going to tell you, oftentimes before you even ask. I'd love it if you gave me the same courtesy. If I come on strong, it's because I feel strongly. We don't have the luxury of playing games anymore. And frankly, I'm too old for that shit."

When I woke up this morning, I didn't think we would be having this talk. But the honesty policy he's instituting has me optimistic. *There's hope.*

"I'll do my best to agree to that." I lean back. "Thank you for making us sit down and have this conversation, I think I needed to know where we were at mentally before I could move forward. I was quick to dismiss your struggle with this when we were arguing, and I apologize for that... Seeing you again brought up a lot of feelings, mostly anger, and I reacted rather than listened. I can't imagine not knowing Arthur, and I'm sorry if I made it seem like you couldn't have a relationship with him. I want him to know his dad, I would never stand in the way of that."

His arms wrap around my shoulders, and he holds me. "I'm all in with you. I'm not going anywhere, and I'm not backing off... So get ready."

My lips curl into a smirk. "Ready, huh?"

"Yeah, we've got a lot of making up to do. I've been waiting a long time for you to come back into my life. No matter what happens, you and Arthur will always be the most important people in my life."

My face feels flush. He's so forward with his feelings. As terrifying as it is, I like his no-bullshit approach—and that we have no more secrets.

"Okay," I agree. "Let's get to know each other."

He licks his bottom lip and smiles. I hate when he looks at

me like that, it puts all those dirty thoughts back in my mind again.

By the time we finish talking, we're ready for lunch. We meet Arthur as he runs toward us, and Barrett catches him, lifting his little body onto his shoulders. It looks frightening being up that high, but Arthur seems to delight in it, no fear of heights, unlike his mother.

"You're very good with kids. Do you have nephews or nieces?"

"I have a brother, Paul, but he doesn't have any kids. I do a lot of coaching with Camp Conway, it's my favorite part of the summer."

"Oh, yeah? I did some research after your little meeting with Method. You've created a very successful camp." It's impressive what he's built in a few short years.

"This summer's session begins next Thursday. I want you

to come with me to check it out. I'll show you how we operate. It's pretty cool."

It sounds important to him. "I can probably get away for a few hours."

"Perfect. I promise you'll leave smiling..." He flashes that flirty grin at me and smiles bigger when it causes me to blush.

Yeah, I bet you will.

THIRTY

Raleigh

"You came on the best day."

"Thanks for inviting me." Barrett texted me earlier this week and put on the pressure for me to accompany him to Camp Conway.

He wants to show me the operations, and apparently, today is the day I really needed to be here. I look around the giant indoor arena. There's dryland training "ice" on half and turf on the other. Boys and girls of all ages, from mites to juniors, sit on the floor in their own groups. Some parents present, some not. I don't think I realized how many kids this supported. And the sheer number of volunteers—holy shit. There's gotta be at least seventy adults running around getting organized.

Someone marches up with a clipboard. "Coach, we're ready, but we're missing a couple of players."

As he chats with a couple of the volunteers, I gesture to the seats off to the side. He nods at me and smiles before turning back to the other adults. I find a place to sit and from my chair, I observe him delegate teams of people. It's kinda hot.

"Which one's yours?" a voice chimes in next to me, must be one of the moms.

"Oh, my son doesn't play hockey. I'm just here to watch."

"You're in for a treat. Barrett is awesome."

"Yeah?" Now I'm curious.

"Kennedy wouldn't be playing hockey without him. She started skating at five, but when they increased the athletic fees, we had to drop out. At the time, Camp Conway was brand new and I was skeptical, but I figured if Barrett Conway was running it, it must be legit."

"Same, the prices for skates are ridiculous, we couldn't do it without assistance," another mom chimes in behind me.

"And the hockey lessons alone brought Grayson up from Bantam A to AA after one summer. It's a dream."

"Wow, that's awesome," I reply.

"Coach Conway would do anything for these kids. How is he not married?"

"Girl, right?" the second mom exclaims. "He's *that* fine *and* has a heart of gold? I mean, he's the most down to earth guy I've ever met. Plus, he gives a huge portion of his salary to the camp."

Are these paid actors? Did he know everybody would be fawning over him like this? Not gonna lie, it's kind of working. I'm keeping my mouth shut and nodding along. He is *fine*. And it's great to hear firsthand how well he treats others.

He's a genuinely nice guy—which makes me love the naughty Barrett even more. It feels like a secret side of him that's just mine.

Barrett takes the center of the turf ice and is handed a microphone.

"Hey, everybody." The parents and kids applaud, and he smiles big. "Who's excited for Gear Day?" Louder cheers.

"What's Gear Day?" I whisper to the woman next to me.

"Oh my God, it's the best!" she whispers. "I don't want to spoil it, you'll see!"

"I'm excited to announce we've got some new sponsors, and I'm going to let their representatives take the mic here in a second. But first, I want to give a short history of how Camp Conway came to be... Youth sports is something I've always been passionate about, and years ago, when I was still deciding how to best help the community, I met this woman—Raleigh."

I try not to gasp.

"She and I hit it off immediately. She played hockey up until college and we bonded over our love of the sport, among other things. She was a goaltender—parents of goalies, you're already familiar with the added cost for specialized gear.

"Anyway, she told me that the only reason she was able to play was due to an athletic financial support program. At the time, it didn't quite hit me, but the more I thought about it, the more I realized how necessary it was. There's a lot of gifted players hiding out there that are trapped due to circumstances outside their control. Camp Conway is dedicated to developing their talent and keeping them in the sport. I know for a fact we have kids playing this season that will someday get scouted.

"If you're here today, it means you care. That goes for everyone from volunteers to parents to players. You are all such an important and integral part of Camp Conway, and I am so happy you're here. Thank you for caring and believing in this amazing program. Okay, now that that's out of the way, we've got some awesome surprises for you."

I'm in awe, speechless, and touched. I had no idea that my hockey playing years would impact something as big and important as Camp Conway.

Who is this man?!

The panties have dropped.

Various brand ambassadors take the "stage" and they each say a few words about their contributions and why they chose to get involved in the camp. There's a short speech welcoming the new campers and huge equipment bins are wheeled out. Barrett takes the mic again and announces all the newcomers get brand-new duffels, one-piece sticks, pads, Camp Conway jerseys, each embroidered with the child's first initial and last name. It's like an episode of Oprah. The returning kids with their hockey duffels still get new jerseys and sticks. You would think it was Christmas morning.

"Oh, there's one more thing," he says, passing the microphone to a representative wearing the logo of one of the top hockey skate manufacturers in the world.

"Hi everybody, I'm Chris. I'm here today on behalf of Bauer. As you know, we've been partnering with Camp Conway for a few years now. About six months ago, Barrett reached out to say there was a big need for skates." There are huge gasps among the families. "We wanted to help make that expense a little easier on you so we can keep these kids on the ice. So today, with help from the Minnesota Lakes and Camp Conway, every player will be receiving a brand-new pair of Bauer skates."

The crowd goes nuts before he can even finish his sentence, and for good reason. My skates in high school were around seven hundred dollars, and that doesn't count the regular skate sharpening every few weeks. The only reason I was able to play was because of the financial assistance I received.

Parents are wiping away tears and smiling. The brand reps are getting choked up too. It's overwhelming. Kids spin around to find their parents and share shocked expressions.

Barrett and Chris laugh, sharing a handshake and slap on

the back. It must feel amazing to give such a significant gift to these families. His generosity astounds me.

Barrett's the real deal. And not only is he into me, he genuinely wants to be involved in Arthur's life. I stare at him as he shakes hands with some of the other men and women I assume are sponsors. When he's done, he turns around and his eyes find mine. He gives me that gorgeous smile and wink. I haven't stopped smiling, and the whole training arena is bursting with joy.

What the hell am I waiting for? Friends are always telling me to get back out there. If I'm looking for a sign, maybe this is it. There isn't a better man than Barrett Conway to take a chance on.

He walks off to the side and speaks to a grinning woman with a clipboard. They nod back and forth and then he hands her the microphone. She sorts the kids by hockey level. Barrett looks at me and crooks his finger. The parents continue to enthusiastically chatter among themselves, allowing me to sneak away unnoticed and meet him on the sidelines.

"Whoa," I say, beaming. "That was something else. You made a lot of people very happy today."

"It wasn't just me, there's a ton of people who are dedicated to the camp. You're a part of this too, Ral. Do you want to help me hand out sticks?"

"Really?"

"Of course. Come on." He holds his hand out for me, and I take it.

We weave through some volunteers and families over to a huge cart organizing sticks by flex and size. There are four carts in a row, each has two volunteers to hand them out to the different youth groups: mites on one side of us and peewees on the other. Barrett hands me a large box of hockey tapes.

"We've got the squirts." I narrow my eyes at him. "Wow, that came out weird."

I chuckle. "I knew what you meant."

One family at a time lines up and we take a paper with their stick flex and player height. I repeat the information to Barrett, then he grabs the junior-sized stick that matches. A couple times, he recommends a longer or shorter stick for the player. When he's done, I hand them a couple rolls of tape, and we move to the next child. Seeing the appreciation, happiness, and hopefulness for these families is so rewarding.

"Hi!" I say to the next child in line, a dark-haired boy bouncing with excitement. He says hi, with his eyes focused on Barrett as he hands me the paper.

I turn to Barrett and tell him the flex and height. "Forty-five. Fifty-five inches."

While he grabs the stick, I make small talk with the players. "What position do you play?"

"Right forward," he says, in unison with Barrett.

Barrett turns around and hands him a stick. "Farrell! I heard you moved up to AA! That's awesome, man." He holds out his hand for a fist bump. The boy taps it with his. There's not one kid who's come through here that Barrett doesn't know. *How the hell does he do it?*

I hand him his hockey tapes. "Have a great season!"

"Thanks!" He's all smiles. The mother presses her hand to her chest and mouths a *thank you* to Barrett as well, and he nods with a smile. Then Farrell and his mother head toward the table passing out jerseys.

"Thank you for including me in this," I say before helping the next player in line.

"Nobody else I'd rather share it with."

I smile at the new kid in line and take his paper, turning to Barrett again. "Forty-five. Anytime. This is awesome, Barrett."

When we're all done with sticks, I help return some carts and float around with some volunteers, assisting wherever I can. Barrett and I get separated at some point, but it's easy to get carried away helping. I'm sorting through some of the registration papers, pulling out the list of kids who didn't make it, highlighting addresses on the papers so we can have their equipment delivered.

"I was wondering where you went." The deep voice makes me smile.

"Sorry, I wanted to make myself useful. I'm almost done." Leafing through the remaining papers, there are no other absences. When I look up, he's got a big smile on his face.

He furrows his brow. "What are you and Arthur doing tonight?"

"Actually, I've got plans tonight with Micky. She invited me out for drinks. Birdie's going too, she said she'd be our designated driver."

His smile grows. "Oh, yeah? A little WAGs night?"

I roll my eyes. "A *girls'* night."

"Po-tay-to, po-tah-to. Who's watching Arthur?" It's bizarre to have another person keeping tabs on my son.

"Babysitter. Don't worry, I've background checked her. Her name is Tabitha. She's a college student going to school for elementary education. She's great."

He looks at his feet. "If you ever need a babysitter, you know... I could—"

"I know."

He nods. His face falls and the hurt expression makes me wince.

"He would love spending the extra time with you. I got this babysitter before our talk, but going forward, your name is on the babysitter roster. I'm sorry, I'm just protective."

I straighten the stack of papers and set them aside, placing a puck on top as a paperweight.

"I'm glad for it. You're a great mom, Ral."

"It doesn't always feel that way, but I do the best I can.

He deserves it." Shouldering my purse, we walk out together.

"They say parenting is only hard for good parents."

Huh, I never thought of it like that. *I must be fucking terrific.*

We finish at the athletic center and say our goodbyes. He wraps me in a big hug, and I lean into it, breathing in his scent.

THIRTY-ONE
Raleigh

After I get back in my car and see what time it is, I panic. I'm running late to pick up Arthur from daycare. The time I was going to use to get ready was just cut in half. I shoot a text off to Micky apologizing and letting her know I might be a little late.

> Sorry, I'm running a bit behind! Mind if we push it back to 6:30 instead?

MICKY

> Actually, I was going to text you. We are not getting together tonight. Rhys just told me you're THE Raleigh.

> What do you mean THE Raleigh?

MICKY

> Runaway Raleigh! You're Conway's "one that got away."

Is this one of those practical joke shows? It's like everyone is conspiring to push us together. The butterflies in my stomach take flight. I gulp, unsure of how to respond.

MICKY

I don't know why I didn't make the
connection earlier. Rhys is locking me down
tonight, I'm not allowed to go out with you.
I've been grounded.

Since when do you let a man boss you
around?

MICKY

Since Rhys

And I agree with him on this one. I insist
you use your babysitter to get laid.

I'm not sleeping with my babysitter.

MICKY

You know what I mean! He's a good guy,
too, Raleigh, and he's obsessed with you.
Jump on his dick and ride it until the sun
comes up.

Micky. Come on. Girls night!

MICKY

You'll thank me in the morning. Go put on
something hot and have fun! You deserve it!
We'll get together soon, I promise

Her messages replay in my head. "*Runaway Raleigh.*" On
the way to the daycare center, I mentally scan through all the
clothing I own. The black dresses I have are all professional
and for work. Although, there is that one black body-
contouring thing. It's been a year since I've tried it on. The
dress came recommended by a plus-size fashion blogger I
follow. It was a gift to myself after getting a raise at work, but
I've never had anywhere to wear it. It might not even fit
anymore.

After picking up Arthur and getting some dinner on the

table for him, Tabitha shows up, and I hustle to my bedroom
to get ready.

> My plans got mysteriously canceled.

BARRETT
How odd.

> Mmhmm.

BARRETT
Look, normally, I wouldn't do this, but I'm
feeling sorry for you. Since you were such a
big help today: yes, Raleigh, I will go out
with you tonight even though it's very last
minute and I have an incredibly busy
schedule.

> You're ridiculous

He responds almost immediately.

BARRETT
I'll pick you up in 30. Wear a dress.

> If Arthur sees you he'll feel left out. Can you
> text me when you're outside?

BARRETT
No problem. I'll be seeing you next
weekend, so we'll get some guy time then.

> Is that so?

BARRETT
I know, it's like you're obsessed with me or
something. Stage 5 clinger.

> Little bit.

After a quick scrub and shave, it's time to try on the dress.
To my utter amazement, it fits and actually looks pretty damn

good. I grab the eyeshadow and upgrade to a subtle, smokey eye. It's been forever since I've seen this version of myself. I'm loving my curves more and more these days. Especially in this dress. Barrett will too. I may not be as hot as I used to be in my early twenties, but tonight I'm a solid MILF candidate.

Dry shampoo adds texture and volume to my hair. I wear it down but keep the side part—they'll have to pry the comb from my cold, dead fingers before I part my hair down the center. It's spring, but the evenings can still get chilly, so I grab a moto jacket and slip on my sexiest heels. One last check in the mirror and then I say my goodbyes to Arthur. He looks at me a little funny with the new makeup as I bend down to give him a hug and kiss.

"I really like your eyes, Mom."

"Thank you, baby! I really like your eyes too!" I stand from my crouch. *Shit, I forgot how hard that is to do in heels.*

"Do you need anything, Tab?"

"All set, have a great night," she calls from the kitchen, picking up dishes from dinner. She walks out wiping her hands on a towel. "Ooph! You look hot!"

I feel myself blushing. I hope I'm not kidding myself with this effort. My phone dings, and I push aside any negative thoughts. This is the new Raleigh.

"Okay, have a good night!"

I walk out the door and find him leaning against the passenger side door. *He's even got manners.* The smile on his face explodes.

"Sweet hell. I can't believe I'm taking you to a restaurant first." He opens the door for me. "You look fantastic." He kisses me on the cheek, and I slink into the passenger seat. He closes my door and walks around to the driver's side, and I kick my feet in excitement before he opens his door.

"What time do I need to have you home tonight?" he says, turning on the car.

"I have the babysitter until midnight."

"We'll have to eat fast, then."

I tuck my hair behind my ear and chuckle. "Oh yeah? What do you have planned?"

He looks at my outfit and back at me.

I laugh. "Subtle..."

"You started it by wearing that fucking dress."

I'm thrilled he likes it. I try not to show my excitement, but the idea of ending up in Barrett's bed makes my heart hammer in my chest. I'm ready. I mentally give myself a pep talk on the way there.

You look hot, you smell great, you are worthy of an amazing man, especially one that's into you. He runs a hockey camp to help underprivileged kids and knows every single player by name. He learns koala facts for your son and carries him on his shoulders. Whatever happens tonight, happens. You have Cinderella liberty, so seal the deal before midnight.

"You okay over there?"

"Huh? Oh, uh-huh."

"What are you overthinking?"

I smile. "Thinking about today."

Leaning my head against the headrest, I face him and narrow my eyes. "What's that like?"

His mouth curves up into a sexy half smile. "What do you mean?"

"Gear Day. Camp Conway. Giving so much and helping so many families. Seeing all that joy and knowing you're the reason behind it. I mean, shouldn't you be out there show-boating or being a smug asshole? *Hey everybody, look how great I am.*"

It was incredible to witness once, I can't imagine what it must be like to experience it year after year. The room was filled with so much positive energy it could have blown the doors off the arena. Radiant smiles on every face.

He laughs and shrugs. "It's pretty great. And yeah, it feels good, of course it does. But it's not just me, there's so many people involved. We have hundreds of volunteers and donors that work much harder than I do to make it happen. It's a cause I started, but it's everybody else that keeps it going."

"God, he's humble too," I groan and shake my head. "Is there anything you're bad at? You're suspiciously perfect. There's gotta be *something* wrong with you."

"I forgot to get this woman's number once. I missed the birth of my son, missed his whole life. I missed years building something with the woman who needed me most."

I suck in air through my teeth. "Well, at least you're keeping it light."

He lifts his shoulders. "You asked. Like I said, I'll always be honest with you."

It wasn't only him, I made mistakes too. I should have left my number, and I shouldn't have made so many assumptions that night. Even if we had each other's numbers, who knows, his PR woman might still have interjected and ruined things for us.

"Barrett, you tried—"

"Not hard enough, Ral."

THIRTY-TWO
Barrett

Getting out of the shower earlier and seeing the text from Raleigh was the icing on top of an already incredible day. I don't want to slow down. I love looking at her in the passenger seat of my car.

"How's pizza sound?"

"Great, but where will we find a place that can incinerate it as good as Top Shelf? And on such short notice. I hope you made reservations..."

"I'm sure we could request it. After all, I'm a celebrity, this town worships me and my big smug asshole." I smile wider.

She scrunches up her nose and tilts her head to the side. "I don't know how some girl hasn't made you hers already."

"She has." I nudge her. "She just doesn't know it yet."

Out of the corner of my eye, I see her staring. Her attention puts me on cloud nine.

"Do you think that's gonna get you laid tonight? Because it might."

"If it does, I'll actually be prepared this time. I stopped at Costco on the way here."

"For what?"

I reach behind her seat and drop the box of 144 condoms in her lap. She holds it up and looks at me bewildered.

"Jesus Christ, Bear! It's too bad you couldn't find a bigger box! What are we going to do when we run out?"

I shrug. "Butt stuff?"

She laughs again, and I swear it's my favorite sound.

We pull in front of the restaurant and get a parking spot right up front.

"Come on, let's eat. I'm hungry."

She mumbles something as I exit. I jog around to open her door, she's already swung it open but takes my hand and allows me to help her out of the car. When she stands, I get another look at that dress up close and those heels. She's much taller than her usual height. I scrub a hand down my face. *Woof, this dinner is going to be a masterclass in patience.*

The restaurant is dim, filled with deep blues and bronze. The wall sconces glow a golden hue, adding to the mood of the space. We are ushered to a C-shaped navy upholstered bench in the corner. I asked for the most secluded table. *No distractions.* I love hanging out with Arthur, but my alone time with Raleigh needs to be used wisely since it's not easy to come by.

We order wine and a margherita pizza.

"To second chances." She holds out her glass, and I clink mine to it.

"Second chances."

She takes a sip of her wine and nods as she swallows, her gaze wanders around the restaurant. "Have you been here before?"

"We've had team lunches here a few times. They're good about privacy. Which I wanted tonight."

"Uh-oh. Does that mean you're going to be grilling me with questions?" She grins.

That's the lighthearted Raleigh I remember. Her eyes drop

to my mouth, and the relaxed smile on my face grows serious. I figured we would have a little more small talk before getting into the heavy stuff, but it seems we've arrived at that destination sooner than expected.

"Can I ask you about Arthur's birth?"

Her shoulders slump, and she tilts her head. "Right now?"

"Please."

"I want tonight to be fun. I don't get to do this often."

I shake my head. "I promise, we can still have fun, but I also don't get to do this often. This is my chance to ask when it's just us. I can't pass up the opportunity."

She takes a drink and sets the glass down. "Okay. What do you want to know?"

I saw the scar on her belly. "You had a c-section..."

My knowledge on the birthing process is minimal, but I know that most women usually don't opt for a c-section on their first baby. *I think.* So either something went wrong or—

"Is there a question?"

"Was that something you planned on or were there complications?"

She nods. "My labor didn't progress. He was late, two weeks past my due date, so I was induced. The induction was useless, my body wouldn't cooperate, I had all the contractions but wasn't dilating, well, not fast enough. The epidural didn't work, and after twenty hours of nonstop pain, I tapped out."

The look on her face is stern. Is this why she didn't want to talk about it because it's a difficult memory? *Fuck.* Thinking about her being put through so much when I wasn't there hurts me in ways she'll never know. I keep my poker face, this is about her, not me. I take a drink and do my best attempt at sounding neutral. "Who was with you when he was born?"

"Heather." She looks down and a small smile pulls up in

the corner of her mouth like she's remembering more joyful parts of that day. Her fingers twirl the stem of the wine glass.

"Who's Heather?" I haven't heard her mention any friends by that name.

"My nurse."

Looking down, I place my hands under the table, balling them into fists. There must have been somebody else. *There has to be.* My throat thickens thinking about her going through this alone.

"Who else? Where was your mom?" I don't mean to sound demanding, but what the fuck...

"She didn't want to come. She knew I was pregnant. I called her when I found out, but—look, you have to understand something about my mom, she's not very... maternal. It would have been worse if she was there. Trust me, it was better this way."

I want to ask her why she didn't have a friend with her, but I don't want to press her and make her feel more alone than she did that day.

"Do you have any pictures?" My voice cracks with emotion, but I clear my throat to cover it.

She smiles. "Yeah. Heather took a short video of him being born, well, being pulled out of the sunroof." She giggles. "Would you want to see it sometime?"

"Can I see it now?" Fuck *sometime*.

She wrinkles her nose and tilts her head away from me. "I don't think you want to watch it now. We're about to eat."

"I don't care."

"Are you squeamish with blood?"

"Raleigh. I play hockey."

She chuckles, and I scoot closer while she pulls out her phone. God, she smells good tonight. I don't know if it's her hair or perfume, but I want to be covered in it. She scrolls through the photo gallery thumbnails until she finds the video. We lean in to watch. She taps play on the center of the screen and suddenly it's like I can't breathe. I'm sent back in time. Raleigh as I knew her then. Still as gorgeous as she is now but *different*. She looks so much younger. And scared. Nervous for what's to come. I can't imagine.

Seeing her on the surgical table, with ambient sounds of doctors and nurses, suction, clanging instruments, and beeping all around her, triggers a dark feeling inside me. It's strange and familiar, something I haven't felt for a long time. And then it dawns on me, it's *fear*. I know she survives this because she's sitting next to me, but the image of her so vulnerable turns my stomach. Her eyes are wide and wild, focused on someone off to the side of the camera. I assume Heather, the nurse.

"You're doing great. Almost there, Raleigh," the woman behind the screen says.

Raleigh rolls her lips together and nods. *She was alone.*

She was fucking alone at the birth of our child. She needed me. And I wasn't there for her. I should have been the one coaching her on and reassuring her.

How the hell did she go through this? She's resilient, but it's because she had to be. And my absence during some of the hardest times of her life hardened her to be what she is today. It smothered the carefree version of her I used to know. When I glance over at her, she's got a big smile on her face, her eyes still focused on the phone screen.

"Okay, get ready," she says, smiling even bigger now.

Cheers play through the speaker, and it pulls my gaze back to the phone.

"It's a boy!"

"We have a boy!"

"He's a boy!"

The camera pans over, just as they drop the blue plastic

curtain and a doctor holds up the tiny Arthur for Raleigh to see. Umbilical cord still attached, covered in red and white.

His little cry is raspy, but mighty.

I watch in awe. He's perfect. The camera pans down and she's smiling through happy tears. They both look so beautiful, and my eyes swell with emotion. I place my palm on her thigh.

"You're doing great, Raleigh! We're going to start stitching you up. We're going to get him measured and swaddled, then you'll be able to hold him."

There's more suction noises and then the video ends.

I wipe my hand down my face. It's my son's birth. Of course I'm going to get choked up.

"Here, I have some baby pictures too." She swipes and taps the screen a few times, opening an album, titled *Arthur* with a bear emoji. She hands the phone over. "You can swipe through them if you want."

"Of course I want to." I smile, getting a peek into the little windows of the beginning of his life. Her sweet face glows in a few of their selfies together. Most are of Arthur, but as I flip through the ones with Raleigh in them, I notice she looks more and more tired with each one.

"Please tell me there was somebody to help you when you got home."

She looks away from me and takes a sip.

You've got to be fucking kidding me. "Ral."

"What?"

I hand her phone back, feeling sick. I loathe myself. My fingers twitch, wanting to punch something. I take a deep breath, hoping for some composure. "How could I have left you alone? I'll never be able to make it up, will I?"

She grimaces and takes my hand, squeezing it. "Don't be like that. We made it fine, and I'm glad you're here now." My heart aches for her. *Pull it together.* "I am too."

"I should have left my number." She snaps her fingers as if to say *drat*, trying to make light of it, but I'm not laughing. Her small hand rests atop mine. "It's okay, Barrett. Let's move forward."

It's definitely not okay, but I'll never be absent from their life again. I turn to face her, and she looks up at me with those big cinnamon-honey eyes.

"I'm always going to be here for you. Even if you find somebody else, it will be me supporting you and Arthur. Always. I don't want you to feel like it's *just you* ever again."

Those warm eyes search mine, and I stare back without blinking. She looks away when the pizza arrives, and I'm half wishing they'd left it in the oven and burned it, to give me the extra time to gaze at her. She's everything I want. I plate a slice and hand it to her before serving myself.

She checks the bottom of the crust and sticks out her bottom lip in a pout. "Ugh, golden brown. This is inedible. Is Banksy still making servers cry? Think we could get him to stop by?" She's trying, but I'm still not ready to jest.

"Thank you for showing me all this, I needed it. I'd like to sit down and look through every photo with you and Arthur."

Her chewing slows as she considers my request. "Sure. We could do that. Arthur likes watching his baby videos." *Good.*

"Tasty pizza," she says, making small talk. She keeps her eyes down while chewing.

"What do you really want to say?" I ask.

She swallows. "Honestly?"

"Of course."

"I'm thinking I'm out with a really attractive man I'm starting to like and I don't want to spend it talking about our history and the mistakes we made. The guilt is coming off you in waves—our situation was fucked because of a force outside our control. I don't blame you anymore, so let that shit go." She takes another bite. "And—" More chewing. "This is our date night. You wanted to take me out and I'm here. So show me a good fucking time, Barrett Conway."

It takes everything in me not to kiss her. My hand drops back to her thigh, and I squeeze her soft flesh, enjoying the way she squirms under my palm. I move to her inner thigh but don't ease up.

She spreads her thighs a little wider. "What do you want to do after dinner?" she asks.

My lips curl into a sideways smile, and I take another bite of pizza while sliding my hand higher up her thigh.

"Tell me about your job."

My fingers slither under the hem of her skirt. Her exhale is sexy as hell.

"My job," she repeats. "Um..."

I work her flesh with my palm. God, it feels so good to touch her. She parts her legs more, her thigh flush against mine. I'm so close. "Where do you work, Raleigh?" I tease.

"Method Marketing."

"Tell me about your boss." *I hate that guy.*

I brush the edge of her underwear, and her eyes close. Pulling my hand out from under her dress, she blinks open again. I look away and continue eating.

"Such a jerk," she scolds with a grin. I do a poor job of concealing my amused smile. It's nice to know she wanted it. "You know my boss. His name is Rob, I've been his executive assistant since, well, since I was pregnant."

"He likes you."

"I know." She rolls her eyes.

"Has he ever made you feel unsafe or uncomfortable?" My voice is hard.

"Unsafe? No. Uncomfortable, meh." She shrugs. That pisses me off. She says it so casually and raises the pizza to her mouth for another bite.

"You don't have to work there."

She practically cackles and has to cover her mouth because she's struggling to chew and laugh at the same time.

"What's so funny?"

"He pays me double what any other executive assistant at Method makes. Yeah, he's a little flirty sometimes, but that job is what got Arthur and me out of a shitty apartment, and pays for an incredible daycare center, and puts food on the table. Besides, it gives me a chance to network with new companies and be involved with the creative departments, advertising is a passion of mine."

All my possessive brain hears is *flirty*—and that *he's* the one supporting her, not me. I want to fly off the handle, I know that's some toxic masculinity bullshit, but it doesn't change how I feel. She's been sacrificing her work environment to make sure Arthur is well cared for. She's a damn good mom. But Rob's taking advantage of the situation by offering an exceptional salary—which she deserves—though I suspect he enjoys making her dependent on him. If she'd let me take care of those things, she could work wherever she wanted.

"If money wasn't an issue, would you still be working for Rob?"

She cocks her head to the side. "Nice try."

"What?"

Her laugh makes me smile. "Don't '*what?*' me. I can see the wheels turning in your head. Laying it on pretty thick, buddy."

Now I'm the one laughing and shaking my head. "We aren't buddies."

She rolls her eyes but keeps the grin on her face. "Why don't you tell me about *your* job?"

I give her the lowdown on how the team is doing after our L, and what Camp Conway's goals are this year. It's a pleasant conversation. I try to keep it brief because there's been an idea rolling around in my head about my plans for the summer, but

I need the right time to bring it up since I want them to be a part of it.

She dabs the cloth napkin against her mouth and sets it on her plate.

"So... what do you want to do next?" she asks.

My arm snakes behind her and I let my hand linger below her hip. "You don't want to know the answer to that." I can think of a hundred things I want to do to her.

"Bet."

I pull my arm back and put some space between us. After swallowing a bite, I sit back and look at her, narrowing my eyes, unsure if this is a trap.

"I've still got..." I look at my watch. "Four hours and thirty-eight minutes until I need to give you back to Mini Bear."

"That's a lot of time to kill."

Not near enough. Fuck it.

"Come back to my place for a drink."

She nods. "Okay."

I get the check, and thankfully, they pick up on the urgency. She adjusts her dress, pulling it back down a little more once she gets to the edge of the booth. With my hand resting above her ass, I escort her back to my car.

Pulling up to my house feels like déjà vu. The last time we were here together, neither of us knew that night would change our lives forever. I park in the far-left stall of the four-car garage.

It may be too soon, but I've already visualized moving them in with me. My mom's been telling me for years it's too much house for one person, that I need to fill it with a wife and kids. Raleigh's the only one I ever pictured here.

"It looks different in the daylight." It won't be long before the summer sun begins to set. I have to remember what changes have been made in the last few years.

233

"Yeah, the shake siding is new. Well, new since you've seen it."

After a bad hailstorm two summers ago, I had the exterior remodeled, though the lakeside is mostly windows. The property is on a private peninsula, which makes the house feel more like a secret hideaway. It makes a good home base.

Other than traveling, I'm settled here. Plus, I love the lake.

We smirk in the entryway, and I'd put money on her thinking about the first time we stood here when I spun her and pressed her against the wall... We pass through the foyer and into the kitchen. It's an open-floor plan and a few lamps are on timers to make my home feel more welcoming when I come home alone. I pull out a bottle of wine and show it to her for approval.

"Oh, that's a good year," she says.

Turning my wrist, I look down at the label. "Is it?"

The corners of her mouth tilt up. "No fucking idea, it just seemed like the right thing to say." I grin and pull a corkscrew out of the drawer. She wanders around, taking in the space. I wonder what she's thinking. Does she like the furniture and decor? Would she ever keep a toothbrush here for herself or Arthur? I'd like to get some things to keep here in case they ever stay overnight.

"Have you dated at all? Since he was born?"

I pour two glasses and pass one to her. Her plump lips match the wine. I stare as she takes a sip. Then blink a few times to clear the sinful images from my head before taking a drink.

"I've been on a few dates."

Not a fan of that answer, but I'm curious.

"And?"

"And..."

"Did you fuck any of them?"

Her mouth drops open in shock. "Excuse me? Rude. Have *you* fucked anyone?"

I shrug. "Yes. Have you?"

She flinches at my answer. That's a good sign, it means she cares.

"Yes, I have." She straightens her shoulders.

I smile at her pride, but take no time to picture her with anyone else. I'm not envious, those other guys will never have the connection we do. They'll *never* have what we have.

"Did any of them make you feel as good as I do?"

She's silent and looks down at the wine she's swirling in her glass. *That's a no.*

"Because nobody has ever come close to how good it was with you." I hope that gives her some reassurance. The smile that creeps onto her face is exactly the response I was hoping for.

"You might have to remind me."

That's all I need to hear to take her hand and lead her through the house and up the stairs. At the top step, I look down, remembering her crumpled dress sitting right in that spot so many years ago. No games this time, she walks into my bedroom on her own, rather than tossed over my shoulder like a caveman.

Exiting the french doors off my bedroom, we step out onto the expansive deck that overlooks the lake below. The fresh, early summer air isn't too hot yet. The spring peepers can be heard croaking near the lilies on the east side of the peninsula. Raleigh walks toward the railing and I kick back on the U-shaped sofa, enjoying the view. She makes herself comfortable, sipping her wine and running her hand through her hair. Not the way she does when she's nervous, it's relaxed and content. She looks like a dream. Aiming the remote at the natural gas fire table in front of me, a small whoosh of flames rise from the center.

The sky is filled with radiant pinks and oranges. This is one of the things I miss most when I'm traveling. Evenings in my own backyard. But the brightest sunset couldn't pull my gaze from her. Goddamn, she's the most gorgeous thing I've ever seen.

"Wow." Her voice is breathy as she looks across the water. "No wonder you like it here."

I set my wine glass on the wide stone ledge that wraps around the firepit and recline, stretching my arms across the back of the sofa on each side, marveling her, taking in every detail. Being here with Raleigh is so surreal. I've envisioned it so many times and it's finally happening. She turns and pads across the deck barefoot, cozying next to me and tucking up both her legs.

Shoulder to shoulder, we watch the sun melt below the horizon as we snuggle and sip wine. *Yeah, this is our 'normal.'* Having my arm around Raleigh feels so natural, like I've done it a thousand times before. Never have I felt so at peace in my own home. I release a deep content sigh.

"Comfortable?" she asks, giggling.

"Very." My thumb brushes her arm, and goose bumps rise from her soft skin. I grab a blanket from behind us and shake it open. Between the fire, the blanket, and our body heat, we're quite warm despite the air cooling as the sun disappears and the evening sky grows darker.

She pulls her phone out and checks her messages, her face lights up and then she holds it out to show me. It's a photo of Arthur fast asleep with an open book of koalas on his chest.

I smile and take the phone to get a better look. "I had a very similar night last Saturday."

"Is that where he gets his partying from?"

"I'm serious!" I chuckle. "I've been reading up on koalas so I can keep up in conversation with him. He's so damn smart."

She smiles and nods. "Are you intimidated by a four-year old?"

I nod. "I want him to like me. If he doesn't, then I'll never be able to sleep with his mom."

Her easy laugh is sexy... but it's nothing compared to when she sits up and straddles me. *Fuck.*

"Good thing he likes you, then."

THIRTY-THREE
Barrett

I push her taut little dress higher to bring her closer, right over my stiffening cock. My palm caresses up her thick thigh—this body blows my mind. So perfect. She's meant to have these curves. My fingers massage the back of her neck, then she sucks in a soft breath and I smile.

The dimming pinks and purples glow behind her silhouette. Everything is more colorful when she's around. I drop my hand to unzip the back of her dress. She frames my face with her hands and delays our kiss with her lips above mine. If she wants this, then she has to make the first move. But she better hurry the fuck up before I take without asking. Her forehead presses to mine, and as she roams her hands down my chest, her breaths grow quicker. Curious fingers trail down my abs, pausing at my belt.

"Bear."

Love that word.

"What do you want, Raleigh?"

I lick her lower lip and then she crashes her mouth to mine, tasting like wine and warmth. Sensitive nerves fire at abandon, buzzing through my fingers. No other woman has ever had this effect on me. I pull her flush against my straining cock, and a sweet whimper slips from her. I missed out on five fucking years of this—kissing her like this every day.

She works my belt with both hands, and I scoot forward to give her more room. Frantically unzipping, she pushes down my boxer briefs, and the second her fingers brush over me, I groan and shove her skirt to her hips and then slide the straps down her shoulders. She wraps her hand around me and rolls the dripping precum down my shaft.

My lips find hers and I grin against her mouth. It's the first time since *her* that a handjob has felt so fucking good. *Just wait until you get inside her.* My hand snakes between her legs and pushes her damp underwear to the side. She's so fucking wet, I want her riding me. It's so hard to hold off.

Pushing a finger inside, her hips grind against my hand. She backs off our kiss and sucks in a big breath, analyzing my expression. Those eyes are hypnotizing. My thumb finds her clit. I add another finger, and her pussy clamps down, but I don't want her to come on my hand.

"I want to fill you up so fucking bad," I say, expelling a breath.

"We left the condoms in the car."

"I don't give a fuck." We're both clean, there's not one consequence that would stand in my way. If she's down, so am I. The thought of having another child with Raleigh rouses a fierce desire deep inside me.

"Let me show you how good it feels to come on my cock."

I grip those fucking lace panties she has on and rip them off.

"Hey! Those—"

"I'll buy you more."

She huffs. "You'll probably rip those too..."

I gaze down and finish pulling off the tight dress so I can watch. "Probably."

On her knees, she bides her time, teasing me. I grip her

waist on both sides, lowering her so I'm pressed against her entrance. Her jaw slacks as she slides me through her folds. I steer myself back to her opening, and with hands pressed against my chest, inch by inch she sinks down on me. My jaw clenches. *Christ.*

"Oh, fuck." I blow out a puff of air. *It's so right.* I only want to be bare with her. Forever.

Her gaze rises from our connecting bodies, and she pauses. Those huge tawny eyes sparkle as we marvel at one another. It's as powerful as before. The rush of lust that rolls up my spine and the things that flood my mind when I look at her... it's almost too much to take on at once.

She dips her chin to see how full she is and looks up at me again. I nod. "It's okay, I promise. I'll take care of you."

Her lips find mine and she lowers all the way. I trap her moan between our kiss. She wraps her arm around my neck and I grip her ass to guide her up and down. Raleigh spends so much time caring for others, tonight it's her turn. Her walls are already closing in on me.

"Right there," she whispers. *Yeah, I can tell.*

Her hips roll and I toss my head back. "Jesus Christ, Ral."

When I look down, she's bracing herself on my knees, leaned back like she's putting on a fucking show. "How am I supposed to make you come first when you do that shit, huh?"

"You'll find a way. I saw firsthand how giving you are today." She smiles.

She has no idea how much I plan to give her.

Her head tilts to the night sky, the warm light from the fire licking her skin.

"That's perfect, love. Keep riding my cock like that." *This woman is mesmerizing.* "Goddamn. You know exactly how I like it."

It's as if she's studied every button of mine, knowing

exactly which ones to push. It drives me wild. Her body trembles, and I palm her ass, speeding up the tempo.

She's about to come. I need to see it. I turn us to the side, the fire illuminating her face more clearly. "Keep going, baby, show me how pretty you are when you come.

Remember how much I love that?" Her teeth sink into her full lower lip. "You are so fucking beautiful."

My thumb sneaks between our connecting bodies, massaging circles where she craves more friction. She bucks and grinds, gyrating on top of me, about to lose control. "Uh-huh, almost there. Ready?"

She nods, and I pinch her clit between my thumb and forefinger. Her lids close, and the sexiest sounds echo off the lake. She's about to detonate.

"Don't you dare close your eyes. Look at me."

She listens, and as soon as our gazes lock, she grips me like a vise.

"That's right, love. Come for me."

Her mouth drops open, and it's like the world stands still. Never has sex felt so right. Nothing compares to seeing the woman I've pined over for years—the mother of my child—filled with pleasure as she comes around me. I flip us over and drop to an elbow, supporting myself above her. She looks up at me while I push one of her thighs up and to the side. I pull out almost all the way and plunge back in again. She cries out, and I grin, loving every sound she makes.

"Ohmygod, more."

Tucking my head into her shoulder, I lick her neck below her ear, and bite. A growl rips out of me. Fuck taking it slow. I want her to scream. The more she writhes, the more I need. I yank down her bra and shove it under her breasts, pushing them higher and closer to my mouth. I swirl my tongue over her nipples and relish the desperate moans. Gingerly taking them between my teeth, I pull. She grips my hair at the base of my neck and pants between small whimpers. Her dewy skin glows in the flames.

"You're going to come for me again, aren't you?"

She releases a sound I've not heard her make before.

"Yeahhh, you are." I smirk. "You're no quitter. I bet you'd let me fuck this pussy all night if I wanted."

Pulling her closer, she expertly wraps her legs around me. After standing, I carry her inside. Inch by inch, I pull out, and the tip of my cock is squeezed as it leaves her tight cunt. I toss her on the bed and shed my pants and boxers that are somehow still clinging to my thighs. After unbuttoning my shirt, I hurl it into the en suite bathroom, closer to my closet. After turning on the lamp on my nightstand, I get a good look at her.

My gaze rakes over her naked body. *Absolute knockout.*

She takes mom bod to the next level. Her stretch marks from carrying our child only make me harder. Grabbing her hips, I bend down to lick each one. I helped in turning her previously slender body into this curvy wonderland I find so fucking sexy. There was nothing wrong with her before, nothing at all, but this version of her makes me feral—gets my pulse pounding and my dick throbbing. She's softer, curvier, more grabbable. I want to claim every inch of her.

She crosses her arms over her chest, but I pull them away and trap her wrists above her head.

"If you *ever* cover your body in front of me again, I'll punish you for it. Understand?"

Her eyes widen and she nods.

Dropping beside her, I plant a chaste kiss on her lips.

"Good. Now ride my face, I'm not done with you yet."

I wrap an arm behind her back, and roll so she's on top of me again.

"Now? But you were—"

I was about to come. And I'm not ready for this to end.

"Now, gorgeous," I demand. "Let me eat that freshly fucked pussy."

She hesitates at first, but rises to her knees and moves up my body. When she reaches my neck, I lean forward and bite her inner thigh while breathing her in. She gasps and pulls my hair—hard—*that's the shit I'm looking for.* I groan and lick the bite all better while watching her face. The smell of sex permeates the space. It makes me salivate.

The scent of her cunt after I've been in it is pure bliss. It's taking serious control to not throw her down and force her to watch as I thrust inside again and again. I don't know what happened to her over the years to steal her confidence, but I'm gonna make sure she finds it. I want this to be all about her, take care of her, like I should have been doing all along.

She holds onto the corner bedpost, and like I knew she would, she hovers. Fuck, this is getting annoying. "Let go of the bed, Raleigh."

"No."

"How the fuck can you grind against my face if you're hovering above me?"

"Come on, don't. I'll suffocate you." Bullshit. If I die with her on top, it'll be from drowning, not suffocation. *Not a bad way to go.*

"I said *sit*. I'm a grown man with a fucking appetite. Get your pussy down here. All of your weight, stop fucking around." Reaching under her legs, my big arms wrap around her thighs and pull her against me. *Oh, fuck yes.* Her taste is everything. She yelps and still tries to push against the mattress to pull up, but I tug her closer.

"Mmhmm." I open my mouth to taste her more, then lift her only for a second to boss her around. "Now grind."

She sits there staring at me, biting the corner of her lips. She does that thing where she pulls inward, trying to hide that sweet body. Her expression is wary and she's overanalyzing again, focusing on those goddamn negative thoughts.

"Raleigh!" I slap her ass and a loud crack echoes off the walls. She jumps and gasps, then rubs the spot. Good. She needed a little redirection. Little by little, her weak gyrations evolve into a gentle grind. Baby steps. Her eyes and mouth soften as she relaxes. Tasting her while she gains back her self-esteem is so arousing. This was supposed to keep me from coming earlier, but now I'm not sure it was a good idea. *She's so fucking hot.*

Her once-stiff shoulders slouch as she surrenders to the pleasure. This time when she grabs the bedpost, she uses it as leverage to grind, and I fucking love it. I grip a handful of her breasts. When I tug her nipples, she throws her head back and moans, with one hand buried in her hair. *Jesus Christ. Marry me.*

She brings her hands over mine as she rocks freely, and I spear my tongue inside her, then she stills and locks eyes with me. My name on her lips is enough to have me smirk beneath her writhing body as she comes. I groan, and she whimpers at the vibrations. When her sweetness hits my tongue, I pull her deeper into my mouth. Tasting her from the source and watching her break apart is ecstasy.

I want to take full possession of what's mine. She reaches behind and digs her nails into my stomach and drags them up to my chest. The feeling must be mutual. My eyes roll back at her aggression. I want all her clawing, scratching, and biting. Untamed. I want to witness her devolve into a fiery goddess while she fulfills her most basic need with me.

Cradling her back, I flip her so I'm on top and finish suckling and massaging her with my tongue. One hand splayed across her chest, between her breasts, and the other sliding fingers inside her. Inhaling a hiss between clenched teeth, she marks my shoulders and upper back with her nails, and the harder she scrapes, the harder I suck. I love that even in this new position, she hasn't stopped grinding against me.

My fingers curl up and tap that spot she loves.

She's closing in on another. I sit up and reach under her ass, pulling her pelvis higher and thrusting my cock inside. She screams out and her body shakes.

"Come on, baby girl. Show me how much you love this cock."

The noises she makes right before she erupts are so fucking erotic.

I bring the heel of my palm to her clit for added pressure and she opens her knees. She pulses around me and it's my name her tongue is begging for while she comes. Seeing her unraveled, flushed, and trembling is the ultimate high, and I'm not long behind her.

My lips curl into a half smile, and I brush the damp locks from her face. She's unbelievable.

"Look down." I nod between us. "See how well you take me?"

She peers to where our bodies meet and props herself up on her elbows so she can watch me fuck her.

"God, that's so hot," she pants.

I nod. "Your body was made for mine."

This time she's the one that grabs my neck, pulling me closer so I can kiss her. I slip my tongue inside her mouth so she can taste herself. She lifts her other hand and falls back. Her mouth claims mine, wanting more from the hot and hungry kiss.

I drive inside her, eager for more while she whispers wicked praises under her breath.

"I love the way you fuck me, Bear."

When she claws my lower back, everything constricts.

"Nobody will ever fuck you like I do. Nobody will ever feel this good," I curse. My breaths are becoming uneven, but I focus. "I don't say that to be arrogant. What we have is special. It's rare. Please, Ral. Tell me you feel it."

Her gaze studies mine, passing back and forth between my eyes. "We're meant to be, aren't we?"

I drop my head. *Exactly.* My mouth finds hers again. Rough and hard. Fuck, I don't know how much longer I can go. Every little dig of her nails into my flesh is pushing me closer to the brink. Her lips are so soft and swollen as I suck the lower between my teeth. My dick is twitching, I need release.

"Where do you want me to come?"

"Um...my back?"

I try not to look disappointed when I pull out. I was hoping she'd let me fill her pussy to the brim. When it leaks, I'll push it back in. I want her gorged with my cum.

Turning her onto her front, I shove three fingers into her cunt and her back arches, pushing her ass out and giving me a delicious view of how snug she is. She moans and grinds with my thumb pressed to her asshole. I grip my dick and pump in rhythm with her fucking herself on my hand.

"I want your cum, Bear. Show me that you own me."

"*You've owned me from the start.*" My groan sounds more like a roar as I shoot onto her ass and lower back.

My hand slows and I knead her cheek where I marked her. "You look beautiful covered in my cum."

A soft laugh leaves her lips, and she turns her head, resting it on the bed, ass in the air. Her arms stretch out above her, and a soft, relaxed smile graces her flushed face. I take in the whole picture, wanting to remember this image for later. *Forever.* Dread sinks in when I realize I can't keep her here tonight. I glance at my phone to see what time it is. She cracks an eye open and spots me.

"Trying to get rid of me already?" she quips.

I slap her ass and toss my phone on the bed, stepping away

to get a wet washcloth from the bathroom.

She sighs when I sweep the warm towel over her skin.

"I'm keeping you until the last second. If it was anyone but Arthur, I wouldn't give you back at all," I mutter.

Afterward, I grab two thick white robes from the closet. I pull her up and wrap her in the fluffy material—she's swimming in its size. But I like it. She raises the lapel to her nose and sniffs. "Smells like your cologne." She snuggles deeper, and that simple gesture does so much.

Gathering the billowy robe in her arms, Raleigh follows me back outside to the fire. She curls up next to me, but I need her closer, so I lift her into my lap. Her cheek rests on my chest, with her head tucked into my neck. I only have about thirty more minutes before I have to take her home, and I need to take advantage of her blithe, post-sex state of mind.

Not sure how I should approach it though...

"I wish I could give you the night I wanted last time." I can't wait for the morning when I can wake up next to her.

Her fingertips meander inside my robe and brush over my abdomen. "I'm sorry I left."

"I should have told you that night I wanted to see you again. For more than sex." I pause. "I knew after the burned pizza that you would never be a bunny to me. You were always more, Raleigh. Always."

She sighs, her chest rising and falling in sync with mine. "Tell me what would have happened if I'd stayed."

A slow smile grows on my lips. "I would pull you against me like this. Kiss your neck and breathe you in. You always smell so fucking good. It's not even perfume it's... I dunno it's just *you*. We would have slept in, and when the sun came up, I would have made you breakfast. Left you at my house while I went to practice and then I'd have come back to fuck you again."

She giggles, but it's probably true.

"And then?"

I know what she's asking. "I've thought about this a lot." I swallow and try to find the words. "If you had come to me and announced you were pregnant... I don't think it would have bothered me. I would have done whatever I could've to support you. I'd definitely have moved you in here though."

Seeing her pregnant is a fantasy. Her lower stomach swollen as she rides me, her body filling out before my eyes. God, it would have been awesome to experience. Knowing there's something so loved between us, a life that we made— half Raleigh, half me—growing under the surface. Unreal. I missed all those moments.

I clear my throat. "You did something to me that night. You made me start thinking about my future and the things I want in life." I hated not knowing where she was. I was worried about her, and even though we had only one night together, I never stopped craving her. The withdrawal was lonely as hell.

"I was on birth control, I swear. But I wasn't great about taking my pill at the same time. I didn't think it would matter —don't worry, I have an IUD now."

"You do?"

"I assumed you knew that... That's why you were okay not using a condom?"

I hum to acknowledge her, but I'd be fine either way. The idea of spilling inside her... *damn.* It wouldn't be careless, every drop would be intentional. Call it intuition, whatever, but I know we have a future together. The three of us. Though, I'd love to add a fourth. Maybe a fifth? It's a bizarre sensation being turned on by the thought of impregnating her.

I've only ever encountered it with Raleigh.

A shiver rolls through her. It's a lot chillier than it was before, but the cool air feels good after exerting all that energy.

She breathes deeply, still in a happy sex haze. It's a perfect night. She looks to the dark sky filled with twinkling stars.

I don't take my eyes off her. Without thinking, the words fall out of my mouth.

"Let's take a vacation together. All three of us." It's not so much a question as it is a plea.

Her arm retracts, and she gawks at me. "What?" she says with a smile... *That's a good sign, right?*

"It's offseason. I have some responsibilities with Camp Conway, but there's a four-week break in between where I'm not needed."

"Um..." She shakes her head, but I don't let her thoughts get too far. We need this time together.

"I think it would be good to take a little trip together." *Like a family.* "Have some time to get a feel for everything without life getting in the way. No work, no schedules, no fans interrupting and asking for selfies, no practices, or obligations."

"Barrett—"

"When was the last time you and Arthur went anywhere?"

She picks at a loose thread on the robe. "We went camping last fall."

"Come on, baby. You deserve a holiday. Arthur would love it."

She laughs. "I'm going to tell you a secret, what a four-year-old likes and dislikes changes hour to hour." She pauses, giving it real consideration. "I mean, how long would you even want to go? I have work and there's daycare..."

"Four weeks."

Her eyes practically bulge. "What?! That's not a *little trip.* That's a *month*, Barrett. I can't take a month off work! I'll lose my job. Even if I didn't, I can't afford a four-week vacation." She laughs, almost hysterically.

"I'll take care of everything."

"It's not just that, I can't afford to not be paid for four weeks. I have a mortgage, utility bills..." She waves her hand around and looks at me with raised eyebrows, like I'm an idiot who wouldn't understand the day-to-day responsibilities of life.

I know she won't give me four weeks, but now we have a jumping off point to start negotiations. *I'm guessing she still hasn't taken that trip.*

I pull her back against me. "You always wanted to go to Hawaii, right? Did you?"

She angles her head toward me inquisitively. "No." *Oh, she's fucking mine now. I've got her.*

"Then let's do it."

"I can't take off four weeks, that's ridiculous. I mean, at most I could maybe do two." I'm sure if she batted her eyes at her boss, he'd do whatever she wanted. But in the unlikely chance I'm mistaken, I'm sure if I tell Rob that our ad deal for Camp Conway relies on her vacation time, it won't be an issue. She rests her head against my shoulder.

My smile can't be contained, but I don't let her see it.

"Two and a half," she says with finality.

I tuck her blonde hair behind her ear. "Three and a half."

"Three."

I'll be the one handling any negotiations in our future. She shakes her head and tucks her tongue in her cheek. *Try and hide that smile all you want, love. I can see your excitement.* I squeeze her, knowing she wants to go. "Arthur could see the ocean... you could relax on the beach while he and I build sandcastles. We could eat fresh pineapple. You deserve this."

"I'd have to get approval from my boss and HR." She'll get it.

"Are you sure you want to do this? Arthur sometimes struggles with change. He'll probably take a few days to get used to the transition."

"Maybe we should do four weeks, then, give him enough time to adjust."

She sits up and pushes my shoulder. "I'm serious."

"Me too! I'm new to this, but I want a chance to see how it works with the three of us together. This isn't meant as a threat at all, and I don't want to scare you, but I'd like to have a little practice with co-parenting. I have a lot to learn." Her searing gaze meets mine.

"It'll be okay," I say, reassuring her and pulling some of her tresses out from the collar of the robe. "Okay."

I bury my hand in her thick blonde locks and bring her lips to mine. Gently swiping my tongue across hers, she opens more, and I deepen our kiss. She doesn't know how much I appreciate her taking this leap. I've been thinking about my retirement now more than ever. Every time we're together, the thought is compounded. We share an attraction, but I need to know what kind of future we might have together. The three of us.

"Thank you," I whisper.

Being on vacation with Arthur is bound to throw some challenges into the mix, and I want to see how we handle them as a team. Ideally, I'd move them in with me—I'm dying to know how we operate as a family. An extended vacation is a somewhat disguised version of moving in together. Am I playing house? Maybe. But what am I supposed to do, be patient? Fuck that.

I think I will make a good husband and father, and I'll do everything I can to be that for her and our son. But she's got an almost five-year head start on parenthood and there's a lot I need to catch up on.

She checks her phone that was left on the cushion, then holds it up to me. I look at the clock and give her one more kiss.

Time's up.

251

THIRTY-FOUR

Raleigh

"Who wants cake?" I say, cutting and plating the slices.

"I love all the decorations! Where did you find koala party supplies?" Brayden's mom, Michelle, asks.

"Etsy!" I bought the digital files and had them printed at work. Then all I had to do was stay up until 2:00 a.m. cutting and assembling. *The sacrifices we make.* But they look great, and I was able to give Arthur the koala-themed birthday party of his dreams. The look on his face when he woke up the next morning made it worth the sleep deprivation.

"It's adorable!"

"Thanks!"

"Mhmm. It looks nice. For being handmade, I mean," Rochelle comments.

Sigh. Rochelle's my least favorite of the moms. She once asked some oddly pointed questions about Danielle being married to another woman, and I haven't liked her since. Unfortunately, her twins are friends of Arthur's, so we see each other fairly regularly.

Six kids come running to the kitchen looking for cake at

the same time the doorbell rings.

"Danielle, do you mind handing these plates out while I grab the door?"

"Of course!" She takes the knife from me. "Give me a hand, babe," she says to her wife, Cora. Cora turns to the kids and pulls open the sliding glass door. "Okay, you monsters, everybody find a spot at the picnic table, and we'll bring out the cake."

Thank you, I mouth, then wipe my hands while exiting the kitchen and hurrying to answer the door. When I open it, I freeze.

"Barrett? What are you doing here?"

He ducks under the doorway as he enters, gift in hand. I shouldn't be shocked he remembered Arthur's birthday.

"It's the twentieth." He cocks his head to the side. "Where else would I be? Shoes on or off?"

I stand there staring at him like an idiot before I remember he asked me a question.

"On is fine—Um, we've kind of got a birthday party going on out back with his friends from daycare. Do you want to come by later?"

"Do *you* want me to come by later?" I see a sliver of hurt in his eyes.

"No, I didn't mean—it's fine that you're here. I'm sorry I didn't invite you, I thought with all the people you might not want—"

"If it's all right with you, I'd like to stay for the party."

I shake my head, trying to ignore how frazzled I feel, and gesture to him to come in. "Uh, yeah. Of course." I tuck the loose hairs falling from my ponytail behind my ears.

As soon as we enter the kitchen, the conversations come to a halt and the moms gawk at Barrett. I can't blame them.

He looks really good today. Who am I kidding, he looks really good every day.

"Everyone, this is Barrett." I turn to motion to the women. "Barrett this is Michelle, Brayden's mom. Jennifer, Caleb's mom. Rochelle, she has twins, Henry and Harriet. And Jill, Lilah's mom."

They all raise their hands and say, "Hi" in unison. Then they shift their eye contact to me while trying to hide smiles.

My face feels like it's on fire.

"Can I help with anything?" he asks.

Just then, Danielle walks through the sliding glass door. "Okay, everybody has cake and one of those stupid healthy organic-whatever juice boxes. Where did I set my White Claw?" She looks around and her eyes catch on Barrett. Two seconds later, Cora enters and halts in her tracks. "Shit, save some pussy for the rest of us."

I roll my lips together and give a pregnant blink. "And now you've met Danielle and Cora, Ezra's moms." I grab a wad of napkins and shove them at Barrett. "Can you make sure the kids have napkins?"

"Sure." He smiles over his shoulder at me as I try to shove him toward the sliding screen door, knowing I'm trying to get him out. "Ladies. Nice to meet you." He nods.

In the backyard, Arthur yells, "Barrett!" The sound wraps me in a hug.

"What the hell, Raleigh! When were you going to tell us you're dating an NHL player?!"

I don't see these ladies often, but we have invited each other to all the birthday parties as a way to get together. We have a text thread we keep in touch in, but it's not something I wanted to start sharing with everyone until he was ready.

"It's still new." I shrug. "We're trying it out."

"Well, we've been here for an hour and all we've talked about are the kids and stupid decorations, no offense, babe. They're cute, but he's *cute.*"

"I'd climb him like a koala."

"Where did you meet?" Jill asks, a big smile on her face.

"A hockey game, we had a work thing at the arena. There was a meet and greet with some of the players." That's our cover story for now. It's hard not to smile just as wide; it's fun having something new and exciting in my dating life. Something for me.

"I'm surprised he goes for, you know, normal women. Don't hockey players usually date models and stuff?" Rochelle asks. The other women glare at her, and the silence suddenly feels heavy and awkward.

"I suppose it depends on the player," I answer.

Jenna rescues the group from the building tension. "He better treat you well. You've been celibate for way too long to break it for some shithead. But I've heard Barrett's a really nice guy, does a lot with charity and stuff. Do you think it's getting serious?"

"Maybe? He's an awesome person. Sometimes it's like he's too good to be true, ya know? And he's been amazing with Arthur, it's like they're becoming best friends," I say, looking outside and watching the two do some secret handshake. *How come I don't have a secret handshake?*

"All I'm saying is that if you think it's too good to be true, maybe it is..." Rochelle adds.

I keep staring out the window at how seamlessly Barrett has entered our life. It's surprisingly been an easy adjustment. But saying it was too good to be true was meant as an expression, *and she's kind of being a bitch.*

"Hey, Rochelle, you might want to check Henry and Harriet's hair later. I saw them itching a lot." Dani scrunches her nose and mimes scratching her head. "You wouldn't want to be responsible for giving the rest of the kids head lice."

"Oof, lice is such a pain in the ass. That would really suck. You have to wash every—"

"My kids don't have lice!" she snaps. Jill turns around,

rolling her lips together, attempting to cover her laugh at the outburst.

"Okay, so he's phenomenal with Arthur," Michelle says, getting us back on track. "What about…" Her eyebrows bounce up and down.

I simply smile. "Also phenomenal. Okay, come on, let's go outside with the kids. He's unarmed."

We walk out to the backyard to find Barrett attempting a poorly done sleight-of-hand magic trick with a napkin.

Caleb wrinkles up his little nose. "You're not very good at magic."

"He's really good at hockey though!" Arthur comes to his defense.

Barrett holds out his fist to Arthur, and he taps it with his miniature one. "My man." *My heart.*

"Baby rabies," Michelle mumbles into her drink, leaning into me.

I smile into mine and nudge her back.

"Call me later, I want to know how your interview goes."

"Oh, I will. Trust me!" Jill says with a snicker.

I laugh and wave as she walks toward her car.

Finally, the last of the guests have left. Well, everyone except Barrett. After the deadbolt clicks shut, I slide down the door and slump on the floor. I need a minute.

Barrett comes out of the kitchen and finds me in a heap.

"There she is." He smiles and holds his arm out. "Tired?"

"Exhausted."

"I ordered us a pizza."

I take his hand, and he pulls me to my feet. "You're amazing."

"I know... Your friends told me so about twenty times." He rolls his eyes and pulls me in for a hug. After a moment he murmurs, "I can't wait to have you and Arthur all to myself soon."

I've been so preoccupied with party planning I forgot to keep him informed of my conversations with work regarding my vacation time.

"I talked to HR about it."

He keeps me in his arms and slips the tie out of my hair, letting it fall down my back. "And?"

"I got approved for three weeks. They said Sondra can cover for me."

An appreciative grunt rumbles in his chest. "Have you talked to Arthur?"

He runs his big fingers through the strands, and I'm not sure if he even realizes he's doing it.

"Not yet," I say with my ear pressed to his chest. I love the sound of his heartbeat. "Wanna do it together?"

Pulling back, he kisses me. "Yeah." He gives me a small swat on my ass and pulls away. I miss his arms around me already.

"Hey, Mini Bear! Come in here, buddy!" I smirk at the nickname.

Arthur meets us in the living room, his head down and focused on one of the presents he got. The koala backpack Barrett gave him is strapped on his shoulders.

Barrett sits down and pats the couch next to him. "Can I see your new helicopter?"

"Uh-huh." He hands it over to him and sits beside him on the sofa. Mini Bear is a fitting nickname. It's exactly what Arthur looks like perched next to him.

"This is pretty neat. What does this button do?"

Arthur presses the button and triggers the sound of chopping helicopter blades through the toy's tiny speaker.

"Man, that's awesome."

"Yeah, and look..." He churns some crank on the side, releasing a tiny gurney on a string. "It has a little thing so they can rescue people."

"Very cool." He hands it back. "Have you ever been on a helicopter?"

"No!" Arthur giggles. "How about a plane?" *This motherfucker is smooth.*

"No."

Barrett looks up at me, and I nod. We're really doing this. "Well, I thought it would be fun if we went for a plane ride."

Arthur sets the helicopter down and hops to his knees, both hands pressed to Barrett's shoulder. "A real one?"

"Yeah. You, and your mom, and me. And we could have the plane take us to an island—"

His eyes grow wide as he grabs onto Barrett's arm. "Like Australia!?"

We both laugh. "Well, we can definitely go to Australia someday. But that's a really long plane ride. I was thinking somewhere a little closer and a lot smaller, like Hawaii. We could go on a vacation."

"Does Hawaii have koalas?"

"Unfortunately, they don't. It's the one downside. Actually, I've heard tourism is down because of the lack of koalas."

"I believe that," Arthur says, scrunching his eyebrows and nodding in agreement.

"Do you think you and your mom would want to come?" He looks back at me for permission, and I nod.

The whole sofa shakes as he bounces on his knees. "Yes! When do we go?"

"In just over a week." Barrett laughs.

"A week?!" I interrupt. I didn't know it was so soon. "A week isn't long." *How am I going to get us ready in a week?*

"It's ten days away. Is that okay?"

My hand rests on my forehead, thinking of the mile long to-do list I have now.

Shit, we don't even have suitcases. Arthur needs a new swimsuit. And I've got to close the loop on a few things at work still. How do you travel with a booster seat? The travel and lodging might be covered, but I'm going to be dropping a few hundred dollars before we even get in the air. The last time I traveled was before I found out I was pregnant.

"Yeah, I'll figure it out. I need to get some things together." I bite my thumbnail, making a mental packing list.

Shit, I need to get a wax, I wonder if there's any openings at my salon this week.

"Raleigh."

"Uh-huh..."

He needs new shorts. And I'll need those little travel bottles for shampoo and conditioner. Do they make hiking boots for five-year-olds? They must. I wonder if I can get them shipped here in time. Where the hell did I pack away those water shoes he has? Will ₁ need water shoes too?

"Okay, buddy, do you mind if your mom and I chat for a little bit about the trip?"

"I'm gonna start packing!" His little legs leap from the couch and he runs down the hall to his room. I'm sure he will start pulling out everything he owns, but I'll deal with the mess later. I need to think.

What about my yard? There's gotta be a high school kid around here that wants to make some money over the summer by mowing lawns. But I won't have time to ask around. And who will pick up my mail? What if something important is delivered? What if packages show up?

"Raleigh. Talk to me."

"What?" I tap my foot, thinking of all the stuff I need to figure out this week. *I didn't even tell HR I would be leaving in ten days. I figured it was at least a few weeks out.*

His palm lands on my thigh, forcing me to look up at him. I swallow.

"Are you afraid to fly?"

I wrinkle my face. "What? No. Why would you think that?"

"You seem a little anxious."

"Barrett..." I take a deep inhale and exhale. "You travel a lot, you're used to up and leaving at the drop of a hat. That's harder for us. I have a lot of stuff to figure out in a short amount of time. Three weeks is—there's mail, and lawns, and tiny hiking boots, and booster seats, and rental cars, and swimsuits—"

"I'm sorry. I should have asked you about dates before I got the tickets. I already talked to my landscaping company about swinging by to cut your lawn. Mail can be put on hold. Don't worry about the car stuff, I've got a rental and have already researched how to travel with his car seat. There's enough beds for all of us. We can order the rest or pick it up when we get there. What else do you need me to do?"

With each solution, the weight on my shoulders lessens. It's like he could read my mind. Tears prick at my eyes. *Is this what it's like having somebody else to pick up the slack?*

"Really?" My hands press together in a prayer against my lips.

"Yeah. I told you I want to be involved. Give me a to-do list."

Sex is one thing, but it's a special kind of pussy throb when he takes care of my errands.

I wrap my arms around his neck and hug him, mumbling, "Thank you" against his warm skin. He smells so good. He puts his arms around me and pulls me into his lap.

"We'll figure it out together." His hand travels up my thigh and grips my ass. "It's going to be okay." And I believe him.

THIRTY-FIVE
Raleigh

"I need some actual advice here," I say over the phone. Jill is a sounding board for me when things get stressful. My mind has started spinning again, and I needed somebody to let my anxiety out to—somebody who isn't Barrett. I pace in my closet with my phone on my shoulder, picking out and moving all the summer wear—that still fits—to one side of the closet to separate it for packing.

"No, you don't. You just want to feel better about your decision."

Jill's right. But she doesn't know what's riding on this trip. This isn't just a vacation, it's three weeks with my son and Barrett. *The three of us.* I've always dreamed about going to Hawaii, and would love to show Arthur somewhere outside the state lines he's never crossed. He could swim in the ocean, see volcanoes, hell, he could pick a fresh fucking pineapple!

I dig through the drawer in my closet that has all my swimsuits, and promise myself that after I get off the phone, I'm going to Target to find a new one.

"And I love you, Raleigh, but I swear to God, if you whine one more time about how you're scared of going on a three-week all-paid vacation to Hawaii with six-feet-seven-inches of sex—Barrett Conway—number thirty-three, star right-winger, and alternate captain for the Minnesota Lakes, I'll kick you out of the activities carpool."

I laugh and nod again. "You're right. I'm overthinking." She's always right.

"Besides, if you're worried about the money, hockey players probably take these vacations all the time during the offseason."

I sit down on the floor and try on sandals that have been hiding in the back of the closet all winter.

That's true. A trip to Hawaii is probably nothing to him. But for Raleigh Dunham, trailer trash from North Carolina who's been trying to rise above her station since she left, Hawaii was always a pipe dream. Arthur has been the center of my universe for so long I may have forgotten about the things I want too.

Like Barrett Conway.

"Thanks for talking me off a ledge."

"I hear the way you talk about him and *girl...* the way he looks at you? Swoon. He's a good guy, Raleigh. Let yourself have this happiness."

THIRTY-SIX

Raleigh

"Mom, I'm driving the boat!"

"You're doing great!"

This man is weakening me by the minute. It doesn't help that he's in nothing but swim trunks and his tanned muscles are on display. His chest, back, thighs, calves, arms... good God. He decided that we, *meaning me*, needed a break from the stress of packing to relax and cruise around the lake. He's been dropping hints about taking us out on his boat for a while now. And you know what? I decided to take him up on that. I'm taking Jill's advice and letting myself have happiness.

Arthur's face remains focused as he takes his captain duties seriously. Over his shoulder, Barrett points out a piece of driftwood that Arthur needs to maneuver around.

"Okay, Mini Bear. See that big log sticking out of the water, can you steer us around that on the right side? Do you know right from left?"

"Uh-huh," Arthur says, turning the wheel.

"You're a natural. Maybe I'll take a nap in the cabin and you can show your mom around the lake." He gives him pointers, and they make conversation as if they're lifelong friends. It makes my heart flip and my ovaries throw a goddamn ticker tape parade.

The hot sun beats down on us, but the breeze off the lake feels like a warm blanket over my exposed skin, and it makes my eyes heavy. I might be the one taking a nap up here in the bow seats—I'd probably sleep better than I do in my own bed. I've never been on a boat this nice.

"Mom!"

"Yeah, bud?" I answer with my eyes closed.

"How come you're not wearing your swimsuit like me 'n' Barrett?" Arthur asks. I sit up and turn around.

"Yeah, good question, Mini Bear!" Barrett winks at me. "Why don't you take off that cover up?"

Previously, I was always very self-conscious in a swimsuit, but lately, I've become so much more comfortable in my own skin. I'm sure Barrett's influence has something to do with that, especially when I catch him checking me out. I went out and got a couple of new suits for Hawaii. Normally, I would've rather shaved my shins with a cheese grater than shop for new suits, but I wanted something cute and sexy.

I grab a handful of my loose sundress and pull it over my head, showing off my new two-piece, and behind me, Barrett chokes on his sparkling water.

"Mini Bear... Your mom is *hot*."

"Barrett!" I shoot a glance at him, and my face heats up. Arthur giggles like it's the funniest thing he's ever heard. I have a feeling it's mostly because he's never heard anyone else be on the receiving end of my "mom" voice."

He wolf-whistles as I sit back down in the cushy seats at the front of the boat.

"Arthur, don't ever whistle at girls like that, it's rude and they don't like it."

That's a lie, pretty sure Barrett could catcall a fucking banana and it would start stripping its peel. My attempt at setting a good example is weak, and I have to smother my grin. I love getting that reaction out of him. When his gaze falls on me, I'm the only woman in the world.

It's an incredible feeling to be wanted the way he wants me. The other night, he came over for dinner and after Arthur went to bed, Barrett licked my stretch marks like he was worshipping each and every one of them. He bit and clawed at my stomach and thighs like he couldn't get enough. Knowing I still turn him on, even after all the changes my body has gone through, digs up the feelings I've had buried and brings them to the surface.

"Raleigh, come back here so I can put some sunblock on you."

Seems like a trap, but he's got a point.

I reluctantly sit up from my relaxed lounging and head toward them. "I can manage."

He slows the boat to a trolling speed, and I walk to the back to grab the bottle. When I pass the two of them, he points at the horizon to Arthur. "Okay, you've got a really important job, I need you to aim us toward that row of trees, way out in the distance, see it?"

"Yup!"

"Good, don't take your eyes off it. Keep us headed in that direction."

He skims his rugged palms up the back of my calves, behind my thighs, until he reaches my ass. I freeze. I should slap his hand away, but I'm loving his attention and Arthur is too busy playing ship captain.

"I'm going to grab us some snacks. Can you keep driving for a minute?"

"Yessir!"

I know a diversion when I hear it. He scoots off the short bench and grabs my hips, walking me backward until my feet hit the stern. One hand tangles in my windblown hair, and the other kneads my ass.

He steals the bottle of lotion from me and blocks my path back to the front of the boat.

"Stand here," he says in a low, demanding voice. "Arthur, keep an eye on the water. Don't turn around until I come back," he says, staring into my eyes like he's about to devour me.

He pulls me hard against him and laps at my bottom lip before biting and pulling it into his mouth. I gasp but it's drowned out by the steady rumble of the inboard motor behind us. His kiss is hungry and explosive. Like he's been thinking about it all day.

His tongue brushes mine. He tastes like watermelon seltzer and Barrett. It's a delicious combination.

He growls against my lips. "New rule, you can't wear this swimsuit in front of me when Arthur is around. I've been running game plays in my head for the last five minutes to distract my dick."

I laugh and give him a small push, but he grabs my bikini bottoms and shoves his hand in. *Oh fuck.* "You're wet. Does it turn you on knowing how hard you make me?" He shoves the coated fingers in his mouth and sucks them clean.

Nodding, my hands cradle his neck and bring him to my lips again to taste myself on his tongue.

He chuckles and grips me harder; I love the feel of his fingers digging into my body.

"Stay with me tonight. Let's make it a sleepover. I'll make you both breakfast in the morning... I'm sick of getting you for only a few hours and having to let go. I fucking hate it."

No way. That's too soon... *right?* Sure, Arthur would love to stay at Barrett's house, he has stars in his eyes when he looks at him. But what message does it send to his little five-year-old brain? Arthur has never seen me share a bed with another man before.

"You said you wanted to live in the moment, right? I promise it'll be fine. Let me wake up next to you. Please."

Ugh, his powers of persuasion are unmatched—or perhaps I have a weak constitution whenever he's around. There's a security with Barrett I can't explain, it's something I didn't grow up with, and I imagine this is what people mean when they say something feels like home. I never had that in North Carolina, I hated the feeling of being at home. But this is different. How can I say no to it? Especially when it's a feeling I spent most of my life craving. This trust we have grows more every day. I like Barrett. And I like the way he is with Arthur—*a lot.*

"What do we tell him?"

"Let's ask him. If he doesn't want to stay, you don't have to."

My head tilts to the side and I roll my eyes. "We both know what that answer will be, of course he's going to want to stay." *What a ridiculous question.*

He glances at Arthur still manning the helm behind me. Sometimes, he looks at him the same way I do. It takes the air out of my lungs every time. It's spooky.

"I would need to get his pajamas and clothes for tomorrow."

He beams at me, and I smile back.

"Already picked up some spares last week."

Unbelievable.

I knew the night we met Barrett was a good man. He's empathetic and has a good heart. It's part of what made him so attractive and why it hurt so much to walk away. One of my biggest regrets.

Opening the cooler, I grab the snacks and nudge him back

to the cockpit. For the rest of the boat ride, whenever Arthur isn't looking, he can't keep his hands off me—*I don't hate it.*

After a spin around the lake, we head back in. As we get closer, I notice someone sitting on the bench attached to his dock. It's a woman.

"Barrett, there's someone at your house."

His eyes go wide the second he sees her. "What the f— what's she doing here?"

"Who is she?"

"Ral, listen to me, babe." He takes my hands in his, and my mind starts swirling. "I don't want you to get all in your head about this, because there's nothing to worry about. But you're about to meet my mom."

His mom!?

"Does she know about—"

He shakes his head. "She only knows about you."

I look back up and stare at my fate and then look down at Arthur. *Oh fuck.* Gliding into the boat garage, my nerves multiply. We hop onto the platform and exit onto the attached dock, where she's as surprised to see us. Arthur stays tucked behind my leg, his usual with new people.

"Hi, Mom. Didn't know you were stopping by, a heads-up would have been nice."

The woman has kind eyes and a big smile. "I know, I'm sorry! But I made this cookie recipe from Amelia and accidentally added too much flour so I had to add more of everything else and now I have sixteen dozen cookies, so I thought I would swing by and drop some off. I saw your car was here, so I figured you were out on the boat, but I didn't know you had company—well, introduce me!"

"Waiting to get a breath in, Mom. This is Raleigh and this little guy"—he looks down at Arthur, who lets go of my leg to cling to Barrett's—"is Arthur."

He pulls me to his side. "Raleigh, this is my mom, Susan."

I'm sweating out of every pore. Does she know he and I had a one-night stand? Does she judge me for being a single mother? She can see right through me, I know it. "It's so nice to meet you!" I say it with a big smile and hold out my hand.

"Oh please, I've heard about you for so long now, I feel like we're already friends." She pulls me into a hug. "I'm so happy you two are finally connecting again. You should know, he never takes women out on his boat, so he's definitely into you. I mean, of course he is, you're the infamous Raleigh from Raleigh! Barrett, she is even more beautiful than you described. Wow, you lucky son of a gun. Better treat her well."

"Hey, Mom?" Barrett interrupts her rambling. "Easy on the overshare, eh? I don't need you to scare her away already."

"Hi, Arthur." Susan uses a comforting tone, bending down and calming her energy for him. "You can call me Big Suze."

"Hi." He wiggles his fingers back at her.

She holds out her fist to him. "Wanna blow it up?"

He presses his small knuckles to hers and then they open their hands and make explosion sound effects.

She straightens and places her hand on my shoulder like we're old friends. I instantly feel at ease. Does every Conway have this magical effect?

"For cryin' out loud, he is just so darn adorable. Can he have a cookie?"

"Sure," I answer with a chuckle.

"Great! Barrett, I'm taking them up to the house for cookies and milk. Grab her bag, will ya?"

Her arm hooks in mine and she holds out her hand to Arthur. Yeah, I can see he's already become comfortable with her too. It must be genetic.

"Whoa, how about you just wait—"

"Chill out, Barrett. Don't have a cow. I'm not going to tell her any embarrassing stories like how you used to smile at the sky during thunderstorms because you thought the lightning was a giant camera flash taking your picture."

My mouth opens in a smile. "Please tell me that's true!" I laugh, visualizing an innocent, sweet, naive little Barrett.

Barrett drops his head in his hands, muttering "Oh my God..."

"Hurry up with that boat, there's no telling how many things I'll remember before you get back!"

"Raleigh, she's confused, I apologize. Mom, maybe you should go sit down for a while, put on one of your programs. How's *Gunsmoke* sound?" he teases her.

She laughs and wrinkles her nose, mouthing, "*He's such a smartass sometimes!*"

"I really prefer *I Love Lucy!*" she yells over her shoulder. His mom and I enter through the lower-level walk-out, the cool air chilling all the sweat from earlier. She heads over to one of the darker rooms, clearly knowing her way around his house. She's a delight. I enjoy seeing the relationship between them. It's fun and lighthearted. And loving. She and Barrett obviously joke around often.

"Do you drink wine, Raleigh?"

I close the door behind me and toe off my flip flops. "Oh, um, sure!"

"Great! You head up and I'll steal us a bottle!" She's got a mischievous streak.

Within fifteen minutes, Arthur is happily sitting on one of the barstools with a couple chocolate-chip cookies and I'm having the time of my life listening to Barrett stories.

"No, Barrett was a fairly normal kid. My other son used to get in trouble for trying to bait seagulls on the playground though."

My cookie pauses on the way to my mouth. "Pardon?"

She nods while swallowing. "Paul would save some of his

lunch and shove it in his pockets. Then, when he went out for recess, he'd use the food to try to lure seagulls."

I finish swallowing the bite from my third delicious cookie. "What was his plan if he ever caught one?"

"Oh, he caught one! He wrapped a string around its neck like a leash. Do you have any idea what it's like signing an incident report that your child almost hung a seagull trying to take it for a walk?"

We're cackling over a glass of wine at the kitchen table when Barrett finally hustles inside.

She places her hand on my arm. "Barrett, she's lovely. And one smart cookie too." Her love language must be words of affirmation or something. She barely knows me, but she's been complimenting me nonstop since we were introduced. She slides the container of chocolate chip heaven over to him. "Speaking of...Here, have a couple."

Before he takes any, he bends over and whispers in my ear, "You good? If you want me to get her out of here, ask me for a glass of water." Like we need some secret code around his mom. I love that he's checking in on me and making sure I'm comfortable; he knows I get anxious when plans change unexpectedly. But this has turned into a fun surprise, it's not formal or awkward. She's welcomed me with open arms.

"No thanks, I've got my wine." I smile back and he seems relieved. I tuck my feet under me and take another sip, enjoying the company of his quirky mom.

We spend the next half hour chatting before we get up to help Barrett with dinner. I chop vegetables while she shucks a few ears of corn.

"So, Arthur, how old are you?"

"I just turned five!"

"That's wonderful! Did you have a birthday party?"

"Yeah, with koalas! That's my favorite animal."

"Arthur knows lots of koala facts!" Barrett cuts in. "He's very smart."

"Oh, I bet! Are you going to start kindergarten next year?" she asks him.

He nods emphatically.

"You're going to love it!" She looks at me with fond eyes and taps her cheek. "You know what's funny, his dimple reminds me so much of when Barrett was..." She looks back and forth between Barrett and Arthur.

Oh fuck. Oh fuck, oh fuck.

I drop my eyes to the vegetables I'm chopping. I'm ashamed, I'm embarrassed.

Looking to escape what must be accusing glances, I turn to wash my hands in the sink while my mind spirals. God, this woman probably hates me. She thinks I kept her grandchild from her. *Shit! What if she says it out loud and Arthur hears!*

"Five years," she mutters. I spin back around to see Barrett grimacing while making a subtle slicing motion near his neck.

She takes a big gulp of air and presses her hand to her cheek.

Barrett gives a swift nod of confirmation. Our story is tangled and twisted, it makes my cheeks burn with shame. I knew a day would come when we would need to tell his family. Barrett pulls me into his side and presses a kiss to my hair. "It's okay."

"And he doesn't...?"

"No," we say in unison.

She looks back at him and tears swell in her eyes. "So he's... Oh my God, he's so beautiful! He's perfect."

"Easy, Mom..."

"What? Can't I say how perfect he is?" She sniffles and wipes her face of the tears she's failing to hold back. "He's so big and so smart and wonderful!"

She's not mad? I was terrified when this day would come,

but it's not at all the way I thought it would play out. She seems more happy with the news than she cares about the circumstances that landed us here.

"It's a long story," Barrett explains.

She sniffles some more. "That's fine. We can talk about it another time," she says in Arthur's direction, unable to take her eyes off him. "Just promise me something?" Her voice is soft and hopeful.

"What's that?" Barrett chuckles at her change in demeanor.

Her request is whisper-quiet and she folds her hands together, pleading. "Can I babysit sometime? Please? You don't even need to be gone! I can help out while you do the laundry or cook dinner or something! Or if you need a night for the two of you, ya know, alone time to get frisky—"

"Stop talking," Barrett cuts her off, and I burst out laughing.

"There's a lot we're figuring out, but I don't think that would be a problem," I answer. I'm so appreciative of her offer, and I want to help him build a relationship with his grandmother when we decide how we will navigate it all with Arthur.

"I have to hug you!" she says, happy-crying when she wraps her arms around me. "I'm so happy you two are working at this. I'm so proud of you both!"

She grabs Barrett's white shirt and pulls him in for a hug at the same time. She lowers her voice when she speaks to him. "Congratulations, baby. You have a beautiful family."

The sentiment causes his eyes to glass up. God, now I'm gonna cry! There's something so sexy about a man getting emotional about his family.

"This is still very confidential, you can't say a word to anyone, understand? Not even Paul. We'll tell him when the time comes."

"Will you come for dinner on Sunday? We don't need to say anything."

"I'm going to be leaving for Hawaii soon, remember? Well, the three of us are going. We thought we could use some time to get closer without any distractions. So I need you to help keep this quiet." She nods and pretends to zip her lips.

"I think that's a fabulous idea. You both are doing a terrific job. But when you get back, dinner at my place." When she lets up, she holds her arms out wide. "Would you like a hug too, Arthur?" she asks him.

He shrugs, oblivious to it all while blowing bubbles into his milk. "Sure."

"Hugs for everyone!" She wraps her arms around him and holds him the longest. Barrett leans down to rest his head on mine, and I slide my arm around his back, needing to reinforce our physical touch a little longer.

After a minute of silence, a small voice pipes up, "Can I have another cookie?"

I snort, and Barrett tells him dinner is almost ready and he can have another for dessert. *Well done, Dad.*

It doesn't take long for the playful mood to return between everyone. Though, Arthur certainly gets his share of Big Suze hugs until she leaves after dinner.

After dishes, Barrett shows Arthur and me the dresser he has in one of the open bedrooms. There's a drawer with pajamas and day clothes. We each have our own toothbrushes. Arthur's has a koala. I don't even know where he found one of those. We go through the bedtime routine. Barrett inspects Arthur's brushing and even remembers to ask, "Clean chompers?" afterward. The attention to detail with that man is something else.

Then we pile into Barrett's enormous bed and watch cartoons together. Arthur snuggles up next to him as much as me. And I can practically see Barrett's heart exploding as he gets to wrap his arm around Arthur. He ruffles his hair tenderly, and after he crashes, pressed up against his side, Barrett kisses the top of his head.

I see it in the way he holds him… You never fall faster in love than with your own child.

In a half daze, I wake up wet. Not in the good way. What time is it? My elbow squishes when I prop up to grab my phone and look at the clock. That's when I see Arthur wedged between us.

Oh no.

"Bear," I shake him. "Bear, wake up. Arthur had an accident, I need to wash the sheets."

He groggily opens his eyes. "Huh?"

"You're sitting in pee."

"Oh, God." He shoots to a seated position, waking Arthur, who's now bawling over the wet pajamas.

He turns and pulls Arthur into his lap. "Don't worry, bud. We'll get you cleaned up." He rubs circles on Arthur's back to settle him while I start pulling back the comforter.

"Tell me there's a mattress protector on this bed."

"There is." He smirks and grumbles under his breath,

"Hoping it was gonna be needed for other reasons…" *Of course he did.* I smile and roll my eyes.

"Can you please strip the sheets while I get him cleaned up?"

"Sure. Yeah. Of course."

Barrett transfers him to me, and I carry his sleepy body into the bathroom and peel off the soaked pajamas. I get him in the shower and use the handheld showerhead to rinse him off, soap him up, and rinse again.

"I'm so tired," he whines.

"I know, sweetheart. We're almost done and then you can go back to sleep." I do a double-take when Barrett walks in shirtless, carrying new pajamas and underwear. Thank heavens for the drawer of spare clothes and sleepwear he set aside for Arthur.

He sets them next to me on the floor and then hands me a warm towel.

"Thank you so much." Turning off the water, Arthur steps out onto the rug, and I dry him off.

"Of course." He drops a kiss to my head. "How's everybody feeling now?"

"Much better," I soothe.

After getting him into clean pajamas, Barrett picks him up and lays him down in the center of the bed with new sheets, pillows, and a comforter. He's asleep by the time his head hits the pillow.

"I'm gonna jump in the shower."

"I'll join you," he says.

I spin around and point a finger at him. "Okay, just know I don't have the energy for anything more than cleaning off."

"I'm wide awake," he says. "God, how was there that much pee? It was on three pillows!" he whispers.

"Was it really?"

"Yeah, it was like he peed out of his head."

I laugh as I pull my top off. "I'll need to borrow something to sleep in. And a pair of boxers."

"Sweet hell. You have no idea the number of times I've thought about you naked under one of my shirts."

The water is still warm when I turn the shower back on. Watching Barrett strip out of his gray sweatpants makes me think twice about how much energy I have left. His body is sculpted art. We each suds up and shower ourselves off in the dual showerheads, stealing glances the whole time. He's half hard, which is already impressive. There's a built-in shower bench along the side, and he takes a seat.

"Come here."

I suck in a breath. He smiles, threads his fingers in mine, and pulls me in front of him. I can't keep my eyes off his growing cock. He sighs. "Ignore that. I won't try anything. I just want to hold you for a minute." Barrett drags me into his lap and nuzzles my neck. It's so warm, I could fall asleep like this.

"You're everything I've been missing," he whispers against my wet skin. We've been so wrapped up in each other today, it's easy with him. Under the warm rainfall, we sit in each other's arms in silence, sharing a quiet, intimate moment.

When we get out of the shower, he dries me off. He blots my hair, then moves to my shoulders and back. He sweeps the towel between my breasts and kisses my shoulder. Then drops to his knees to dry off one leg at a time, pressing more kisses to the back of my thighs. Every touch feels like a sensual caress.

I run my fingers through his wet hair as he does it. When he stands, I return the favor, drying off his chest and back. He wraps the towel around his waist, going into his dark walk-in closet and coming back with a huge Lakes hockey T-shirt with a big thirty-three and Conway on the back. It almost reaches my knees. If he weren't a giant, I doubt I'd be able to pull the boxers he gave me over my thighs. They fit, but barely.

"Mmm. Damn."

I chuckle. "Come on, let's go to bed."

He smacks my butt, then we crawl under the new, dry, fresh-smelling sheets. It's so comfortable and safe here. He drapes his arm across Arthur and me, and the weight of it puts my body into deep relaxation. All three of us in this bed, I've never felt more whole. It's a feeling I've been chasing all my life.

The drowsiness swallows me up, I'm two seconds from

falling asleep when he whispers my name. At least I think it was him. I can't tell if I'm dreaming or awake.

"Hmm?" I mumble, unable to open my eyes.

"I love waking up next to you, baby... even when we're covered in piss."

THIRTY-EIGHT
Barrett

The sun is just coming up, it's probably only been a few hours since we went to bed, but my internal clock is an early riser. Waking up next to the two of them floods me with a feeling of contentment I can't put into words. I'm enraptured by them. I gently brush the hair out of Raleigh's face so I can watch her sleep. The most beautiful woman in the world is in my bed, with our son sandwiched between us. It doesn't get better than this.

The more time I spend with Arthur and Raleigh, the more I realize I have a decision to make. I missed out on five years; do I want to travel for the rest of my career and miss out on more time with them? More mornings like this?

Especially Arthur, this is a critical time in his life, I want to be here for it. Leaning over, I press a kiss to the top of his head. I love how much he looks like me. I never thought I would ever feel happiness like this. Hockey has never made me feel the way this does. And let's be honest, how many more years do I have left in this sport? My body is tired. I'm thirty-eight, I'm fucking lucky I've made it this long. Gretzky retired at thirty-eight.

I haven't talked to my agent yet. But if I'm going to pull

the plug, I have to give them a heads-up. I love the Lakes; they've been my home for the last fifteen years. I don't want to leave them high and dry.

When I turned thirty-five, I opted for an annual one-year contract with performance bonuses. It gives me a little more freedom to move around if I need to, but now that's the opposite of what I want to do. Previously, I waffled back and forth about retirement, I didn't know what I'd do. Now when I think of retiring, I'm relieved. I know exactly what my focus will be: my family. Even Camp Conway would be a much better use of my time—and I need all the time I can get.

I need to call Sully, as I have no idea how to navigate this and I'm not ready to break the news to my agent and excite anyone, especially until I talk to Raleigh and get her opinion. If I bring it up now, she'll freak out; I know how she is. She won't want to be the reason for me retiring. She'd want me to continue my career. But if it's between her and Arthur or my career, it's them. Every fucking time.

I lift the sheet and slip out of bed. I'll get more mornings like this, but my head is swimming and I need to get some of my thoughts off my chest before they wake up.

Unplugging my phone from the charger, I take it downstairs and go outside. As I walk toward the lake, I call up my best friend. "Hey. How's retired life?"

"Boring as hell. I need some hobbies or something. I'm getting sick of golfing. I need something else, a project or hobby or something."

I laugh. "Maybe you need a woman."

"Ha! Maybe. Speaking of, how are things with Raleigh? She hasn't gotten sick of your ass yet?"

The sound of the water lapping at the shore calms some of my nerves. "Actually, that's kinda why I'm calling. I need some advice."

"Uh-oh. You calling me for relationship advice is never good. What's up?"

No reason to beat around the bush. "I want to retire."

Silence.

"...You there?"

"Yeah...yeah, I'm just... wow. Shit, retire? What's driving this?"

"Seriously? You know what's driving it." It's her. It's *them*.

He lets out a long whistle. "It's that serious, huh?"

I shake my head, trying to find the words to describe it, but I can't. There aren't words big enough. "Christ, Sull. It's like nothing else. I missed out on so much. I don't want to lose another second with them. They're my everything, I've fallen so fucking hard. For both Raleigh and Arthur... I want them more than the game or championship trophies, more than performance bonuses. More than anything I've wanted before. I can't explain it."

The sound of coffee mugs clinking comes through the line and then the sound of pouring. It's early to be laying this much on him. "Do you think you're getting ahead of yourself here?"

"Fuck, probably. But what's my alternative? Wasting more time? I know she's it. So why delay the inevitable? I need to be here for them. I don't want to miss out on Arthur's milestones. I'm already irritated I'm making her a hockey widow for the upcoming season. I have a contract for the next year, but after that, I'm out."

"Conway, hockey wives parent solo anyway. It's what they sign up for."

I shake my head. "No. She never signed up for this. Our situation is different."

It's quiet again, except for the sound of him sipping coffee.

"Holy shit." He pauses. "You're really gonna do it, aren't you?"

Rubbing the back of my neck with my palm, I peer across the lake, squinting to see through the morning fog coming off the top of the glassy water. "I still gotta talk to Ral. This is a decision she should be included in. Afterward, I'll reach out to my agent."

"You better do it soon. But whatever you need, whatever you decide. I support you."

I nod even though he can't see me. "Do you think I'm crazy?"

He laughs. "Yes. 'Cause you're in love."

THIRTY-NINE

Barrett

The day before we leave, I stop by to assist with making sure she has what she needs. The plan is for me to stay the night at Raleigh's since she lives closer to the airport and then in the morning, we'll get a rideshare to take us to our terminal. I've never wanted to get on a plane so fast.

I'm barely in the door when she rushes up to me. She gives me a chaste kiss. "Do you want to take him for a couple hours so I can finish getting us packed?" Raleigh asks, frantic. "It would be a huge help." Her hair is falling out of a ponytail, she's clearly been rushing around, trying to pack the last-minute items.

One-on-one time with my son? Fuck yeah, I do. I roll my suitcase into her house and push it to the corner. "I'd love to. Sure you don't need any help here?"

"That is helping me here. He's *very* excited for the plane ride." She stares at me with a forced smile through clenched teeth. *Message received.*

Arthur darts through the room with a plane in his hand. "Barrett!"

"Hey, bud!" I kneel and he jumps on my back. "How about we get out of the house and pick up some lunch for your mom?"

Raleigh's shoulders relax, then she adjusts her messy ponytail. "Let me grab my keys for you. The booster's still in my car."

"No need, I had one installed in the BMW."

She freezes and looks back at me. "You did?"

Shit, maybe that went too far. I didn't discuss it with her beforehand. I'm inserting myself into their lives with force, but I'm not willing to waste time or hold back. I want to make things easier on her for once. If her life is more convenient with me in it, she might see me as a benefit rather than an invasion.

Raleigh and I have a resilient connection, but having a connection with Arthur is as important. She needs to see I'm as good for him as I am for her. This time away will show us how well we work as a family unit. It should be startling how quickly I've come to care for them both, but it feels so natural.

"I thought it would be easier for this kind of stuff, save some time so we don't have to switch yours around all the time. Are you okay with that? It's a good one. I did my research and the woman at the store said it had the highest safety ratings. If you want to inspect my installation—" The more I ramble on, the bigger she smiles.

"Thanks, Bear. I really appreciate you doing that." She looks around and holds her palms up when she shrugs.

"Okay, I guess that's it, then." Pointing a finger at Arthur still hoisted on my back, she tells him to behave.

She plucks his shoes off the floor, and he giggles while she shoves them on his dangling feet. His hands are clasped around my neck. Any tighter and he'd probably collapse my windpipe.

I lean down so he can reach out one of his arms to give Raleigh a hug and then we are on our way. She gives another thank you and squeezes my bicep.

Getting Arthur in the booster seat is a breeze. However, on the road, my fear kicks up a notch. I'm suddenly so much more aware of the people driving around me. I trust none of these assholes. I've got my kid in the back seat. I need to keep him safe.

"Your car smells different than Mom's car," Arthur comments, oblivious to my newfound parental anxiety.

"Good-different or bad-different?"

"Different-different." I smile. "That's fair."

"I'm hungry. It's good we're going to lunch or my tummy will explode."

"Explode?"

"Yes, Barrett. Explode."

Better get this kid some food. "What are you hungry for?"

"Cereal."

"Cereal?"

"Why do you keep repeating me?" I laugh.

"Cereal is my favorite food." I know it's his favorite, but shit, where the hell do they serve cereal for lunch?

I pull into a drab hole-in-the-wall twenty-four-hour diner. If any place has cereal, this is it. When we get inside, the restaurant is practically empty. A few seniors sit around one table, but we're the only other people here. I grab the menu and flip it over. *Cereal.* Perfect.

Arthur chooses which empty booth looks best and we barely sit down before we're greeted, well, acknowledged, by an older waitress holding a coffee pot.

"Can I get you something to drink?" She sighs and sets down a paper kid's menu and a single yellow crayon. An upside-down coffee mug sits on a saucer in front of me. I flip it right-side up and she fills the cup.

"Chocolate milk, please! And a bowl of cereal." Arthur sits up with pride. I smile at his boldness, he's normally shy around strangers, but he's been coming out of his shell so much more since I've met him. He's got such a great personality.

"Frosted Flakes or Cheerios?" The waitress asks. His little forehead wrinkles. "The good Cheerios or the gross ones?"

That coaxes a half smile out of our battle-axe of a waitress. "The gross ones."

"Let's do the Frosted Flakes, then. But can I keep the menu? I still have to help the pig through the maze so he can find his boat." He taps the illustration on the corner of the paper. I try not to laugh at his earnest request.

"Sure, hun." Her eyes crinkle as she smiles bigger. He's a charmer, like his dad. She turns to me, and the smile fades away. *Then again, maybe the charm comes from Raleigh.*

"And you?"

"I'll have the same, chocolate milk and Frosted Flakes. Thanks."

"Easy enough." She takes my menu and walks off. Arthur scans the dining room of the dingy café. Peeling wallpaper, there's patched holes on the vinyl bench we're sitting on, and a steady hum coming from somewhere. Possibly an old commercial freezer...or maybe it's one of the flickering fluorescent lights above us.

He genuinely nods in approval. "Nice place."

I bark out a laugh. I love that he sees the good everywhere he goes.

"Are you excited for tomorrow?"

"Mmhmm," he says. His eyes trained on the maze. *How can he even see what he's doing?* The shitty yellow crayon barely shows up on the white menu, I'm half convinced it's just an old birthday candle wrapped in paper.

"Me too. It's going to be a fun trip for all of us. Do you think your mom will like it?"

"Uh-huh. She likes you." He scribbles where he ran into a dead end and starts back at the pig again.

"How do you know she likes me?"

The waitress returns and sets down the tray with two bowls of cereal and two glasses of chocolate milk. One tall and one short. We say thank you, and she wanders toward the table of older men to check on them.

"Mom smiles when you're around." It pleases me to hear, but it makes me wonder if he thought she was unhappy before.

"Maybe she's being polite."

He shakes his head and talks with his mouth full. "No, she has a different smile when she's polite. She has a real smile with you."

He's observant as hell.

"Does she use her real smile more than her polite smile? Is she happy?"

"Sometimes."

"Just sometimes?" I push the cereal around in my bowl.

"Yeah. We're all happy sometimes. And we're all sad sometimes too. Mom says there's lots of feelings inside us and we have to listen for when they need to come out. Happy ones come out more than sad ones, but she says even the sad and angry ones need to get air every once and a while."

He lifts another heaping spoonful of cereal into his wide-open mouth. He has a better grasp on emotions than most adults I know.

"You have a very smart mom."

"Yeah, she's the smartest. I love her." *Shit, I think I might too.*

Raleigh has done such an incredible job raising him. And she did it all on her own. *But who takes care of her?*

"Is your mom more happy than she is sad?"

"Yeah. But sometimes she stares at the air and gets this line between her eyes and has a serious face." He jams his finger between his eyebrows and wrinkles his nose. "I ask her if she's letting her sad feelings out, but she just says it's her thinking face."

I nod, it doesn't surprise me, I've seen her stuck in her thoughts firsthand.

"She says I'm better at listening to my feelings than she is."

He stuffs in another spoonful, and milk trickles from the corner of his mouth. I hand him a napkin from the dispenser and take a bite of my cereal.

"That's hard for a lot of grown-ups." She doesn't know how badly I want to care for her. I want to be a safe space for Raleigh to feel however the fuck she wants. No more brave-face bullshit.

"Yeah."

I sip the chocolate milk and sit back, placing both my palms on the table.

"Can I tell you a secret?"

"Yes!"

"Between me and you, I like your mom a lot."

He mirrors my posture and slaps his hands on the table like mine, then does his best impression of an eyeroll. "Everybody likes her." *I bet they do.*

"Well, I really, *really* like her."

He sits back and giggles. The giggles turn to laughter. It's contagious. "What's so funny?"

"Do you want to *kiss* her?" He teases.

I chuckle and shrug. "Do you think she'd let me?"

"I dunno, maybe. I've never seen her kiss anybody. But she might." He taps his chin. "She paints her lips when you come over."

I know that lipstick well, kid.

"You should ask her if you can kiss her, and if she says yes, then you'll know."

Swallowing my bite, I nod. "That is great advice, I'll try that. You're smart like your mom."

FORTY

Barrett

He rustles in his sheets as I slip the storybook back on his bookshelf. "Okay, Mini Bear. We have to get up early. So *big* sleep tonight, ya feel me?" Raleigh tucked him in, and I got to do the story and final good night.

"Yup! And it's going to be dark when I wake up because we are waking up before the sun so we can go to the airport." He's clung onto the *waking-up-while-it's-still-dark* thing.

"You got it, bud. Sleep tight." I walk to the door and turn off the light. "Open, cracked, or shut?" I ask.

"Shut." He yawns and pulls his koala under the covers, snuggling it close. "Good night, Barrett."

"Good night, Mini Bear."

Stepping into the hall, I click his door behind me, then smile and take a deep breath. *Fuck, today was a great day!*

I'm less than twenty-four hours away from being in Hawaii with the two people I care about most. I had some one-on-one time with my son. When we got back, Raleigh had a big, refreshed smile on her face, all the suitcases neatly lined up by the entryway. She looked sexy as hell curled up on the sofa with a glass of iced tea and her book, it was like peering into our future.

The sound of the dishes lead me to the kitchen where she's cleaning up from dinner. I grab her hands and pin them behind her back, sliding my knee between her legs.

"I want you."

She angles her head to the side and a smile forms on her lips.

"Right now?"

I spin her around and place a kiss on her lips. "Right now." Pushing up her sundress and dropping to my knees, I peel off the thong I know she wasn't wearing earlier. "This for me? I like it."

From my knees, I settle her legs over my shoulders and draw my tongue across her inner thigh.

"Bear, we can't—"

She gasps when I stand, her fingers gripping my neck for dear life. "Oh my God, put me down!"

I hoist her higher to get my mouth on her. Another gasp. Fuck, she tastes good. I chuckle against her clit as she squirms.

She squeaks when I push her back against the tall cabinets.

"Barrett!" she whispers-shouts. "Put me down, this is too high! I'm too heavy!"

I swat her ass. "Don't insult me like that. Are you scared of heights or me?"

"Heights, Bear. I'm scared of heights! I'm going to fall."

"No you won't. Now be quiet while I eat my dessert or you'll wake our son."

I grip her thighs, dip my tongue inside her, and growl. She moves one hand from my neck and braces her arm against the ceiling. Her gaze reaches mine, and the fear in her eyes is gradually being replaced by pleasure.

"That's it, keep those pretty brown eyes on me."

She gives a subtle nod.

There's that trust. I love that her walls are coming down.

I rub my lips side to side over her pussy. I want my face covered in her. When I suck, her mouth drops open and she cautiously circles her hips, the pressure increases when she pushes off the ceiling, grinding against my mouth. *Thatta girl.*

My cock twitches when she moves her other hand to the ceiling. She hums as I dip my tongue inside her again.

"Oh my god."

I adjust my position to gain more access and knead the back of her thighs under her ass. My middle finger slides between her cheeks and presses against the tight knot. I can hardly take it anymore. Seeing her fear from heights mixed with lust is sexy. It's fucking hot when she's at my mercy like this. I bring my focus back to her clit and she flexes in my palms.

"I'm gonna come."

No, the first time she comes better be on my cock.

I back up and push her off my shoulders, catching her around my waist, and safely bringing her feet back on the floor. I'm not finished with her. She yelps when I bend her over the kitchen table.

"*Shhh.* If you make noise like that again, you won't get to come at all."

I flip her dress up and sink my teeth into her ass before slapping it. She groans against her forearm, trying to muffle the sound. Pushing down my jeans, my erection springs out. I spread her legs wide and slap my cock on her ass. She squirms and tries to push against me. She's soaked.

"Please," she whispers.

"You want this?"

"Yes," she whines.

"Beg for it."

She slouches over the table, but looks back at me. "Please. I need to feel you in me." Those fucking eyes are really doing it for me. "Fuck me, Bear. Fill me up."

Jesus Christ. I grab her neck and push her cheek into the table. The pulsing head of my cock thrusts against her entrance and she stretches around me so beautifully. She sighs, and I kick her feet apart to watch my dick inch into her plump, bare pussy.

This cunt was made for me. "How much are you going to give me, Ral?"

"All of it," she moans.

"And why do I get all of it?"

"Because it's yours."

"My brilliant girl."

I wrap her warm-blonde hair around my fist and crane her neck up. My other hand locks her shoulder in place. I make good on my word and make her mine without mercy. She grunts, taking it so well. She's trying so hard to be quiet. Her muffled sounds and garbled whimpers only make me more unhinged. Hearing her try to keep it together when I know she's falling apart... it's magnificent.

"Oh my god," she mewls. I release her hair, and when she looks back at me, emotion floods my senses. Those trusting, pleading eyes make me want to give her the world. For now, I'll have to settle for a little piece of ecstasy.

"As soon as I saw you in this sundress, all I wanted to do was bend you over and take you against this table. I've been dreaming about it all night." She likes it when I talk dirty to her. "From now on, when you wear this dress, I'm going to fuck you in it. Just like this."

"Please."

"Mmm, that's right." She's going to explode. "Let me feel that cunt throttle my cock. You want to come?" She moans.

"Do it, Raleigh. Come on this cock."

She turns her head again and there's a hint of a smile on

her lips as she prepares for her climax. Every time we make eye contact, I almost lose it. Plunging deep, I slap her ass right as she combusts. She gasps and pants, trying so hard not to scream. She's such a champ.

"*Oh, goooood girl*. That's it, deep breaths."

She inhales through her nose, and a low growl escapes me. My hands run up and down her back and then I grab her waist, fucking her over and over again, chasing my orgasm.

"Can't believe we lived without each other for so long. Never again, you hear me?" I don't want to go a day without her for the rest of my life.

"Promise?" she asks, breathless. My chest pounds at the single word.

I lean over her and kiss her neck. "I will always keep my promises to you, Ral."

I can't hold back any longer. I wish she wasn't on birth control. The possessive part of my brain wants to fill her up and impregnate her again. How fertile is she right now? I want another child to tie us together for the rest of our lives. I'll be present for all of it. My imagination takes over, and I don't censor my fantasy.

I want to be there when she takes the test and kiss her over and over again when she tells me it's positive. I want to rub her feet and buy her ice cream at one in the morning. I want the doctor's appointments and the ultrasounds. And then I want to bring her home and watch her ride my cock while I fill her up again. I want to go to the classes and read the books. I want to hold her hand when she delivers and be there to introduce Arthur to his new brother or sister. I want it all. All of this. All of her.

I've got it bad.

If I'm being honest, I think it happened while we were apart all those years. I knew we had something the first night we met. My attraction never stopped growing, even while she was absent from my life. She's gone from *the one that got away* to just *the one*. I'll do whatever I have to do to make her mine.

I heave when the last of my cum spills inside. My arms on either side keep me from crushing her when I fall forward. I sweep her hair to the side, pressing kisses to the back of her neck and shoulder. A relaxed, happy sigh slips out and it's such a comforting sound.

When I sit up, I lean back to watch my dick slide out of her. A string of cum hangs between us, and I grin. *"So hot,"* I mutter.

"What is?"

"You..." I squeeze her ass, pushing a cheek to the side so I can watch it leak out of her pussy. "...filled with my cum."

"Clean me up," she demands, reaching behind to deliver a flirty little slap.

"Do I have to?" I ask, still staring. "It looks pretty good like this."

"Yes!" She giggles. I reluctantly trudge over to the sink and wet a paper towel with warm water. I wring it out and slide it over her pussy, thighs, and ass. We made a mess.

She pushes off the table—her dress falling over her ass and making me pout—then saunters toward her bedroom. "I'm going to get ready for bed. Don't forget to wipe down the table when you're done." I hear the playful lilt in her voice. My mouth curves into a half smile at the sassy little retort.

"Someone's feeling brave."

I do as she asks and then meet her in the bathroom where she's brushing her teeth, already in pajamas.

"At lunch today"—I pull out my toothbrush to begin my nighttime routine—"he asked me if I wanted to kiss you."

She spins to look at me. "He did? What did you say?"

I brush my tongue and laugh. "I said yes." She weakly shoves my shoulder.

"What? I'm not going to lie to him! He knows we're more than friends. I think he likes it too," I assure.

She nods while rinsing with mouthwash, then spits. "You're probably right."

I stand behind Raleigh and envelop her in my arms. "We look damn good together." She smiles while stroking my arm. I kiss her cheek before we leave the bathroom and climb into bed. Before long, I'm drifting off to sleep with a smile on my face, knowing when I wake up, she'll be next to me.

FORTY-ONE
Barrett

My phone alarm vibrates, and for a second, I forget where I am. Then the warm, soft woman next to me stirs—my woman. *Raleigh. Hawaii.*

I wrap my arms around her stomach and pull her into me, her ass secured to my pelvis. She sighs, the sound wakes up my lower half. I push her hair to the side and press my lips to the back of her neck. If there wasn't a plane waiting for us, I'd probably turn off the alarm and go back to bed. Forget everything else.

"It's so early. Didn't we just fall asleep?" she croaks.

"I'll get some coffee made. You've got twenty more minutes to sleep, but after that, I'm coming in here to haul this fine ass out of bed." I slap her backside, and she jerks.

My feet hit the floor and I get moving.

She yawns and lifts her head. "I better not, I need to get Arthur ready."

"I've got it," I say as I exit the bedroom, pulling a shirt over my head.

Caffeine first. After digging around the kitchen for a minute or two, I find the coffee, flip on the machine, and set out a couple of travel mugs.

When I enter Arthur's bedroom, I sit on his bed, but delay waking him for a moment, he's so peaceful. He sleeps like Raleigh does, splayed out on his tummy, and the comparison makes me laugh. With my hand on his back, I rub small circles until his little limbs stretch like a lazy cat.

"Is it time to go on the airplane?" he asks, his voice scratchy with sleep. His eyes aren't even open yet.

"Not quite yet, we have to get ready and eat some breakfast. Your mom has your clothes already picked out, can you handle getting dressed on your own while I get you a bowl of cereal?"

He sits up and scratches his arm, nodding. "Uh-huh."

"Atta boy. I'll be back to check on you in a few minutes."

He stumbles across the hall to the bathroom.

I don't even have to ask what cereal. It's always Cinnamon Toast Crunch. I even know how much milk to add, not too much and not too little. The sound of coffee percolating echoes down the hall as I make my way back to Raleigh's room. For once, I don't have to go to the airport in a suit—I could get used to this. I throw on some joggers, a T-shirt, and a baseball cap, hoping it will provide us with a little anonymity during our travel.

While brushing my teeth, Raleigh enters the bathroom and turns on the shower. I shut the door and lock it. She strips, and my toothbrush hangs out of my mouth while I enjoy the show. *I will never get sick of this view.*

I grab her and set her up on the counter, spreading her naked thighs.

"Bear!" she squeaks, laughing.

"What?" I ask. As if she thought I could keep my hands to myself.

She flips my ball cap backward, then snatches the frothy toothbrush from my mouth and kisses me—then puts my toothbrush in her mouth.

"That's gross," I say, chuckling. I palm her ass and pull her into me. *Damn, this body.*

She takes it out and holds it out for me to see. "This is my toothbrush. Mine's blue. Yours is green." Her gaze falls to the other toothbrush on the counter.

Shit, she's right. "Well, at *my* house, mine's blue...This his-and-hers situation is getting old, babe."

Her finger wags, and she narrows her eyes at me. "Don't joke about that."

I smile. "Who says I'm joking?"

She hops off the counter and spits in the sink, then steps into the shower without saying another word.

"We'll continue this conversation another time. But, while you're in there, why don't you think of what color we should paint Arthur's bedroom at our other house." I walk out before she can protest, but she cusses at me on the other side of the door. We already share a child, we might as well share real estate.

If I play my cards right, it won't be long before she's making herself at home there. I've finally got a woman who can fill up that other walk-in closet with her clothes. The first garage stall will need to get cleared out so she's got a place to park, while I'm at it, might be time to hang up some hooks for bikes and scooters for Arthur. It's all figured out in my little cartoon bubble.

After everyone is ready to go and the car service arrives, we pile in and make our way to the airport. I didn't get time to get Raleigh set up with PreCheck clearance, but luckily the lines are short and it's not too busy. Boarding the plane is easy, and we settle into our seats with no issues.

"I've never flown first class."

"Never?"

She shakes her head and looks out the window and points at the different provisioning trucks to Arthur. I love that I can give them some of their firsts. Especially Arthur's first time flying. Fuck, I'm over the moon about that one. I remember my first time on a plane as a kid, it was a big deal.

When the flight attendant stops by to get a drink order, she looks to Arthur and comments on his cute, cuddly koala tucked under his arm.

He looks up at her with innocent eyes and a big smile and says, "Did you know that half the koalas in Queensland are infected with chlamydia?"

Raleigh and I freeze in horror. Arthur keeps his big smile, unaware of any social awkwardness. I think it might be time to limit his exposure to nature documentaries.

There's no coming back from that, so I simply turn to the flight attendant and ask if it would be okay to bring him up to the cockpit, with the promise of not sharing any more koala "fun" facts. She blinks at us, and I try not to laugh knowing Arthur likely ruined koala bears for this poor woman. She slowly nods, staring, but eventually peels her gaze away from us to assist other passengers. I make a mental note to discuss with him what bits of trivia are okay to share with strangers and which aren't—like marsupial STD statistics.

I lead him toward the front of the plane, praying we don't attract any attention. The pilots are more than happy to oblige Arthur. They let him push a button that lights up all the switches.

"Holy fart feathers," he mumbles under his breath. His eyes are gleaming. "Do you know what all of the buttons do?"

"We sure do," one pilot answers. "And these are the thrust pedals here... This is the control yoke, we pull up to go up and push down to go down."

"Cool!"

"Do you want to welcome the passengers on the PA system?" He hands Arthur a small telephone. "Just push this button here. Maybe your dad can help you. Say '*Welcome aboard Flight 1127.*'"

I hold my breath for a second, waiting for Arthur to correct him and say I'm not his dad, but he either doesn't notice or doesn't care with all the excitement. I'm thankful for it, because if anyone ever asked me point blank if Arthur was my son, I wouldn't have the strength to deny it. I'm his father, and I can't wait for the day when I can tell him.

Before we head back to our seats, they ask for a selfie, and I'm happy to return the favor after how accommodating they were. Arthur runs back to his seat to join Raleigh. He holds out the small pin with wings on it.

"Look what I got! Did you hear me on the speaker?"

"I heard! You did great! What was it like?"

"There were buttons everywhere! It looked like a Christmas tree!"

"That's so awesome!" She cocks her head to the side and mouths, *thank you*. I smile.

"He was a hit," I answer.

I keep replaying the pilot's words, referring to me as *dad*.

FORTY-TWO

Raleigh

"This is where we're staying?"

Barrett clears his throat. "Do you like it?"

When we pull up to the rental house, I almost don't believe my eyes. I laugh in response.

"Arthur, what do you think of it?" There's no answer, and when I turn around, he's crashed out in his booster seat. Not surprising, he slept less than an hour from Minneapolis to LAX. But after we transferred to the second plane, he was wide awake and chatty for the whole flight to Maui.

Mostly with Barrett, who kept up with the conversation like a pro. They discussed cereal, koalas, pre-k drama, and the books and cartoons he enjoys. It was impressive, considering it's no easy feat. He even came prepared with his own koala trivia game for Arthur—none involving koala chlamydia—*thank Christ.*

When Arthur played on his tablet and got stuck in a game, he asked for *Barrett's* help, not mine. It made my heart flip. His, well, parenting, allowed me to get a little sleep myself.

I'm able to relax so much more when Barrett is with him, it's really nice. And after seeing how great they are together, I trust him with my son. *Our* son.

Stepping out of the car, even the warm, breezy, mid-seventies air smells sweet. My cheeks are puckered from smiling so much. Scanning over the gorgeous stone exterior of the beach house, I already know this place must have cost a fortune to rent. And we're here for three weeks! He didn't need to get such a luxurious house. A bungalow or budget hotel would more than suffice.

Barrett keys in the code on the door and carries in a sleepy Arthur ahead of me. When I step inside, my jaw drops to my feet, along with my bag.

"Holy shit."

Kicking off my sandals, I wander through the gorgeous interior while Barrett rests Arthur down on the huge white wraparound sofa. The whole back wall of the space is windows, highlighting blue waters and the lush, tropical mountains in the distance. *Wow.* The kitchen off to the side features stunning koa wood cabinets, matching the rich trim that carries throughout the rest of the house.

I step inside a bathroom to freshen up and pull out my phone, plugging in the address. I tap the screen on the rental property and when I see the price, my phone clatters to the floor. It's almost two thousand dollars a night! I'm reminded of how different our lives are. Barrett is so down to earth that sometimes I forget he's a celebrity. He's not like the other hockey players I've met. He has a good heart. He's selfless and kind. He's giving. *Loving.*

When I return to the main living space, Barrett flips a latch in the center of the windows, and when he hits a nearby light switch, the massive windowed wall starts moving. It separates from the middle, and each side accordions flat, flush along opposite walls. Outside, the open-air patio butts up against an infinity pool that overlooks the aquamarine cove below. *Is this real?*

Now that the wall is gone, it's hard to tell where the

indoor ends and the outdoor begins. I wander outside in a trance and admire the scenic panorama while Barrett leaves to put away our luggage. He already knows his way around.

Minutes later, he comes up from behind and wraps his arms around me.

"You didn't answer me before. Do you like it?"

I puff out a breath of air. "I didn't answer because I'm speechless. I didn't even know places like this existed... You know we would have been fine with a run-down hotel room, right? I don't want you to think you had to spend all this money on us. I'm happy to be here with you, so is Arthur."

His arm wraps around me while the other hand pulls my spaghetti strap down, then his lips press to my shoulder.

"Mmhmm." He chuckles against my skin. I reach behind his neck to hold him closer and notice his hair is wet.

"Did you take a shower?"

How long have I been standing here?

He nods, and I enjoy the feel of his touch while taking in the incredible view in front of us. I close my eyes, listening to the hushed waves lap against the sandy beach below and committing this moment to memory. *In paradise with Barrett.*

My stomach rumbles and ruins it. He laughs and pulls me inside toward the kitchen, stepping into a narrow hallway tucked away behind the built-in refrigerator.

"There should be some snacks stocked in here," he mutters.

When I follow him around the corner, the whole space opens into an enormous hidden butler pantry that's almost the size of my kitchen at home. I spot the wall of cereal and instantly laugh. Above a long marble counter, a series of tall clear tubes are mounted to the wall. Each filled with a different cereal.

Arthur is going to lose his goddamn mind.

"Oh my God!" I say, pointing at the ridiculousness. This

place has every amenity possible. Including a chic, aesthetically pleasing breakfast bar, complete with cereal dispensers. Unreal.

"What?" He laughs along but doesn't quite seem to get what I find so amusing.

"That!" I wave my arms, gesturing to the whole contraption.

He inspects the tubes, and gently turns one of the X-shaped dials, a few pieces of cereal fall from it and he pops them in his mouth. "Thought it'd be a fun surprise, I had them installed last week."

I stare at him for a long second. It takes that long for me to comprehend what he said.

"*You* had them installed?"

"Yeah." He turns a dial on one of the other tubes and catches some cereal in his hand, holding it out to me. "Want some?"

My brow furrows. "Wait, are you saying this is *your* place? You own this? This is your house?" I rattle out the questions one after the other.

"I originally bought it as an investment property. My wealth manager suggested. All the other guys on the team were buying up real estate, so I figured what the hell, why not." He shakes his palm holding the sugary cereal, shuffling more mini marshmallows to the surface and picking them out before his eyes meet mine. "Then I remembered you saying you always wanted a beach house in Hawaii." I stare back slack jawed and unblinking.

He didn't. No... there's no fucking way he said what I think he did.

"Barrett, that was our first date!" *I'm not even sure if it qualified as an actual date, we ran into each other at the bar one night!*

He shrugs. "I couldn't get you out of my head, Ral... And at the time, I didn't think it was going to be years before I saw you again. But I always said when that day came, I would bring you here."

I'm speechless. I don't know whether to swoon or suspect mental illness. Barrett wasn't lying. He's been all in from the start. Since the very beginning. If I needed any more evidence of his feelings for me, I'm fucking standing in it.

FORTY-THREE

Raleigh

L ast night, we were so tired from traveling, we mostly focused on getting situated for bed. But today we got out of the house and did some exploring. We ate an absolutely delightful lunch at one of the local restaurants and then spent the afternoon down on the beach. It was wonderful. The look on Arthur's face when the saltwater splashed in his mouth will go down as one of the funniest things I've ever seen. His eyes popped open and he stuck his tongue out, slapping at it like it was on fire.

We promised him an evening pool party, but a rare rainstorm came through. I'm not sure he would have had the energy for it anyway. Instead, we've opted for an indoor picnic dinner with a movie. Barrett's fingers are intertwined with mine and I noticed Arthur looking at our hands curiously.

We're about twenty minutes into the movie, when Barrett scoots off the "picnic blanket" and leans against the front of the couch, dragging me between his thighs. I try to pull away, but he holds my back to his chest.

"Bear, he doesn't—"

His lips brush against the shell of my ear and we whisper

to keep our conversation below movie volume. "We talked man-to-man on the plane while you were sleeping."

I crane my neck as much as I can. "About us? What did you say?" I whisper.

"I said I liked his mom a lot, which he already knew. I told him that you two have a special relationship I'll never break or get in the middle of, but explained I also have a special bond with you."

"What did he say?"

"He asked if he had a special bond with me too. I was truthful, and told him yes. But that's all I said. Promise." *Oh, my heart.*

"He really asked that?"

Barrett sighs. "Yeah—shot me right in the feels with that one."

I wince, knowing he's holding back all the things he wants to say to Arthur because of me. He's probably feeling tortured, but it has to be the right time for Arthur. I'm not ready to unleash the truth on him yet.

"Me too." I swallow.

"I told him I'd be hugging and kissing you more, but that it wouldn't change anything. It's because we like each other. Then I said if he hears you making strange, loud noises all night—"

"Shut up," I whisper, nudging him with my shoulder blade.

He locks our fingers once more, and this time, wraps my arms with his around my waist. I relax and lean against him.

"Your hair smells good."

"Thanks," I respond, chuckling. "It's your shampoo." The products stocked in the showers are nicer than what I brought. My post-airplane shower felt like a day at the spa.

Arthur points at the television and laughs at some hijinks

the talking animals have gotten themselves into. He turns around to see if we saw it too.

"Mom, did you see that?" He giggles more.

I nod and laugh with him. He doesn't seem to notice or care that Barrett is holding me in his arms. Knowing he had the foresight to bring this up with him ahead of time earns him major points. I snuggle deeper against his chest, and he hums in approval.

His giant palms graze over my arms and shoulders. He digs his thumbs into the tense knots and massages my muscles through my cotton sundress. With each pass over my thighs, I swear he's purposely moving higher up my legs.

Light caresses become petting. Massages become gropes.

My nerve endings are lighting up like little sparks, stoking the sexcitement. I grip his knee, needing a place to squeeze and ground my breathing. His hands travel lower, and he runs his fingers over the side of my panties through my dress. He fists them through the fabric and pulls until a small tear can be heard.

I smack his leg and he smiles against my neck just before he nips with his teeth. Damn it, I know he's doing this to torture me. He thinks it's funny to turn me on and leave me squirming, knowing there's nothing I can do about it when Arthur's in front of us.

"Look, he crashed."

Sure enough, he's curled up with his pillow and koala, conked out. I'd be willing to bet there's a puddle of drool dribbling out of his mouth. "He didn't even make it halfway through." I snicker.

He grabs at my sides again. "Go to your room. I want you naked, lying face down when I get in there."

I suck in a breath. I'm unsure what he's planning on doing, all I know is I need it. Last night we were so tired from

310

traveling, we mostly focused on getting situated for bed. With each touch, I've become more and more restless.

"What about him?"

"I'll get him tucked in. Go."

Normally, I'd rouse him first so he doesn't wake up in the middle of the night and not know where he is, but after our hike today, I have a feeling he'll be out until morning. Slightly dizzy, I stand, but before I take two steps, he snatches up my hand and pulls me to his chest, the grumble under his breath is low and threatening.

"Raleigh, I mean it, if those panties are on when I get there, I will finish what I started and rip them off of you."

He's not bluffing, and he's certainly capable. It wouldn't be the first time.

Smiling, I practically skip to our room to brush my teeth and wash up. When he comes in, I'm lying naked on my stomach, as he requested, though my knees are bent and bobbing with crossed ankles. I can't risk losing any underwear when I'm on vacation. He huffs through his nose and locks the door behind him. He strips down but leaves on his boxer briefs.

"That's not fair."

He goes to the bathroom and walks out with a bottle of massage oil, and I bite my lower lip in anticipation.

"I'm not fucking you tonight." A rain cloud bursts over my sex-fueled parade. His voice lowers again when he whispers, "I'm helping you relax."

"Well, that's *not* the reaction my body is having," I gripe, disappointed.

"What reaction are you having?" He pushes apart my thighs, and I startle. He must see how wet I am. Knowing I'm exposed to him only draws more heat to where I need him most.

"You're the worst."

He chuckles and drips oil down the back of my legs and

arms. He starts at my hands, pressing his thumbs into my palms and dragging them away from the center. He works between my fingers. Then from my wrists to my elbows and up to my shoulders. The scent of the massage oil is calming, it's fragrant, but not overpowering.

While he works, I admire the beautiful bedroom we're in. The bed faces a huge set of panoramic windows that span to the vaulted ceiling. Exposed beams showcase more of the native wood from the island. The bed is as massive as the one he has at home. Everything in this house exudes luxury and comfort. This is the experience of a lifetime.

He sweeps my hair to the side and massages there, moving higher, grabbing a fistful of hair near the nape of my neck and pulling. I don't know what he did, but it causes my shoulders to slump in relaxation.

"Oh my god." I groan.

He laughs a little at my reaction. "You like that?"

"Uh-huh. Do it again."

He slides the heel of his palm up my bare back and into my hair once more, tugging, and I moan before he releases and repeats it a third time. I'm so turned on, I'm seeing stars. I know I'm wet because the air is cold between my thighs. I can't believe he won't give me his cock tonight. His hands work their magic on my back. He's good at this. Occasionally, his fingers brush the sides of my breasts when he spans over my ribcage, and it drives me wild. I crave gratification.

After finishing my lower back, his breaths come quicker as he reaches my ass. The way he gropes and kneads is agony. He grabs a handful on each side, under each cheek, and massages the flesh. My pussy twitches.

If he's even half as needy as I am, it won't be hard to make him give me what I want. After all, I'm his greatest weakness. Hoping to entice him to take what he wants, I arch my back and wiggle my ass. He smacks the top of each cheek and then scoots away from me and starts on my feet instead.

That's fine, I can give him a view from down there.

The foot massage is great, but his calf massage? *Sensational.*

Once he gets to my thighs, shit gets real. He spreads them wider. *What I must look like from his angle.* If he leaves me like this, I'm going straight into the bathroom and finishing the job myself. There's no way I'm not coming before I fall asleep. I might make him watch me for good measure. At the top of my thighs, he grips my ass with firm hands, and I picture the marks he's leaving on me. It's hard to slow my exhale into something more respectable, so I stop trying.

When he spreads my cheeks apart, I unconsciously reach for him.

"Keep your hands above your head or I'll have to tie them up."

I consider ignoring the request but know he'll only delay my gratification more, so I stretch my arms over my head and cross my wrists.

"Good... Now arch your back again. Let's see that pussy you were so desperate to show me before." *Oh my god. I love his mouth.*

I gasp and arch my back. *Please, please, please.*

He continues massaging my thighs, moving to the insides. The higher he goes, the faster I breathe. By the time he reaches the top, I'm panting.

"Oh, sweetheart. Is this difficult for you?"

"You're evil."

"Aww..." he mocks. "You don't mean that."

His thumbs massage circles outside the wet seam. My body is trembling, literally shaking with need, and I can't catch my breath. I whimper.

"Please, Bear. Don't tease me like this."

Both hands move down my ass to either side of my pussy, and I want to scream at him to fuck me. My arms begin to slip lower. I'm losing control.

"Keep your hands up."

"I will, I will, I will." I stretch them out in front of me, hoping he rewards my good behavior.

The sound of his boxers being pushed down thrills me, and I practice being perfectly still. My eyes are clenched shut, waiting... *waiting...*

He slaps his hard cock where I'm most sensitive, and the sharp sensation shatters me. I cry out. My back is arched so hard, my quads burn as I keep my ass as high as possible while trying to keep my chest flat. I need more. *Fuck, I need so much more.*

He mutters something, but I can't hear it over the pulse roaring in my ears. Another slap makes me jerk. Then he slides his cock through my folds. I attempt to back into him but his hands are on the back of my thighs, holding me in place. One arm wraps around my stomach.

"Please, Bear. I need you so bad. This is cruel."

"You're walking a fine line."

I'm walking the fine line? *He's rubbing my clit with his dick!*

"What are you going to do about it?" I'm becoming agitated.

"I'll leave you like this and walk away."

I'd rather he walk away and let me get myself off than go through this torture any longer. He said I needed to keep my hands up, but he said nothing about my legs. I keep my shoulders down, but push to my knees, showing him what he's missing out on.

"You're really going to walk away from this?"

It's silent for two beats, and I hold my breath waiting for

his next move. I look back and he regards me like a man starved.

"Go on. Walk away, Barrett. I can make myself come."

All I hear from him is "Fuck it," before he plunges inside me.

Oh my god.

I gasp, the way he fills me up has my entire body vibrating. He slaps my ass and propels inside me again. My eyesight blurs, and I'm blinded by the rush of adrenaline.

"This what you wanted?"

"Fuck me, Bear. Harder," I rasp.

He grabs me and flips me on my back like I'm nothing. The soft sheets feel like silk on my back. His palms skate up each arm as he pins my hands above, pounding into me and asserting his physical dominance. He drops to his elbows and leans in to bite under my ear. He runs his nose up my neck and inhales. His whisper is gruff. "I wasn't going to fuck you. I *told* you I wasn't going to fuck you. But when you look like this, make those sounds, I can't control myself—I don't want to."

"Then don't." My voice is desperate. "I like you unleashed. Haven't I earned it?"

Rising above me, he wraps his hand around the base of my throat and growls. *Holy fuck, I'm going to come already.*

Pulsating bursts of energy spread from my core to my fingertips. The anticipation did me in, and now that I'm filled to the brim with him and he's talking that way with a hand on my neck, I can't take it.

"Already? Come on, you can do better than that. At least try and make me work for it."

I can't answer, my mouth gapes and I prop up on my elbows to watch him drive inside me as my pleasure explodes.

"Yeah..." He slaps my clit, and I bite down, trying not to scream. "That's it, milk every inch. Show me how good your cunt feels when I'm the one fucking it. Tell me, do I get you off better than you do?"

Wincing, I nod and roll my lips together, trying to keep my voice down.

He leans down and purrs in my ear, "You will only come for *me*."

I've never heard him talk this way, and I never want him to stop.

"Bear, Bear, Bear!" I'm babbling, he's fucked the vocabulary out of me.

He merely laughs and slaps between my legs, making me jolt. As I slump from my climax, my surroundings are still blurry. Every touch feels amazing, and I tell him so. He kisses the relaxed smile on my face.

"You plan on getting your way all the time?"

I moan under my breath, trying to keep up. "Yeah...You better get used to it."

"Shit, you're such a weakness." He pinches my nipples and I arch into him. "I'd give you anything to make you happy."

A wicked smile forms at the corner of my lips. "Then give me your cum," I beg.

He drops his head between his shoulders and shakes it back and forth.

"Fucking incredible," he mumbles. Sitting up, he holds my knees open, showing no mercy as he hammers into me, rendering me speechless. His giant palm wraps around my throat again.

"Is this the way I need to fuck you to make you beg like that?" He bites my breast, and I suck in air between my teeth.

He bites again and again, devouring me.

Spots form in my field of vision as a bigger wave builds, and this one might swallow me whole. I cover my face, and my thighs shake. He pushes my arms out of the way and smiles like he knows something I don't. I'm lightheaded and can't think straight. My body is squeezing him like a vise, he pulls out and a quick spurt of warmth shoots from me. "Oh my god!"

"Fuck yes!" He drops his mouth to my clit and sucks as I finish squirting. Then pops back up and shoves his cock back inside where he pulls and pushes in long strokes. *I can't believe that happened!* He speeds up, sweat glinting on his brow. "You were made for me," he grunts.

His words wrap around my heart and my life feels complete.

"No more pulling out. From now on your pussy takes it all." He says it like it's a threat. Of what, I have no idea, because there's nothing I desire more than to be claimed by Barrett Conway.

With a furrowed brow, he bursts inside me with a deep snarl. His expression is dark, feral, possessive. It's so erotic. My fingers dig into his flesh and I pull him close. I love feeling his cum inside me.

His arms slide under my back, and he nuzzles my shoulder. My hands travel to his neck and I bring his mouth to my lips, kissing him. His tongue is gentle but his hold on me is not. I'm forever his.

"I'm not cleaning you up. You wanted my cum, so you're going to keep it. *Every drop.*" He pulls out, and the warm sticky fluid leaks from me. He swipes it with his thumb and pushes it back inside. *Holy.* Afterward, he gets off the bed but brings one knee up on the edge. His cock is glistening, slick with the mixture of us. He looks down at it and back at me like he's waiting. *Does he expect me to...?*

"Crawl." He nods and takes a slow inhale through his nose. "Every drop, love."

FORTY-FOUR
Barrett

S o far, Raleigh and Arthur are having a blast. Today we took a hike to one of the small waterfalls on the island, it was an easy trail for Arthur. He looks so cute with those little hiking boots and the koala backpack. It's given us the chance to see his adventurous side.

The forests are lush and deep, and the canopy of trees keep us shaded for most of the hike. After a good thirty-minute walk, the trail opens up and the waterfall comes into view. It's picturesque. This is the first time I've been able to actually enjoy Hawaii and all its natural beauty. A sheet of water cascades and spills into the plunge basin in front of us. Giant, charcoal boulders circle the perimeter of the huge aquamarine pool of water. There's no one else here, it's perfect.

"Wow," Raleigh muses, wide-eyed. Arthur bolts to get a closer look, his backpack swishing side to side as he runs, and when he gets to the edge of the rocks, he holds his arms out wide as if he's greeting the water with an open hug.

"Can we go swimming?!" he yells over his shoulder.

I laugh. "Sure!" He throws off the backpack and tears at his shirt. "But wait for us before you get in." He knows how to swim, but there's no way he's jumping into that water until one of us are with him. Raleigh touches my arm, she knows how protective I've become.

"You're moving like turtles!"

Raleigh and I catch up, and the three of us strip down to our swimsuits. There's a wooden platform to enter the water. It doesn't look deep. I jump in first, it's a little over five feet. The bed of rocks at the bottom isn't too bad. The water is cool and refreshing when I dunk my head under and come back up again.

Arthur is waiting for me on the platform, and I hold out my arms for him to leap into. Raleigh hops in after him and treads water. Her hair is piled on top of her head in a messy knot, and thank God she's wearing a different swimsuit than the one she wore on my boat, or I'd never be able to get out of here without having to answer some questions. It still shows off her figure and cuts high on her hips, which makes me bite my cheek, but once she's in the water, it's no longer torturing me.

"Can I swim?" Arthur says, practically paddling in my arms, like a dog being held over water. "Throw me like you do in the pool!"

"Okay, ready?"

I thread my fingers together and he places his foot in my hands while grasping onto my shoulder for balance.

"Mom, watch!"

Raleigh smiles. "Let'r rip!"

He adjusts his position and then springs off my hand like a diving board, making a cannonball and splashing the both of us. He comes up for air, giggling and blinking the water out of his eyes.

He does the most adorable sidestroke I've ever seen, paddling around in circles, occasionally dipping underwater, just so he can flip his hair back when he comes up. While he swims, I pull Raleigh closer, and she wraps her legs around my waist. A ray of sunlight hits the waterfall, and a small rainbow appears over us. Arthur gasps and points, and we laugh at his excitement.

He passes under it with bright eyes and exclaims, "I swam under a rainbow!"

Resting my head on hers, we watch our son in amusement. Surrounded by greenery, tropical flowers, and a misty rainbow above us. It's the perfect day. She looks up at me smiling, and I kiss her... almost saying the three words.

FORTY-FIVE

Raleigh

Halfway through our vacation, Barrett got his first taste of real fatherhood when Arthur had a fucking conniption over having to get out of the swimming pool to take a nap. He was practically dozing off, but as soon as we suggested some sleep, all his little five-year-old rage came out to play—which only confirmed how bad he needed rest. He's been swimming so much, he'll be ready for the Olympics by the time we get back.

"Jesus Christ." Barrett wipes the sweat from his forehead and closes the door to Arthur's bedroom after finally getting him down. "I had no idea five-year-olds could have meltdowns like that. Will he be okay?" He sounds concerned, it's sweet.

"He'll be fine, he's just wiped out. I knew it would hit him eventually with everything new that's been happening. He's overstimulated." I pat him on the shoulder. "You handled it really well."

I gave him the opportunity to get some dad practice, and he rose to the challenge. He wants to be a part of our lives, he's gonna get the good and the bad. He stayed calm throughout the whole thing. Barrett was so patient despite not knowing what he was doing. Even when Arthur took a swing at him.

"That was well?!"

I chuckle and nod.

"And how is he so strong? He's five! Shit, he was thrashing around so much, you'd think he was getting sent to the fucking chair. What the hell?"

My shoulders raise in a shrug. "Ain't no 'hood like parent-hood. So...wanna get down?"

I bite my lip and start unbuttoning my shirt.

He furrows his brow and pulls his head back like I'm crazy. "What?! No, I don't *wanna get down.* After that? No way in hell I have the energy, I'm exhausted! How can you even think about sex right now?"

I break out into a fit of laughter. "I hate to break it to you, but this isn't going to be the first time that happens, and with a kid running around, our chances of getting privacy are limited, so I'm going to need you to pull your shit together." I clap him on the back twice. "Let's go, sport."

"I'll soundproof every wall in the house and build you a sex room, but babe, I'm taking a rain check. If you need me, I'll be in the kitchen stress-eating a bowl of Cinnamon Toast Crunch."

"Better make it Honeycomb. If you thought naptime was bad, wait 'til he sees you've eaten his cereal..."

"Too soon," he says, shaking his head. He gives me a soft slap on the ass as he walks past me. "You'll pay for that later."

"Probably shouldn't make threats before you've got the soundproofing done."

He spins around with an exasperated smile on his face and pushes me against the wall.

"Now you're gonna get it." I giggle as he presses his lips against mine. "You love running your mouth, huh? If I fill it up, I won't need to soundproof, will I?"

Hm. *Plot hole.* That's fine by me, I'll take it however I can get it. My sex drive is through the roof since I've started getting it regularly.

"Only one way to find out," I tease.

He pushes off the wall and continues his mission for food. I follow him to the butler pantry where he's plucking a ceramic bowl off the shelf. He fills it with Cinnamon Toast Crunch from one of the dispensers on the wall, and adds milk from the fridge under the breakfast bar. *Come on!*

After he grabs a spoon, he leans against the cabinets to eat it.

"Get on your knees."

The command catches me off guard, and I cock my head to the side. "Do you really think I'm going to suck your dick while you stand there and eat cereal?"

"That's exactly what you're going to do. Get on your knees, Raleigh."

A smile creeps on my face, and I step up to the plate. I push down his joggers, leisurely dropping to my knees. He leans against the counter and grips my ponytail in one hand while balancing a bowl of cereal with the other. I look up at him and could melt into a puddle with the way he gazes down at me.

Wrapping my fingers around him, his cock thickens and I look up at him through my lashes while I lap at precum covering the tip. His pupils are blown, and he barely blinks as he watches. When I kiss the tip, he blows out a puff of air.

"Don't wake our son." I remind him.

"Better hurry up, I don't want soggy cereal." The burn on my scalp heightens my anticipation. I love that he can barely contain his aggression when he wants me. *I fucking love it.*

Taking him deeper into my mouth, his head falls back before he peers down at me again, like he doesn't want to miss a second of this. I let him set the pace by bobbing me over him.

I swirl my tongue on the underside of the tip, and brush him over the ridges on the roof of my mouth. He lets go of my hair and goes back to eating his cereal. My hands scratch down his thighs, and he shivers.

Pulling off him, I lick and suck the side of his cock. The power dynamic is exhilarating as I work to steal his focus. I fist his base and twist, bringing him back to my mouth. It's entertaining to watch him tense literally by my own hand.

"So lovely on your knees." He swallows. "Show me," he demands through gritted teeth. I gaze up and open my mouth to paint my tongue with his cock. "Dirty girl."

Still pumping him with one hand, I tug on his balls with the other. He groans and drops his spoon in his bowl with a clang, then goes back to gripping my hair, sending a frisson of pleasure through me. My cheeks hollow as I take him deeper, my lips stroking his cock as I go. I want all of him. It's as if he can read my thoughts. He pulls my head closer, pushing himself to the back of my throat.

He feels when I'm about to gag and pulls my head back, and I gasp. Then shoves me back down on his length again. My mouth salivates for him.

"Take it nicely for me." Those blue eyes turn to dark storm clouds when he enters my throat. *"There you go."*

I moan around him when he fucks my mouth. Every part of me is aching for more. My thighs press together as I squirm. He must notice. "You want to touch yourself?"

I hum in agreement, and he picks his spoon back up for another bite.

"Rub your clit."

Slipping one hand beneath my waistband, I do as he says, and my whimper reverberates around him. He strokes my cheek with his thumb, and I grind against my fingers.

"Show me how wet you are."

I pull out my hand, and he snatches up my wrist, then

leans over and sucks my fingers while I suck his cock. God, I'm head over heels for this man.

After tasting me, he reverts to eating his cereal, consuming a couple bites while I roll my lips over his length. His casual body language turns me on even more, it's become a game and I want all his attention. He takes another bite of cereal and chews, watching me.

"Oh, baby, you're going to have to work harder than that if you want my cum." *Holy hell.*

I rub my thighs together, trying to stave off my own orgasm. I pop off him and suck one of his balls into my mouth while my hand corkscrews up and down his shaft. My free hand travels back between my thighs. Barrett stops midchew to watch me work.

He swallows and drops his spoon back into the bowl so he can brush my temple with his knuckles. "Look at you earning extra credit. Now the other..."

I move to the opposite side and suck again, still stroking him.

When he returns to eating, I go back to the crown and wrap my lips around him, suckling as hard as I can while tugging his sack. The cereal bowl is dropped to the counter, and milk sloshes over the side. I brace both my hands on his legs as he cups my face and gathers my hair into his clenched hand. Barrett snaps his hips, pushing deeper into my mouth.

"That's my mouthy fucking girl," he rasps. "Take it all." *That voice.* It's like he turns into a beast whenever things get heated. It does something to me. I nearly sob around his cock at his demand, and my core clenches. He sees me struggling and holds eye contact, giving me something to fixate on while his dick pushes down my throat, blocking my airway. His movements become more erratic, so I know he's right on the edge. I gag and he smiles, pulling me out enough to see me drooling.

He bobs me over him again and again, growling praises. Tears pool at the corner of my eyes, and every once in a while they stream down my cheeks. The power exchange, his words, and the taste of his precum send me over the edge. I dig my claws into his quads and tremble all over as my body gives in to him. No man has ever made me orgasm from giving a blowjob. *Until now.*

His eyes darken, and he grips my chin. "Fuck, Ral! Are you coming?"

I moan louder around him, and my eyes roll back. I'm not sure how I must look, because it takes every bit of concentration I have to continue on while my lower half is spasming. He groans while fucking my mouth and takes my head in his hands. "I've got it, you keep riding that wave... *Goddamn you are so pretty when you come.*" His voice sounds far away as my climax rolls through my bones. Three more dips into my throat and he stills his movement. *I want it.*

"Drink, love."

My taste buds are hit with salty victory as he unloads in my mouth while I finish coming. Getting off while on my knees for him is one of the hottest experiences I've had. I let him coat my tongue before I swallow.

When he's empty, he lifts me into his arms, locking his lips on mine and no doubt tasting himself. Then without warning, Barrett tosses me on the counter like I'm nothing, yanking down my shorts and shoving his face between my legs to lick me clean. My clit pulses every time his tongue drags over it, each pass makes me surge with sensitivity. I thread my fingers into his hair and scratch his scalp. He's so gorgeous.

"I thought you said my pussy was going to take it from now on."

A lop-sided smile forms on his lips and his eyes sparkle. "Did I say I was done?"

FORTY-SIX
Raleigh

"He looks like you," I tell him.

Barrett smiles beside me, and I sink my toes in the warm sand of the secluded beach while Arthur plays about twenty feet away. I don't remember the last time I felt so content and at peace. Maybe never. The waves lap on shore in regular intervals, and palm trees sway in time with the breeze. He's quiet while we watch on.

The more I observe the two together, the more I want to tell our son who Barrett really is. That's what this vacation is about, right? Finding out if we have a future together. A chance to see how he does with us. There's always the possibility we scare him away, but I don't see that happening.

"He looks similar to me when I was his age. But I see a lot of you in him too."

"Hmm," I muse. We have under a week left in paradise. I'm so happy we did this. Barrett and I have learned so much about each other. Arthur has become even more enamored with him. This vacation was more essential to us than I realized.

He clears his throat and pulls me into his lap. "I want to be more involved in his life. In your life. I've missed out on so much. I know how I feel about you. And about Arthur. I get that there's a lot of trust still being built, but you should know my intentions. I want to be a family, Raleigh... When you're ready."

I swallow. He's so forthcoming, and I like that he leaves no room for miscommunication between us. If this is going to work, we need to be clear with each other. "Which brings me to something else..." *Something serious.*

"You said you wanted to be included in the decisions I make that involve you, granted this is a bit bigger than plane tickets, but... I want to retire."

Whoa. I scramble off his lap and look at him. "You're thinking of retirement? Is this because of us?"

He takes my hands in his and brushes his thumbs over the top of my palms. "It's not the only reason, but it's my favorite one." He winks. "My thought was to finish up my contract for this season and retire next spring. You two are a part of my life now. I'm going to be thirty-nine this year, my days of playing hockey are numbered anyway. My body's tired and I want to focus on us. Plus, I'll be able to commit to more involvement with Camp Conway, maybe get into coaching. It's important you and Arthur can depend on me, and for that to happen, I need to be home. I'm already not looking forward to traveling this season, but I think it's best for all of us if I finish out my contract."

There's a long pause while I consider his words.

"Would you still retire if Arthur and I weren't in the picture?"

"I don't know. But if I didn't retire now, I'd probably be retiring in the next few years because my body couldn't keep up with the sport. I don't want to retire because I'm too old to play, I want to retire because I have something better waiting for me."

The things this man says and the way he says them... I love

the idea of him being around for us and I've seen how animated he is when he mentions coaching—it would be a great opportunity to explore something he's passionate about.

"Then..."—I thread my fingers with his—"I think you should retire."

He searches my eyes and then nods. "Okay... I'll make a call in the morning," he states.

Just like that? "Well, wait—I mean, how do you feel? Now that you've made the decision, does it feel right?"

"It feels fucking fantastic." A genuine smile splits his face. I trust he would tell me otherwise. He does about everything else.

"Then you made the right decision." I kiss his cheek, and he turns to kiss my lips. He scoots behind me, bracketing my body between his massive thighs, this man is built like a tank. He brushes sand off his knee, and in my peripheral, I see him nod toward our son. Arthur is busily digging up the white beach, filling in the holes, and then shoveling new ones, repeating the whole process.

"What's he doing?"

I shrug and call out to Arthur, "Hey, buddy! What are you looking for?"

"Pineapples!" he yells back.

Good grief. "Find any yet?"

"Not yet!"

"Okay, better keep digging!" Barrett hollers.

I shake my head. "He knows all that shit about koalas, but thinks pineapples grow underground."

His arms engulf me, and I lean into his embrace, inhaling deep.

"Can it be like this all the time?" I ask, sighing.

"If this is what you want, I'll give it to you, baby."

I kiss him again with a smile. His tongue darts out and laps at my lower lip.

He retreats briefly and cups my face, gazing down at me through hooded lids. His thumb strokes my temple and I angle into his hand.

"I'm so in love with you, Ral."

Any remaining walls around my heart collapse into a heap of old insecurity. My lips part, and I can't breathe. I'm frozen. It's the first time a man has ever said those words to me. The second they fell from his lips, my entire soul reciprocated.

He loves me.

His voice drops an octave. "Say it back."

My mouth opens, but I'm unable to speak. I thought Arthur would be the only person to ever have my heart, but Barrett has made me capable of loving beyond what I thought possible.

"I know you feel it too." His voice is calm. He's so patient. "Say it back."

His thumb swipes a stray tear from my cheek, and my world clicks into place.

"I love you," I whisper.

As soon as the words are out, his mouth crashes to mine and he sinks his hands into my hair. I kiss him back with the same intensity and know right then that Barrett Conway is the man I want to spend my forever with. We're getting our happily ever after.

FORTY-SEVEN
Barrett

I get in my six o'clock morning run, and after five miles, I'm ready to make the phone call. I know it's the right decision, but it doesn't make it any easier. I pace outside near the pool. Arthur and Raleigh aren't awake yet, now's as good a time as any. I dial my agent, Jeff Henderson.

"Barrett! How's my favorite client?" He clicks the pen in his hand. He's been my agent for over a decade.

"Yeah, yeah." I chuckle. "I'm good. Say, I want to talk to you about something."

"What a coincidence, I want to talk to you about something too. With the playoffs last year, we can negotiate a bigger bonus for this upcoming season."

Well, this should be fun. I take a deep breath and stare out at the horizon stretched across the ocean. The sky is painted with pinks and oranges as the sun comes up. The bright colors and stunning beauty remind me of the woman in my bed. "Okay, I'm gonna stop you there. I want to retire."

"What?!"

"After this season, I'm done."

"How come you didn't bring this up last year when I

asked about retirement? I mean, this feels very outta left field? Can we talk this through? Is this about Sully?"

"This is confidential, got it?"

"Shit," he exclaims. "Are you in trouble?"

"I found out I have a son. He's five."

Jeff coughs on the other end. "Jesus Christ... Have you told anybody?"

"Fuck no! Well, Sully. And my mom figured it out on her own, but she won't say anything."

There's a loud noise, and I'm pretty sure he slammed his fist on his desk. "Why the hell didn't you call me sooner? We need her to sign an NDA, I'll fax a copy to you. What's the mother's name? When did you get the paternity test?"

"Her name is Raleigh Dunham. I haven't done a paternity test."

"Wait...like Raleigh-Raleigh? As in, puck bunny Raleigh?"

Easy, motherfucker. "She's going to be wife Raleigh soon, so take that word out of your mouth."

"Look—" He sighs. "Don't take this the wrong way, but... we need to have a paternity test done. Do you know for a fact it's yours?"

How am I not supposed to take that the wrong way?

"No test. He's mine. Trust me," I respond through gritted teeth.

"You're not putting me in a good spot here."

"I'm sorry. I know it's a lot."

"Ya think?! Goddamn it, Conway... You call me up and suddenly you're retiring, a dad, and getting married. You can't keep secrets from me like this. What if the press found out first! We need PR brought in on this so they can get ahead of it in case anything slips. Who have you told about retirement?"

I run my hand through my hair. "I briefly brought it up to Sullivan that I was considering it. And Raleigh."

He breathes a sigh of relief. "I assume she's in support of it. Did Sullivan try and stop you?"

I don't like how he phrased that. "First of all, Raleigh pushed back when I told her. And Sully doesn't understand it, but he's got my back."

"Yeah, well, it doesn't make much sense to me either. Are you sure you want to quit after this season? After this last round of playoffs, we can negotiate some killer bonuses. I just think—"

"I'm fucking tired, man. I'm thirty-eight. I don't want to be on the ice after forty. I'm done. I want to focus on my family and Camp Conway."

He's quiet for a while, but makes a hum of understanding. He knows there's no point, my mind is made up.

"You know I love you, bud. Hell, I'd probably do the same if I were in your shoes. I'm here to advocate for you. But I need to know, are you absolutely one hundred percent sure this is what you want to do? If I tell them you're done and you change your mind, there's no way we'll be able to negotiate the same contract. They may not even take you back at all."

"It's what I want."

"Okay. Let me make some phone calls and get back to you."

I scuff my foot over some of the landscaping rocks. "Thanks, Jeff. I know I'm not making your job easy."

"Not even a little, but I still love ya. I'll be in touch."

As soon as I hang up it's like an enormous weight has been lifted from my shoulders. I didn't expect the massive relief I'm feeling. With both fists in the air, I let out a whoop and toss my phone onto one of the lounge chairs before diving into the pool with my clothes still on. When I break the surface and inhale, it feels like the first breath of my new life. Floating on my back, I watch the gold and bubblegum sky fade into soft blue. It took them to make me realize what I want in my life.

What makes me happy and fulfills me—one more thing I've gained since they've come into my life. As cliché as it is, they make me feel complete.

When I get out of the pool, I clean up in the outdoor shower, washing the rest of the sweat off me from my run. My soaked clothes fall to the tile with a slop. I wrap a towel around my waist and do my best to tiptoe across the house, grimacing as I look back and see all the wet footprints I've left on the wood floor. Goose bumps rise on my skin from the loss of body heat. In our bedroom, Raleigh is out cold. I throw on a fresh pair of boxers and a T-shirt and crawl back in bed, only to be surprised by a Mini Bear snuggled under the covers. He must have come in here sometime when I was out on my run.

Climbing under the sheets, I drape an arm over them and their warmth soothes my chill. I welcome the relaxed smile that forms on my lips. Life is so fucking good.

They are my world now.

It only reassures me I'm ready to close that chapter and am making the right decision.

I've had a solid career. I'm in the 400 Club. I've got a Ted Lindsay Award and a King Clancy Memorial Trophy for my work with Camp Conway along with various other charities I've been involved in over the years. We closed out last season with playoffs, but after this next one, it's time to hang up my skates. *When you know, you know.*

Arthur turns over and snuggles into my side, still sleeping. *Yeah, I definitely know.* My chest expands with love for the two most important people in my life. I tuck my head down and press a kiss to the top of his little head. I'd do anything for them. My hand brushes the hair out of Raleigh's face. She's so beautiful.

I'll be damned if I don't make her my bride before the year is up.

"I found this out by the pool, it was ringing," Raleigh says, strolling inside and handing me my phone. Glancing at the screen, I see three missed calls. Two from Coach. One from Jeff. *Here we go.*

"Thanks, babe. Why don't you jump in the shower and then we can go explore or grab something to eat."

She nods in understanding and gives me privacy. I know who I need to call first.

He answers and I smile. "Hey, Coach."

"Conway... So, retirement, huh?"

I run my hand through my hair and walk outside, closing the door behind me.

"Yeah, it's time."

"We wanted to offer you the captain spot—I don't suppose that changes your decision at all. You must have known that was coming."

Yeah, I figured as much. I'm already the alternate.

"I took that into consideration. It's nothing personal, but this is the right move for me. Besides, somebody's gotta babysit Sullivan." I laugh to break the tension.

"Losing two caps in two seasons. Son of a bitch. What do you think about getting together for lunch to discuss this a little more?"

I run my hand over my facial hair. "I'm actually in Hawaii."

There's a pause and I pace.

"You took a vacation? You never take vacation."

That's not true. But I don't take trips as much as some of the other guys. Sullivan and I have always been homebodies like that. We travel enough with the team. I'd rather stay home when I'm near my base. "Yeah. I needed to clear my head." *Didn't take long...*

"Just answer one question for me. Is it worth it?"

"What?"

"Whatever it is that's driving this decision. I know you didn't wake up and decide to retire."

I smile and look through the glass windows at Arthur eating cereal at the island countertop.

"Yeah. It's worth it. It's worth everything."

"Well..." There's a long pause, but I don't fill it. He knows I'm set in my decision, and once I make up my mind, I don't often change it. "Ya know, I love this organization... but I love the players more. In the end, you gotta do what's best for you. I trust that you're making the best decision for yourself. And I'm glad you're giving me one last season."

That's why I love Coach. He's a good guy. He knows hockey has been our life since we were young kids, and he understands there are other things that exist outside of it that are just as important. Like family.

"I've loved playing for you over the years, and when it's time, I'll help wherever I can with the transition."

"Oh yeah? You're gonna find a new cap for me?"

I chuckle. "Sure. Banksy." He laughs, but I don't.

"*Teller*? Are you serious? I have a hard enough time keeping him out of the sin bin, the last thing we need to do is add to his ego. Don't get me wrong, he's a natural talent, terrific athlete, but the org would never go for it. He's too much of a wildcard."

I plead my case for Banks. He's a good guy, a little misunderstood. "He only ends up in the box because he's protective of the boys, it's part of his intimidation. He's an enforcer. You put a C on his sweater, and I guarantee he'll surprise you. He needs something to challenge him, make him grow the hell up, focus on something other than women and whatever else he

IN THE GAME

keeps himself busy with. Banksy's ready, he just doesn't know it yet."

"I think that vacation has gone to your head." I laugh.

"Okay, well, look, I'm going to sit on this for a week. If you happen to change your mind between now and then, you call me. We'll pretend this conversation never happened, got it? But if I don't hear from you, I'll put the word in and we'll go from there. Let the paper pushers handle the offboarding. But let's still get that lunch when you're back in town, eh?"

"Sure, Coach. That sounds good."

"You take care now. And enjoy that vacation. It's about time you fuckin' relaxed."

Smiling, I nod. "Will do. Bye Coach."

I tuck my phone in my pocket and weave my fingers behind my head as I look out at the ocean panorama. I can't wait to tell Raleigh. Soft arms enclose around my waist from behind. I smell her scent, and smile. "Thought you were in the shower."

"I was watching from inside... So? How'd it go?" she asks.

"I did it."

337

FORTY-EIGHT

Barrett

It's been two and a half weeks of heaven with Raleigh and Arthur. We've fallen into a routine: I get up with him, supply him with some cartoons and cereal, and then Raleigh wakes up with me between her thighs. I hope nothing ever changes.

After grinding beans, the coffee maker starts to brew a fresh pot. Arthur sits at the kitchen island in his palm tree and pineapple pajamas. We got them from one of the souvenir shops. I slide the cereal in front of Mini Bear, and he shoves his face in the bowl like a Miami drug lord. *Jesus Christ, this kid loves Cinnamon Toast Crunch.*

"How did you sleep last night, bud?"

"Good," he says with his mouth full. "I had a dream that we went surfing with koalas!"

"Dang, that sounds awesome. Do you want to learn how to surf? We still have time."

He shakes his head. "Not really, I only did it because the koalas wanted to."

I chuckle. "That's fine too. Do you need anything else?"

His little fist holds the spoon in the air. "All set!"

"Okay, I'm gonna wake your mom up. Can you hold down the fort until then?"

"You got it!"

Back in the bedroom, Raleigh lies on her side. She blinks awake with those sexy-as-hell golden brown eyes I love so much. I take in every detail from her messy hair to the small ash-colored smudge of mascara at the corner of her eye. She's so fucking gorgeous I can't believe she's mine.

"How's he doing?"

"Good." I crawl in behind her and bring my hand between her breasts to pull her close. "He had a dream about koalas. They went surfing together. He only went because the koalas wanted to."

She snickers and it makes my smile bigger.

"Did you lock the door?"

"I did..." I answer.

"Good. Lay on your back, I want to ride you."

I withdraw my hand from her shirt, she grasps the hem, and pulls it over her head. No underwear. *Fuck me.*

She tucks her hands into each side of my sweats and pulls them down, causing my rock-hard dick to spring back up. Leaning down, she spits on my cock and slides her tongue over it, coating me. My palm brushes the top of her head, and she looks up, smiling.

"Mmm... get up here."

She climbs over me, and I lick the tips of her nipples before closing around them and kneading her breasts. I've got big hands and she fills both of them. Biting her lip, she straddles and sinks down.

"Ugh, there you go."

Her lips part, and she exhales at the same time I groan. Light filters in from the windows, haloing her in a soft morning glow.

She seductively rolls her hips while I palm her ass. I love that I can grab and squeeze every delicious inch of her whenever I want. This woman is spectacular.

I tuck some loose strands behind her ear. "I love you."

Dropping to her elbows, she cradles the back of my neck and pulls me toward her. Her nose brushes mine. "I love you too." We smile, and my lips take hers in a kiss I never want to end.

She sits back up and plants her hands on my chest, grinding her body on mine. *Heaven on earth.*

"I've got a proposition for you." I've only got three days left with them in Hawaii, and I need to make plans for when we return.

She raises an eyebrow. "You want me to spin around?"

Laughing, I shake my head. "That's not what I was going to say, but I'm not opposed to it."

We've always been able to joke around during sex and it's part of what makes it so comfortable.

"I was going to say..." *What was I going to say? Focus, moron.* "...going to say that I'll be traveling a lot next year. Arthur will be starting kindergarten. I understand we've still got some things to figure out, but...I'd love to have you both move in before the school year starts." She halts her grinding and clears her throat.

"What do you think?" I ask.

"I'm still processing what you just said. You want to move in together? Are you sure we're ready?"

I shrug. "I know all I need to know."

"I have a house." Her hips begin their lazy gyrations again, and I grit my teeth, praying I can maintain some blood in my brain to keep up my end of the conversation. It's not easy when a naked Raleigh is riding my dick.

"You can keep it if you want. I have no qualms about it if

that makes you feel better. But you asked me if it could always be like this. It can, baby. You can wake up and fuck me like this every morning until we're old and gray."

Her fingers run through my hair. "You're already old and going gray."

I slap her ass. "Aren't you funny..."

Her head cocks to the side, flaunting a sassy smile. It earns her another swat—she bites her lip and yelps.

After rubbing away the sting, Raleigh leans back, bracing her hands on my thighs, her breathing becoming more labored. "The schools are good in your area."

"Ohhh!" I laugh and sit up, wrapping my arms around her back, drawing her to my chest. "You've looked at the schools in my neighborhood, have you?"

She waves me off and continues grinding at a leisurely pace.

"I may have looked them up, for curiosity's sake."

"You're such a liar." I cradle her shoulders and flip us so I'm on top, enjoying her squeal.

She holds me close while I drive in and out, her soft lips tracing my jawline. "Where do you see yourself in five years?"

My brows knit together. "Is this a job interview?" I ask.

"Kind of, yeah." She says it with a smile, but her earnest eyes tell me it's an important question.

I sit back and massage her clit while lazily thrusting. I love our morning sex. "That's easy... Here, with you, celebrating our five-year wedding anniversary."

She scoffs and smacks my chest. "I'm serious!"

I lean forward and kiss her neck. "So am I. I would marry you today, Ral."

Her eyes study my face, as if she's waiting for me to give a serious answer, but I wasn't joking.

"It's only been a couple months!"

"All I know is there's no ring on your finger,"—I point out toward the door—"that's our son, and we have time to make up for. Since the moment I laid eyes on you two, I've been all in. I want to make a home for you, *be* a home for you —and Arthur—the three of us... And maybe add a fourth or fifth."

God, I hope she wants more kids.

The soft pads of her fingers run over my lips, down to my jaw, and circle behind my neck. "How can you be so sure about us?"

"All these years, you were never far from my thoughts. I think I fell in love with you while we were apart." I nip at her shoulder. "And then again when you did that thing with your tongue..."

She giggles and kisses me. "I fell in love with you when I saw your work with Camp Conway. And Arthur did when he saw the cereal dispenser." I swallow.

"Do you think he'll ever forgive me for being absent in his life? Love me like a real dad?" I know Arthur feels comfortable around me, but I've never verbally expressed to him that I love him. Never told him how badly I want to say he's my son. To hear him call me dad.

Her eyes soften. "Let's tell him today."

My eyebrows shoot up. "Yeah?"

"He already loves you like a dad. You both need this." I crash my lips to hers and pull her close.

Thinking about it makes me nervous as hell, so I push the thought aside and thrust harder to finish the job.

"Yeah, right there," she whispers. I keep the rhythm she likes. "God, Bear..." Her knees quiver and she purrs when I thumb her clit as she comes. It triggers my own orgasm, and I fall after her, spilling inside, and stealing every moan from her lips.

I love Raleigh and Arthur more than words could ever say. And today, I get to say I'm his dad.

After taking the fastest shower ever, we go out to the kitchen, where Arthur is on his, at least, second bowl of cereal. I couldn't wait any longer. I've been wanting to say it since I first discovered I was a father. Raleigh and I each fill a bowl of cereal, then I sidle up next to him on one of the barstools.

I hold up my spoon, and he clinks his to it. "Cheers." *How the hell do I say it?* I've had plenty of time to think about it, but my brain is blank. How do you explain some-thing like this—to a five-year-old?

"Can we talk about something important, Mini Bear?"

"Is this about the koala chlamydia thing?"

I bark out a laugh. "No, nothing about koalas. Or... *that.*" I continue, "Um, so I want to discuss us. Have you ever wondered where you came from?"

"They opened Mom's belly and pulled me out. Like when you open Easter eggs and candy falls out. Except it was a baby."

There's an image. Raleigh rolls her lips together, holding back a giggle. She seems as eager to hear what I've got to say.

"Well, I knew your mom before you were born, the night I first saw her, I thought she was the most beautiful woman I'd ever seen—she still is. But after the night we met, we didn't know how to find each other again. We were lost.

"Then you were born. It's been you and your mom for a long time, but it shouldn't have been that way. I was supposed to be with you too."

He stares at me wide-eyed and blinking. *Okay, new tactic.* "Um..." I rub the back of my neck. "Have you ever seen Cinderella?"

"Uh-huh."

"Well, your mom is kinda like my Cinderella."

"My mom doesn't drive a pumpkin. She drives a Corolla." Raleigh snorts.

"True. But, the night of the ball, after the prince meets

Cinderella, she takes off at midnight and the prince chases after her but she's long gone, right?"

Arthur points at me with his spoon. "She leaves her shoe behind."

"Right! Except for me there was no shoe. There were no clues. And I looked all over, but couldn't find her." He nods. "Yeah, she's really good at hide and seek." *Fuckin' tell me about it.*

"And that night we met, me and your mom..." *Shit, this is not going well.*

Raleigh clears her throat and interrupts. "Arthur, do you remember that time you asked me if you had a dad? What did I say?"

His attention turns to Raleigh. "You said yes. And that he loved me very much wherever he was."

I swallow—so grateful she never spoke ill of me. Time to rip it off like a bandage.

"I'm your dad, Arthur. And I haven't been here, but not because I didn't want to be, but because I couldn't find you. I wanted to be with you and your mom so much, and I'm sorry I wasn't." *Please don't hate me.* If he does, I'll spend every day proving that I can be the dad he deserves.

"You're my dad?" He looks between Raleigh and me.

I nod. "I'm your dad. The three of us"—I point to each of us—"we're a family."

"Holy fart feathers. I knew it!"

I rear back to look at Raleigh, but she shakes her head.

"What do you mean, you knew it?"

"I guessed it. Three reasons." He counts on his fingers. "You call me Mini Bear, and you're the Big Bear. Following me?"

I nod, holding back laughter at his seriousness.

He continues. "We both like the color red. And because you act like my dad."

344

I scoop him up in my arms, and he lunges for his cereal bowl, grasping for his spoon that's just out of reach.

"Dad! Put me down. My cereal... it's getting soggy!"

My voice breaks, and I squeeze him tighter, flooding with emotion after hearing him call me *dad*.

"Can't do it. I love you too much."

FORTY-NINE
Raleigh

I've hit the jackpot, and I can't figure out what I've done to deserve a man like Barrett Conway. It's been two weeks since we've returned to normal life, and while I miss being in Hawaii, Barrett makes our everyday feel like a vacation.

We're still adjusting to getting things moved into the new house, but he's done so much of the work on his own, allowing me to get caught up at Method. We've decided to keep my place for now, but only because there are some updates I'd like to finish before we put it on the market. The back steps need to be redone, shutters need to be painted—honestly, the whole house needs to be painted, and the garden out front needs new plants before any photos are taken. All the stuff I didn't have time to do when it was Arthur and me. Today, he's at my house packing up my stuff so I don't have to do it after a long day at work. I love him so much.

Susan has been incredible too. She brings us dinner a couple times a week and babysits while we unpack and get a bedroom set up for Arthur. The first time he called her Grandma Suze instead of Big Suze, she broke down to tears.

We all got a little choked up. She's a fabulous mother-in-law. I hope someday I have a relationship with Arthur like the one she has with Barrett. I'm taking notes.

After perusing the "number one interior paint colors home buyers love most," I close the tab on my internet browser. Okay, I'm done planning for the day. I need to get back to work. Rob has realized I'm no longer single. I can tell he's bummed out about it. I should have said something long ago. Looking back, it was pretty fucked up of me to not draw a line in the sand. The door to his office opens and he steps out.

"Hey, Rob, is there anything you need from me?" I keep my eyes on my screen, still going through the correspondence from my absence. Sondra did a fine job covering for me, but I want to catch up on where all of our projects are at.

"So, you and Barrett Conway, huh?"

I turn in my chair to face him. "Yeah... me and Barrett. We have history."

He nods and leans against the wall, crossing his ankles and stuffing his hands in his pockets. "I see. So there's no use in trying to talk you out of it, then?"

Wincing, I shrug. "I should have made it more clear earlier."

He shrugs. "I should have taken the hint. I'm sorry if I ever made it weird." He claps. "Well, I'm happy for you... Arthur too."

"Thanks, Rob, I appreciate it."

He pushes off the wall and strolls back to his office, holding up his hand. "Just invite me to the wedding."

We're not quite there yet. Though, things are headed that way.

"Will do. Oh, and I got you booked for the leadership summit in Aspen in September."

"Good to have you back, Ral!"

FIFTY

Raleigh

I've got most of your kitchen packed up and Arthur's books. Want me to start on the bedroom?

You're amazing. Thank you! My brain is fried, I'm heading out early. I'll swing by and grab some boxes. I need to go through my closet before I pack up, I know there's a lot I can get rid of.

BARRETT

Cutting out early? Slacker.

...Says the guy who skipped dryland training to take Arthur to the zoo.

BARRETT

THE KOALA HAD A BABY, RALEIGH!!!

I laugh and drop my phone in my purse. As soon as the news reported that one of the koalas at the local zoo had a baby, Barrett was loading up the car to take Arthur. They had a blast.

Once I collect all my things, I say goodbye to Rob for the

day and head out, hoping to get a couple hours to go through my clothes before I need to pick up Arthur from daycare.

When I get to my house, Barrett's truck is in the driveway and he's already loaded up a couple pieces of furniture that will be going to a donation drop-off. Dating a guy with a truck has come in handy during this move.

"Hey, I'm here," I call out to the empty living room, setting my purse down by the entryway and slipping off my heels. I wiggle my toes with sweet relief. This place is already transforming so much. The living room has been staged with the few nice pieces I have. There's so much space once you get rid of all the toys and bookshelves. Who knew?

"Bedroom!" Barrett shouts back.

Walking down the cramped hallway feels new and old at the same time. I love the blue upholstered headboard on my bed. We're using it for real estate photos, but after that, I told Barrett I want to put it in one of the guest bedrooms at his house. I can't give it up yet. I asked if there was anything he wanted from the bedroom and all he said was that he wants my bedroom mirror for *sentimental* purposes. Big surprise there.

When he meets me at the threshold, I swoon. He is such a welcomed sight. His shirt spans tightly across his chest and arms, showing off his strong physique, and his pants give away any secrets about his size. *Is he hard?* He leads me over to the bed. I stand between his open legs while he kisses me.

"I missed you," he gruffs.

"I missed you too. Thanks for loading up the furniture into your truck."

He nods and wraps me up in a sensual hug. "How was your day?" he whispers next to my ear.

I don't want to talk about work. "Argh, it was mind-numbing." I groan. Large hands span across my ribs and drop down to my skirt where he drags the zipper down. *Okay.* I use the last of my brain cells to continue on about my day. "We had this new client and spent the afternoon going over their various services. Data storage and recovery. It was information overload, and the presentation was so dry. I'm exhausted."

He presses a line of kisses down my neck.

"What do you need, love?" His voice is low and growly and suddenly I don't care about responsibilities or packing up clothes or any of the other things I'm supposed to be doing.

A slow smile forms on my lips. "I'm bored... Play with me."

When he says nothing, I pull back to get a read on his face. He's biting his lower lip and smiling—wheels turning in his head. It spurs my racing thoughts.

"What are you thinking?"

He chuckles, tipping up my chin to kiss me. I'm such a sucker for him. The look in his eyes tells me I'm not leaving here without at least a couple of orgasms. *Who am I to stand in his way?* Getting alone time without Arthur around is a rarity, and when we do, he enjoys making sure we use that time wisely.

Although there's a wild beast behind those hungry eyes, he's being so patient as he strips my clothes. He unbuttons my shirt, focusing on one button at a time, then nudges it off my shoulders, letting it fall to the floor. The lace bra I'm wearing, a gift from him, makes my boobs look awesome. It lifts and separates, and gives me confidence.

Barrett pushes the skirt to the floor, and wetness pools between my thighs. He looks satisfied that I'm wearing the matching undies. I'm happy I wore the set today—the rod stiffening in his pants says he is too.

He delicately grasps the front of the new underwear.

He's a gentleman about it—no ripping of my new garments. Then he pulls them up and I sigh as the material separates my folds, giving me friction where I need it. It feels so good.

"I'll play with you. But we're playing with your toys."

I cock my head to the side, and he holds up his closed palm. When he opens, a string with a key at the end dangles from one of his thick fingers.

"Guess what I found today?"

That key belongs to a secret box I keep hidden under my bed. Still fisting my underwear, he bends over and pulls out said box, setting it beside him on the mattress. Like some street dealer showing off stolen wares, he flips the lid, revealing my collection of silicone vibrators in an array of colors. He's clearly already been snooping since I never leave it unlocked.

He smiles. *I know that smile.* He's up to no good.

This man better not give me any shit for my hoard of battery boyfriends. I push down any embarrassment and bat my eyes at him. "Found your competition, I see."

"Competition?" He cocks his head to the side, quirking an eyebrow. "No, love. Collaborators. We're joining forces. When our powers combine—"

"Thanks, Captain Planet. I get the picture." He tugs the underwear higher, and I gasp.

"Good." He releases them. "Lay on the bed. I get first dibs."

Holy hell, *yes.*

I practically leap onto the mattress and flop on my back.

I'm so ready for whatever he decides to dole out.

Reaching for the hem of his shirt, he pulls it over his head and then unzips the fly restraining his erection. That's what I want. After he shucks off his pants and boxers in one swoop, he pumps his cock twice. Sometime, I hope he'll let me watch him get off. I bet it's hot as hell.

I think he's going to crawl over me, but instead, he grabs my ankles and pulls me to the edge of the mattress and drops to his knees. He drags my underwear off my legs, with a wicked grin, then brings my legs over his shoulders.

"I want to try something new we haven't done yet. Do you know what I'm talking about, Raleigh?" Adrenaline courses through me, and I nod. I've never taken him there, though I desperately want to. "You ready?"

I nod again. I have been preparing for this anytime we might get a chance.

He gets closer to my sex, and his beard scratches my inner thighs, making me shiver with anticipation. I prop myself up on my elbows to watch. While peering up at me through hooded lids, his tongue slips out to open kiss my clit. My eyelids flutter shut as he laps at me again and again. The visual is so sultry and intimate, but the way he licks and sucks makes it impossible to pry my eyes open.

"If it gets to be too much, you tell me and we'll stop."

"Mmhmm."

In one movement, he pushes my thighs higher and spits on the tight knot. I gasp, and my eyes pop open. The corners of his eyes wrinkle as he tries to control a smile.

"Oh my god," I mewl, "we're finally doing it."

He returns to feeding on me, but this time brings his left middle finger to my second entrance and pushes until he invades me. I moan and tension wraps around my core. I love the sensation of his lips sucking my sensitive nub while he fucks my ass with his finger.

When the adrenaline blooms in my chest, I grip his hair and hold him close while I come. He licks me, dipping his tongue inside my pussy and I close in on it. I'm dripping everywhere. He stands, smirking, then pulls the box closer and finds the bottle of lube.

"Spit on me again," I beg. The first time, I only heard it, this time I want to see it too. With perfect accuracy and total dominance, he does, looking down at me with darkened eyes. I feel like his personal toy, and relish the idea of being used. *Fuck yeah, it's on.*

He coats his throbbing cock in lubricant. "Flip." I roll to my stomach, bent over the bed. He slaps my ass and spreads my cheeks, the head of his cock pressed to my asshole. I wiggle my hips, needing him, wanting him to fill me up.

"Always so eager to be fucked," he mutters, then speaks louder. "Just relax, take a slow breath."

Breathing in and out, my shoulders droop into the mattress. With his palms gripping my hips, he pushes the crown inside me, and I turn my head to the side, resting it on the soft comforter while he stretches me. "Breathe, baby."

After another inhale, he pushes deeper. When he pauses, I glance back to see him shaking his head, disbelief painted on his face.

"Fuck me, you are so tight," he growls. "I want to see you take every inch of my cock up your ass." I grin and sigh.

He instructs me breathe until he's all the way inside. "I'm going to move us." He wraps his hands under me and moves so he's sitting on the bed, and I'm straddling his lap, facing away from him. I glimpse at us in the mirror. The same mirror he finger-fucked me in front of a couple months ago. Now that I'm in his lap, I sink down a little lower and my eyes nearly roll back. I am absolutely engorged with his cock.

"Oh my god." I sigh. "I've never been so full."

"Not yet, but you're about to be." He reaches into the box and pulls out one of my vibrators.

Oh fuck. I was wrong, I may not be ready for this. When the U-shaped toy comes buzzing to life, he holds me still while grazing it across my sensitive flesh. The vibrator provides clitoral and G-spot stimulation, and I shudder.

I turn my head to look at him, his jaw is clenched, but he takes a moment to stop and kiss me. His mouth is soft, yet firm.

"I love you, baby," he says, his voice lower and more aggressive than usual. I love seeing this feral side of him. "

"I love you too."

When the vibrations pass over that bundle of nerves again, I turn my face forward and lean back, resting my head on his shoulder. After coating the toy in my wetness, he plunges it inside me. My mouth drops open the same time he groans. "Fuck, I can feel it on my cock... Breathe, Ral."

I take a deep inhale through my nose and squirm as I'm being overstimulated from every angle. He chuckles. "You're trembling like you're about to come. How's that fullness now, baby?"

My legs aren't trembling, they're *quaking*. "It's more, so much more."

Everything feels so beautifully excruciating and stings in the best way possible. I love being stretched like this. I moan, and my fingers dig into the forearm across my abdomen, securing my back to his chest.

"Mmm." He points at the mirror and brings his face next to mine. "Tell me what you like."

I look at myself, really look. And for the first time in a long time, I see what he sees. A small smile curls at the corner of my lips, and he notices my change in demeanor this time around.

My eyes are soft and sultry, lips swollen from his kiss.

My hair is mussed from lying on my back earlier, but it's a reminder of his mouth on me. The lace bra accentuates my full, heaving breasts. And my stomach and sides are striped with stretch marks, but they're evidence of the months I carried our son. My parted thighs are thick but powerful. The curves on my hips are feminine and sexy.

"I'm beautiful," I whisper.

He smiles bigger, and it's hard to tell, but I think his eyes turn slightly glassy.

"That's right, love." He dips his chin to kiss my shoulder,

and I can't keep my eyes off us. This man has not only made me feel more loved than I ever knew, but he's shown me how to love myself.

My sappy feelings are brushed aside as my body tingles. I sit up on my knees a little bit and sink back down again.

"Fuck," he barks out. The muscles in his face are tense.

"Relax your jaw," I remind him. I'm afraid he will crack a tooth. His mouth forms an O, and he blows out a long breath.

"Good boy."

He raises an eyebrow. "...Open your mouth."

His right ring and middle fingers invade my mouth. Wrapping my lips around them, I suck.

He whispers behind my ear, "I'm not your *good boy,* Raleigh. *I'm your Bear.*" He bites the back of my neck, and the assault of pleasure in every hole makes the building pressure inside me burst *like* a levee. I moan around his fingers and grind into him.

"You like this, don't you?"

"Bear," I pant. The nickname he loves.

"That's my dirty fucking girl." I wrap an arm behind his neck and pick up and drop down on him again. My hips undulate as my climax rolls through. *Holy shit.* He hisses and grumbles in my ear as he struggles. I fucking live for those noises. He grips me and releases his orgasm in my ass. It makes me feel so powerful.

As soon as my climax dissolves, I squirm, the vibrator overstimulating me after my orgasm. I reach down and pull out the thing that's torturing me. It flies out of my fingers and skitters across the wood floor. Barrett laughs against my back. "That's okay, we have a whole box to go through."

My eyes widen. I glance down and see six more in the box. *No fucking way.* "Didn't you just...?"

"Yes. But that doesn't mean we're stopping."

"I can't."

"You can. You're going to take every one. Do we need a safeword?"

"Yes!" I yell. "Obviously!"

"What's our safeword?"

"Koala chlamydia." I attempt to say with a straight face.

"Hard veto." He smacks the side of my ass. "Pineapple."

He's already getting hard again. *How is that even possible?* One by one, he test drives each toy on me while my ass warms his cock. Sweat is beading at the nape of my neck. Orgasm after orgasm. I'm four in and am getting closer to my threshold of using the safeword. It's a delicious torment. He takes a wand from the box and slides up my clit. My thighs begin to quiver. I try to ride, but don't have the strength. "I need..." My body goes limp, and he removes the stimulation to give me a short break.

"Lean back." His hand snakes up to my neck, and I relax back onto his shoulder again. "That's it, let me do the work."

The mirror shows one hell of a view, I'm spread wide open for him.

"So pink..." He gently thumbs my clit. "So wet..." His thumb lowers and traces my opening. I'm soaked. Then without warning, he slaps.

"Fuck!" I cry out, squeezing my eyes shut and jolting forward. I'm at his mercy. Literally putting my pleasure in his hands. I nearly crumble.

He snickers. "Even buried in your ass I can feel every flutter of your pussy."

He changes the rhythm to a steady pulse and slips the wand inside, pulls it out, circles the bundle of nerves, and repeats. Over and over and over. The wet smacking of my arousal growing louder with each pass.

"That's my messy girl. Look at you being so good for me. Letting me keep my cock in your ass while I play with your pussy." My hips roll, and he hums his approval. I won't last much longer, I know it.

He circles again and it feels like I'm being compressed into a tiny ball. I whimper his name, and he pulls me into him. I love the feeling of safety I have when his arms are around me. Everything pulls inward more and more until this strange euphoria comes over me and I almost feel like I'm floating.

My ears ring and I know I must be on the cusp of the biggest orgasm I've ever had.

"It's—Something's—"

Right then, it's like a tidal wave capsizes me. Pure nirvana rolls through every nerve. It feels like an out-of-body experience. My eyes fall to the mirror. Barrett drops the vibrator and it buzzes across the floor. His right hand takes over fucking my pussy with vigor. Nothing but love in his eyes as we regard each other in the reflection.

It's so much all at once. I hear his voice through the fog telling me to let go, and when I do, fluid gushes out of me. He continues pumping his fingers in and out while bouncing me on his dick. All at once, it's like I'm thrown back into the living, breathing world again. I scream out and burrow my fingers into his thighs like I'm holding on for dear life. I've squirted before, but never like this. He roars—*and I swear it sounds like a bear*—when he comes a second time.

I'm frozen, surrendering to the oblivion. He growls in my ear, "That's it, baby. Oh my god, you are beautiful. Keep going, keep going. You're doing so good, sweetheart." He rubs my clit until I'm drained in every sense of the word. As soon as I'm done, he reaches down to turn off the vibrator clattering against the hardwood, it sends ripples through the pool of fluid at his feet.

"Fucking hell. Pineapple." My chest heaves, and I finally let go of his thighs, my knuckles white and his legs probably bruised. I'm limp and spent. *And high as fuck.*

"That was intense." He sounds as tired as me. "Raleigh you are—fuck, I'm speechless. You are all my goddamn dreams come true." He shakes his head. "Okay, baby... I'm going to pull out now." He turns us on our sides so we're spooning and slides out before picking me up and carrying me into the hall bathroom.

I'm sore. Not just my ass, every muscle feels like it's locked up after a cramp. "But we didn't get through the last toy?"

He stares at me with raised eyebrows. "Did you want to keep going?"

I give a swish of my hand. "Fuck no. That was a joke. Pineapple. All the pineapples."

He laughs and fills the bathtub. His cum is leaking out of me while I sit in his lap on the side of the tub. Once it's full, he deposits me into the soothing water, I exhale the tension, and it dissolves almost instantly. He strides out of the room.

"Hey, where are you going?"

"Forgot something, one sec."

When he comes back in, he holds out a glass of water for me. The cold drink is a delightful refreshment in contrast to the hot water I'm soaking in. He climbs in behind me, leaning forward and kissing my temple. Caged between his arms, he holds out a necklace with a gorgeous gold pennant in the center. It's a locket. He opens it up to a photo of the three of us on the beach in Hawaii. I sniffle, trying to hold back tears. There's so much adrenaline and post-sex feels happening. I'm overwhelmed with all these competing emotions flooding my headspace. Happiness, melancholy, love, shame. I'm crashing. He places the necklace around my neck, and I press it to my chest, needing to touch it. Barrett simply holds me close and lets me cry.

"I've got you. You're safe. I'm not going anywhere." I shudder through a sigh, getting some of the tears under control. "I texted my mom, she's picking up Arthur from daycare. We'll pick up some takeout on the way home. There's this place I know that has pitas that feel like fluffy clouds. How does Greek sound?"

It sounds amazing. "I love you" and a nod is all I can muster.

"I love you too," he says, a slight chuckle in his voice when he massages my shoulders. "So much. You and Arthur are my everything. You're my world."

His words eclipse the strange, confusing feelings and replace them with comfort and security. I spent much of my life feeling alone, but Barrett has become my safe space. And he's how I want to spend the rest of my life.

FIFTY-ONE

Barrett

"Okay, ready for my koala trivia?"

"Sure." He giggles. I've been trying to school him on koala facts since I first saw him. I'm bound to do it one of these days. I'm feeling good about today.

"Did you know… that koalas can gallop as fast as twenty miles-per-hour? That's like three times faster than I can run."

Arthur's eyes get wide and he turns to me. "Really?"

It stops me in my tracks. "Wait, you didn't know that?"

He shakes his head with a big smile on his face. He looks just as proud of me, which makes me feel like a king.

"Hell yeah! I got you!"

He laughs, and I scoop him up to set him on my shoulders. We're having guy time while Raleigh spends the morning getting brunch with the WAGs. Afterward, we'll go to my mom's, and she's going to take Arthur for the night, his first sleepover at Grandma Suze's house. For now, there's something we need to talk about man-to-man. "You said the H-E-double hockey sticks word!" *The H-E double…what? Oh! Shit.*

"Oooh, I'll work on that. Sorry, buddy."

"I won't tell Mom. It will be our secret."

Holding my fist up, he taps it with his. *Raleigh didn't raise no snitch.*

"Hey, so I know things are really hectic with the move and having me around more. How are you feeling about all the new stuff happening?"

"Good!" He seems genuine. There's a happy lilt to his voice. "Except..."

"Except what?"

"When are you going to ask Mom to marry you?"

A laugh explodes from my chest. "What do you mean?"

"Aren't you?" He leans over my face, and actually looks worried. I nod to reassure him.

"That's why we're having a guy's day today, so I could consult with you first. I want to make sure you're okay with me asking your mom to marry me. What do you think?"

"I think you should hurry up and do it—you need a ring. Do you have one?"

The smile on my face can't be smothered; the things that come out of this kid's mouth...

"Not yet. Wanna help me pick one out today?"

RALEIGH

"Holy shit!" Birdie exclaims!

I run my fingers through my hair and nod. We've told the rest of his family, and now I'm sharing the news with Micky and Birdie. I figure we'll be spending a lot of time together this fall in the WAGs box, so Barrett and I decided to come out with it to the team and their wives. Well, I decided. Barrett's been ready to scream it from the rooftops from the get-go. It's nice releasing those secrets.

Barrett is letting me share it with the WAGs first. He said if he told the guys, they'd share it with their wives before I got a chance. We hope that by doing this before the season starts, we'll be able to get any awkwardness out of the way when we sit in the box suite. Although, talking with Birdie and Micky doesn't feel all that awkward. They are both so honest about their own stories, that it makes me feel comfortable in mine.

"So where is this woman now?" Birdie asks, referring to Julia.

"No fucking clue, but truthfully, I don't want to know. I don't want to meet her—God, I'd probably take a swing at her." I roll my eyes. "Barrett's lawyer is looking into it. It doesn't matter. No money will ever be able to make up for the time we lost, but it makes Barrett feel better."

"You know, now that I think of it, Lonan mentioned her calling him into her office a few times on false pretenses for work too. She never touched him, but it definitely made him uncomfortable, enough that he refused to speak with her in person and everything had to be done through email."

"Damn, I'm glad she wasn't there when Rhys started. The last thing he needed was more pressure from outside shit." Micky stares wide-eyed as she drinks through a straw and listens.

"Anyway, that's our story. That's why I was weird at the soft launch. That was the first time I was in the same room as him since everything happened."

Micky and Birdie throw an arm around me.

"I'm so happy you guys reconnected," Birdie says, her eyes welling up. "I'm sorry, I'm so emotional these days. And I know what it's like to reunite with people you lost contact with, it's such an intense thing to go through. And to do it with a child? God, I can't imagine."

"And you saw him at my opening! I helped!" Micky coos.

Birdie narrows her eyes at her. "The fuck are you talking about?" She laughs, sipping her mocktail. "They didn't even connect until the Lakes-Method event."

"I brought a *fam-il-y* together." Micky enunciates, punctuating each syllable in the air with pinched fingers.

"You're *de-lu-sion-al*," Birdie responds, mirroring her.

She turns back to me. "So now that you're back together, how is it? Is it awkward? Is it hot? How is Arthur with everything?"

"That's what's so wild, it's like we're picking up right where we left off. It's... *easy.* He makes life seem so simple. Before him, I was responsible for everything, but he's stepped in and taken care of things without even being asked. It's become such a seamless transition. It's almost too good to be true, and sometimes I think I don't deserve all this happiness."

"Fuck that, you absolutely do! And Barrett's obsessed with you. He loves you both, I can see it. I mean, you're Runaway Raleigh—" Birdie says.

"How's the sex?" Micky interrupts. "Please tell me he wears your pussy like a gas mask. After all that time, I hope you're getting it on the reg. Hockey-player sex is next level." Her eyes roll back in her head.

I've had plenty of hockey-player sex in my life, but *Barrett* sex is next level.

"I laugh. The stamina is ridiculous. God, he's so amazing. It's not even just the sex, he's always doing these sweet gestures, he's so giving. I want to do something nice for him too."

"Blow him," Micky says around her straw, at the same time Birdie asks, "What does he like?"

I chuckle. "I do blow him! Honestly, he might like being a dad more than blowjobs."

"You're not doing it right." Micky shakes her head, and I laugh.

"I swear to God! He's so fucking proud of being a Dad, and all he talks about is having more kids."

"Did you see this photo he posted on Instagram?" Birdie

holds out her phone to show me. It's a picture of us in Hawaii with the caption *"Finally got her."* I clutch my locket. I know he hates social media, so to see that small act makes my heart burst. Fuck, I love him so much.

I swirl my glass and the delicious Micky-made POG juice coats the sides. And then it hits me.

I have the perfect idea.

"So get him something dad-like. Maybe Arthur can make him something."

"Or I could surprise him and get his name put on the birth certificate."

They "Awww" in unison. Micky slaps the table. "Yes! That's perfect!"

"You could use the same genetic testing company I did, Stellar Genetics. They do paternity testing."

Micky rolls her eyes. "Yeah he won't find you asking for his DNA suspicious at all..."

"Tell him you want to get his genetic history done, say you want it to find out about Arthur's ancestral background."

"No, that takes too long. Just swab his cheek while he's sleeping. Way easier and less complicated," Micky argues.

"Has Rhys ever mentioned having trust issues with you?" I ask, and Micky barks out a laugh.

"Girl, you could harvest his organs in his sleep but as long as he woke up and you were the one holding the saw, he wouldn't mind."

"A saw!? What organs are you harvesting with a saw?" I ask, laughing.

"Knife, whatever. I didn't go to medical school."

Birdie chimes in. "You went to culinary school, so I'm also questioning why you went straight to saw."

"I skipped class the day they covered organ harvesting, okay? I feel like we're getting off topic."

Birdie rolls her eyes and turns her attention back to me.

"If you were a psycho ex-girlfriend, yes, absolutely it would be creepy. But it's to get him on the certificate. He'll love it."

After brunch, we spent the afternoon with Barrett's family and had dinner with them. It was a gorgeous day, so we spent most of the time playing in the backyard and chatting. Arthur was so excited to get Grandma time in that we chose to let him sleepover at her house. He's probably a half-dozen cookies into a sugar coma right now. He's gaining this whole new family, it fills my heart. We plan on getting some counseling started for all three of us to help with the transition, but so far, it's going well.

When we get home, Barrett goes straight upstairs while I jump on my laptop and order the paternity test. When I'm done, I meet him in the bedroom. The French doors are open, and the cool summer breeze makes the curtains billow. *Mmm, I love summer nights like these.* The gas firepit is lit on the deck and he's got the lid off the recessed hot tub.

"Hey, sailor, looking for a good time?"

He spins around and smiles. "Fuck yeah. Come here."

I strip my clothes. He drifts to the other side of the hot tub and stretches his arms over the ledge behind him, watching me with a sly smile.

"How did the news go over with the team? I saw your Instagram post."

"Team who?" he says, playing dumb while watching me unhook my bra. He holds his palm out while I dip my toes in the water, my hand takes his and he hauls me into his arms. I hiss and suck a deep breath as the hot water envelopes me. "It went well. I made a bunch of phone calls, they're all pretty psyched. Sorry, I couldn't wait. You said you didn't mind if I shared our selfie, that was okay, right?"

"Of course. I like you laying claim to me." I run my nails up his thighs while his cock hardens against my back.

"Mmm. Good. You're mine and I'm telling everybody. It has 122K heart thingys—didn't realize I was that popular. Anyway, how was it telling the girls?"

"Great, they're very happy for us. It was really lovely getting to know them better. It'll be nice having a couple friends in the WAG box."

His palms travel up to my breasts, and I lean back, covering his hands with mine.

"The stars are pretty tonight."

"Hmm." He drags his nose over the shell of my ear, and I smile. *This is my life.*

Lifting me to the edge, he pushes my legs apart. I lean back on my elbows and look up at the sky while he licks and nips my inner thighs. *Fuck. Receiving oral sex while stargazing is my new favorite foreplay.*

When he reaches my clit, I slip my hand into his hair to pull him closer. He groans, and the vibrations add to the fervor of his tongue. The cold air makes my nipples harden into peaks. His hands slide up my chest, pinching and tugging. Hot hands on my chilled skin is a wonderful combination.

I arch into his mouth and the hungry eye contact from him makes my pulse ring in my ears.

"Oh fuck," I whisper.

He pops off me and shoves two fingers inside, tapping at my G-spot. I throw my head back with a moan.

"That's right, I don't want you being quiet tonight. I'm gonna have this whole house soundproofed next week so I can hear more of those."

I smile, amused that he's making good on his word in Hawaii.

The lights from the Jacuzzi and fire bouncing off his glistening muscles adds to the sexy scene playing out in front of me. He grips my ass and drags me against him, his tongue delving inside. Right before I'm about to come, he hops out and pulls me up with him, hauling me off to the bedroom.

Tossing me across the bed like I'm nothing, he prowls closer. That body's a work of art. When he stands near my head, he shoves his fingers back inside my pussy, and I cover his fully hard cock with my hand.

"You know what I want from you, love. Open up."

Ugh, his gritty authoritative voice is my weakness. I part my lips, and he sweeps his cock over my tongue. He fingers me while I suck, and I whimper with my mouth full.

"That's it, moan around my cock."

With each sexy praise he bestows, I make more noise and am rewarded with more attention from his hands. Before long, he bends my knees and drops them open, dipping his head down to feast on me. I groan and feel him smile against me.

"Hum around me like that again."

He flattens his tongue against my clit, varying the speed and pressure. It's so hard to focus on anything I'm supposed to be doing with my mouth when his tongue plays with me. I gag slightly and he raises enough for me to get a deep breath in and then plunges back inside. I wrap my hand around the base of his cock to give myself a buffer.

"Every inch, Raleigh," he instructs.

This time I remember to relax my jaw when he pushes down my throat. With his fingers shoved back inside, he fucks me on each end, and the dual penetration has my head spinning. I'm so busy paying attention to his cock I almost don't notice how fast my body tightens up.

"Such a good girl for me," he mumbles, feeling my body about to lose control.

FIFTY-TWO

Barrett

I want her. And when her eyes dip below my waist, she can see it. She's getting fucked so hard tonight.

"What's the safeword?"

She smiles. "Pineapple."

I've never met a girl like Raleigh before, who can let go like this and drag me into a new level of connection. It plays into the most basic, caveman part of my brain. Like we share this evolutionary need to act like hunter and prey. A push and pull of *fight me* and *fuck me*.

I pin her hands above her head, but she wriggles out with a satisfied grin for the second time.

"You want to play that game?"

She nods and pushes my hands away, somehow getting to her knees on the bed. I grab her thighs, pulling her to the edge, and she yelps in surprise when I flip her on her stomach and cover her body with mine, my cock between her wet thighs.

"I win," I whisper in her ear, sliding my arm under her and crawling it up to her neck.

She gives up and lets me show physical dominance over her, establish control, and make her mine. I have to work for takedown, and I fucking love it. She's panting, but it's not exhaustion—it's lust. She tries to push off me, but I flip her back again. I love watching her expression, eyes wild and full of sex. She moans at my touch when I restrain her, and stroke the wet cunt that's got me seeing stars.

Holding her legs open. I thrust my cock inside her. Her whimper goes straight to my balls. *Jesus Christ this woman...*

Raleigh leans forward and grazes her nails over my thighs, toward my groin.

"Hold on to me." She wraps her legs around my waist, and the need to drive inside her is overwhelming. My free hand dives to her pussy. She rocks against me, increasing the friction. Bouncing her on my dick, she cries out and I want more.

I bring my mouth to her ear. "You're going to take all of it." I slam inside her again and she stiffens around me. She grunts and scratches, it feels so good. "Harder," I say. I want to feel her intensity.

She digs her nails in and drags them across my skin slowly. "That's it, baby." I growl in response. I pummel into her over and over, feeling her body shake. Her next whine is one I've never heard her make before. It's demanding and desperate at the same time.

"Shit, I've got a cramp!" She laughs and lifts her leg. I can fuck her and massage her calf at the same time. It's oddly intimate that we can laugh together during sex. Even when we're rough and aggressive. Her shoulders relax some and we're back on track again.

Spreading her knees apart, the view is unreal. I love watching her take me. Her cheeks are flushed. Raleigh is the most stunning thing I've ever seen.

"I love you so fucking much."

Her plump lips part on a soft smile. "Tell me again."

I grin wider. "I love you. So. Fucking. Much."

My hands palm her flesh, squeezing and gripping her like

it will never be enough. She makes everything in my life feel complete.

I drop down and suck her pert nipple into my mouth, swirling my tongue around it. She pulls me into this gentle embrace that counters the roughness of each thrust. When I rub her clit, I'm pulled deeper. Her breaths heave, and I lock my eyes on her, needing to watch her break. "Let go."

Her cry is choked when she gasps my name. The thrumming pulse inside her sends me over. She cups my face and brings my mouth to hers, then nips at my lower lip as she rolls those sexy as sin hips under me. I groan and spill inside her, pretending her birth control doesn't exist and letting myself feed into the fantasy. I come harder than ever before.

"It's so good, Bear." She's right. What we have is pure goodness. My mouth takes hers—she's so sweet—we are perfect together.

I grip her chin so she looks at me. "I love you." Her eyes gloss over, and she smiles.

"I love you too."

That's my girl, soon she'll be my wife... my forever.

FIFTY-THREE
Raleigh

Three weeks later...

The doorbell rings and I glance toward the front hall. Barrett's still at the gym, and I'm not expecting anyone. I've never answered his door before when he's not home. Walking to the entryway feels strange, but I suppose it's my house too, so...

I open the door and nearly fall over. *No.*

"Hey, sugar!"

"Mom. Um, hi... what are you doing here?"

"What the hell kinda greeting is that?"

Who travels over a thousand miles without calling first? I'm acutely aware of Arthur's presence somewhere behind me and want to hide him.

She tries to push past me, but I block her. "Mom, no. I'm sorry. You can't come in."

The look she gives me makes the hair on the back of my neck stand on end. This time she puts her weight into her suitcase and shoves her way in. Arthur jumps behind me. "Is this my grandbaby?! Hi, cutie! I'm Grandma D, what's your name?" I've told her his name over the phone.

I slide him farther behind me to create a barrier of protection. There's no way she's just showing up out of the blue to meet him. She's had five years to come and didn't. She doesn't get the privilege of looking at him. Doesn't get to talk to him. There's some other reason she's here. I know it.

Spotting Arthur's tablet on the end table, I pick it up and tell him to go to his room for a few minutes so I can talk to *"Grandma D."* What kind of bullshit moniker is that? Like she's able to come in and pretend she's his grandma? Fuck that. Susan is his grandmother.

Arthur checks my face, and I plaster a smile on, hoping to hide my anxiety over her arrival.

"Okay, Mom," he answers, before scurrying off to the bedroom.

My fingers fumble as I work to unlock my phone and tap out a message to Barrett.

> I know you're busy training, but can you please come home? My mom showed up and I need you to get Arthur and take him to your mom's while I figure out why she's here.

BARRETT

Why?

> Because I don't want her around him.

BARRETT

No, why is she there Raleigh???

> I don't know, but I don't trust her and I don't want her around Arthur.

BARRETT

Are you safe? Can you leave?

I've told Barrett about my history with my mom. That she's never forgiven me for chasing off her cash-cow boyfriend after I reported him to the social worker at school. How she accused me of trying to seduce him. The fight that sent me running. I can still hear her yelling, see her pointing at me with a cigarette between her fingers as she told me I ruined her life the day he ran off. That she chose a rich sexual predator over her child's safety. It wasn't until I had a son that I started to see my childhood through the lens of motherhood.

Now I know how truly fucked up my upbringing was.

Barrett's not a fan.

> I'm acting normal and keeping things civil until you can get him out of here. I don't want her to become angry and put him in danger.

BARRETT

Already on my way.

"I've only been in a car for twenty hours, but please, continue your texting. That's more important than your own mother."

"Mom, I'm sure you traveled a great distance, but I wish you would have called instead—wait how did you even know I was here?" She curls her lip up at me, not liking that response.

"Unbelievable. I'm trying to have a relationship with you, and this is your reaction, Raleigh Jean? Still ungrateful for all I've sacrificed for you."

She means the *men* she's sacrificed for me. The ones who would track me with their eyes when I was only fourteen. Her presence triggers the repressed memories.

"Why now? Why after all this time?" Then it dawns on me. She found me at Barrett's. Is she still keeping tabs on my Instagram?

I don't know what my mom has up her sleeve, but it must be motivated by money. If she saw the photo of Barrett and me in Hawaii, now she's seeing dollar signs. Whatever she's up to, it's bad news—and sure as fuck isn't to see her grandson.

"I thought you would be happy to see me, what's it been, eight years? Jesus, you think you could come home once in a blue moon. Looks like you can afford the plane ticket." Her eyes glance up to the sparkling chandelier over the table.

Taking a deep breath, I relax my hands. I can't let the conversation escalate. Not until Arthur is gone. For now, I make an attempt at small talk. She follows me into the kitchen. I gesture for her to have a seat at the table.

"No thanks, I've been sitting a while in the car. I'll stand."

"How was the drive?" We regard each other without blinking. Heaviness hangs in the air, the tension expanding wall to wall.

Pursing her lips, she bobs her head slowly. "Slower than a bread wagon with biscuit wheels," she deadpans. She's trying to get in my head. Make me feel small. I won't do it. And I won't feel bad for not coming home. Why would I?

"Where's Jerry?" Her latest boyfriend.

She rolls her eyes. "Where do you think? Thought I taught you better than to ask stupid questions. *Men. Always. Leave.* Except in your case, I see." She looks around the kitchen. "Lucky you." She points to the smart fridge. "That's a pretty fancy fridge. Must be nice…"

"Hm." I stare back.

"Better enjoy it while it lasts."

"It's a new fridge. It's going to last."

Her scoff is like nails on a chalkboard. It's so patronizing. "Don't play dumb. Things these days aren't built like they used to be. Just because it's new and shiny doesn't mean it will last. I get new refrigerators every couple years. They all break eventually. Or your kid'll break 'em." She shrugs.

"Stop it, Mom," I snap.

She cuts her eyes at me. "You think because you get to play house and have whatever you want, that you can live like this forever? You can't. You're no exception. I don't know what put this idea in your head that you're better than the rest of us, but you're not. Barrett Conway might be a dumb jock, but he'll figure it out eventually and then you'll wish you listened to me." Figure out what?

The door to the mudroom slams. "Ral!"

My shoulders relax. "He's in his bedroom," I call back. *Please get Arthur out of here.* This conversation is already getting too heated, and it's probably going to escalate before she leaves.

Barrett walks in with Rhys on his heels. "Top of the stairs, left hallway, first door on the right," he instructs.

Two seconds later, I hear Rhys taking the stairs two at a time. Thankfully, Arthur has been around Rhys and Micky Kucera enough at this point that he won't be alarmed by seeing him. A minute later, Rhys hustles down the stairs. He's busy telling Arthur all about the desserts that Micky has whipped up and how she needs a taste tester.

Barrett tosses him the keys to the BMW, where we keep the booster.

I give Arthur a hug and speak close to his face, murmuring so she can't hear. "Be good for the Kuceras. I'll see you in a little bit. Afterward, we'll go out for ice cream!"

"Cookie Monster kind?"

"You bet. I love you!" I squeeze him extra tight. Barrett hugs him, and when he glances back at me, he nods and mouths, *I'm here.*

I'm relieved Rhys is taking Arthur away from here. Whatever happens now, I know he's safe—though I'm not loving that Barrett is about to get a front-row seat into my fucked-up upbringing. The front door slams, and we turn to our unwelcome guest.

Now she decides to sit at the kitchen table.

"Hi, Barrett! It seems my daughter doesn't have any manners. I'm her mom, Darlene."

He sits down across from her. "I know who you are."

She narrows her eyes at him. "Oh, good, then we're all acquainted."

I pinch the bridge of my nose and choose the chair next to Barrett. "Mom, I think it's time you leave."

"I'm not here for you, Raleigh. I have business with Barrett."

He scoffs. "What business could we possibly have?" Takes the words right out of my mouth.

"I thought you should hear the truth about Arthur. You have no proof he's your child. Raleigh doesn't know who Arthur's father is. She's like her mama that way." Her scratchy laugh makes me cringe.

"Oh my God, I'm not you. Barrett is Arthur's father. Nice try."

He jerks his head back and laughs. "What are you talking about? Arthur's mine."

"You and I both know Raleigh's past. The likelihood is slim."

Barrett puts his hand on my thigh, but the way he's looking at my mother—he's about to rip her apart.

"Just for fun, let's say you were right. Do you think I would love either of them any less? You're wasting your time trying to plant seeds of doubt. I know he's mine."

While he finishes his speech, I stand up and walk over to my purse and slap the paternity test results down on the table for her. This is not how I wanted to surprise Barrett, I hate her on a whole new level now for ruining this moment of ours.

"You're disgusting. It's his kid. What else do you want?" I'm seething.

"Don't give me attitude! I'm trying to help you!" she snaps at me, and Barrett stands up. I'm not sure I've ever loved him more than I do right now.

"What part of that was helping me? The calling me a whore part or telling him that his son isn't his?"

"Well now that you have proof, then he owes you. How many years didn't he pay you child support? Not a fucking penny. This man abandoned you! He owes you for all those years you—"

"Oh! So now—" I start. I reach for Barrett's hand under the table. She's hit him right where all his guilt lies. How dare she.

Barrett throws his arm in front of me and cuts me off. "What the hell are you even talking about?" He screws up his face and looks at her like she's crazy. "I've always been here! I've never abandoned her!"

I don't know where he's going with this, but I'll follow his lead.

She points her finger at him. "That's bullshit. You left my baby alone while she took care of your child. You've got five years of unpaid child support you owe her. And I'm here to see that she gets it. I've seen the text messages from her that you sent. They are heinous. And I'm sure some news outlets would love to get their hands on them." She's here for blackmail. Then I freeze.

I never showed her those messages.

"Oh my God."

She sits back in her chair and purses her lips.

I'm in shock. I knew my mother was a shitty parent, but I never realized how truly evil she was until this moment.

"You sent those messages."

"No, I said I *saw* them. You sent them to me, remember?"

I shake my head. "No. I only ever showed them to one person—Barrett."

This time the claws come out when she speaks. "You're an opportunist just like your mama, you're still the same Raleigh from back home. Shake your ass and get whatever man you want. You may have learned how to take care of yourself when you get yourself into a bind, but you've forgotten who you learned that from: me! I've got the texts either way, tabloids aren't gonna care. Family first. So we can do this under the table, or loud enough for everyone else to hear. The ball's in your court."

"I fucking knew it." His smile doesn't reach his eyes.

"I've been waiting for you to show up."

She blinks at him, trying to act cavalier but deep down she wants to know what he means as much as I do.

"Oh, did you think I haven't been keeping tabs on you? The minute Raleigh told me you weren't allowed to see Arthur, I did a background check on you. I'm smarter than I look. Even for a dumb jock."

He points up to one of the security cameras in the far bookshelf. "See that? If you think it's smart to threaten black-mail or slander my or Raleigh's name, you better believe I'll bury you in a lawsuit so deep that by the time you surface, you won't have credit to buy a pack of fucking Newports." He lowers his voice to barely over a whisper and leans over the table. "And if you ever try to contact or step foot on this prop-erty again, I'll shoot first... You understand, right? Isn't that how you people do it in the south? This is my family now. Not yours."

Holy fuck. I have never had someone stand up for me like this in my life. This is an entirely different level. I'm seeing Barrett in a new light. Fierce, protective, and unhinged. I do everything I can not to gawk at him, but my thoughts are interrupted by a knock at the door. Barrett keeps his eyes on her, but speaks to me.

"Get the door, Raleigh."

"Who is it?" I ask. He seems to know something I don't.

"It's her ride."

FIFTY-FOUR
Barrett

I called the police on my way home to make sure when she left the house, she left for good. At the time, it was for trespassing. However, now I get to tack on the charges for assuming a false identity—mine. And all the years it cost me with Raleigh and my son.

While they read Darlene her Miranda Rights, I pull out my phone, snap a copy of the results, and begin tapping the screen.

"What are you doing?" Ral asks.

"I'm texting our lawyer to tell him it's not Julia we need to go after, it's your mom. And I want an order of protection against her."

I was ninety percent sure she had a warrant out for her arrest. It doesn't make sense to drive instead of fly. I saw the North Carolina plates, and her background check says she's got a habit of not showing up to her court hearings. I wanted to make sure she was removed from the house before she could peel out of here like a bat out of hell. Or a cunt out of... well, our driveway. Turns out, I was right, color me stunned.

"When did you call the police?" Raleigh mutters. Her voice sounds small, and is muffled with her chin dropped to her chest. She has no reason to feel shame over her mother. I slide my arm behind her and squeeze her side.

"On my way home." As soon as I saw her barge in on the doorbell cam, I knew I had her. "It'll be okay."

"Thank you for having Rhys take Arthur so you could stay with me."

I nod as Darlene is escorted past us to the waiting police car outside. Another officer stays behind to take our statement. It feels like forever to give all the information we can to police, and I let them know I was already in touch with my lawyer because we would be pressing charges. After he leaves, we both take a heaving breath. *Holy shit.*

The second I shut and lock the front door, I walk back to the table and hold the paper confirming the paternity test results.

"You did a paternity test?" *Did she doubt he was mine?*

"I wanted to surprise you, so we could get your name on the birth certificate. Make it official." She sounds so disheartened, like all the effort she went through was ruined. I kick myself for thinking she had doubts. I love that she went through the trouble to do something so thoughtful, she knows how bad I wanted that certificate.

I walk back to the front door, peering out the sidelight to see if the police have left. They have. We were told a truck would be by later to tow her vehicle away. I'll feel better when every trace of Darlene is gone.

Raleigh steps next to me and pulls me away from the window.

"I can't believe she came here. And seeing you go all papa bear for us back there, *oh my god—*"

My phone rings and my lawyers name flashes on the screen. I need to take it..

"Hey."

"What the fuck is going on over there? Did you give a statement?"

"Yeah, I explained as best I could. Took them a minute to understand how it went down. It was all on camera."

"Send me the footage so I can add it."

He goes over some legal jargon, but eventually I have to cut him off and explain that I need to tend to Raleigh. As soon as I hit the end call button, I wrap her in my arms. Her shook body trembles.

"No one has ever protected Arthur and me like that." Her chest heaves.

Parents are supposed to protect their children. The stories Raleigh has told me about the close calls she had as a kid with grown men, men three times her age, make my skin crawl. It enrages me. I will always put her and Arthur first. Even against the people that were supposed to protect her all along. I'll be that person for her and our family.

I sink a hand into her hair. I still can't believe she did a paternity test to get my name on the birth certificate. *How fucking sweet is she?* God, I love this woman. My mouth takes hers in a soft kiss.

"I don't want to be like her," she mumbles, hurt flickers behind her eyes, and I wish I could take it away. I saw the way she flinched when her mom compared Raleigh to her.

"You are so incredible. You're *nothing* like her. You are kind, thoughtful, caring, empathetic, selfless. You are her polar opposite. You're a fantastic mom and a loving partner and a *good* person."

A fat swollen tear builds in the corner of her eye, and I brush it away. Her gaze meets mine, and it's so full of love.

Because that's what Raleigh is, she's love.

I rub circles on her back and hold her in my arms, letting her grieve for all the things she should have had. All the things I promise to give her.

FIFTY-FIVE
Raleigh

B arrett sits at the table while I work around the kitchen getting ready for dinner. We're talking about our day, the simplicity of it makes me smile.

"I worked out with Banksy today. He's all bent out of shape over being the best man in some wedding from a childhood friend. I'm sure he sees monogamy as an affront to everything he believes in. He's such a whor—" Arthur bounds into the kitchen for dinner. "—*rrible gift wrapper.*"

"Who's a horrible gift wrapper?" he asks.

"Camden Teller, you know, Banksy."

"What number is Banksy again?" Arthur asks. Memorizing the players on the team has become very important to him. We keep talking about all the games he will go to this fall, he wants to be prepared.

"Forty-six."

"Do you get to pick your numbers?" He grabs his spoon and rolls up his sleeves. He's about to go ham on some Cinnamon Toast Crunch.

"Sometimes," Barrett answers, taking the bowl of cereal from me. "Thanks, love."

Arthur and I rock-paper-scissored for dinner, and Arthur won. *Cereal it is.*

"Lonan Burke, number fourteen, he picked his number." He nods. I'd love to know what he's thinking about.

"Did you pick *your* number?"

Barrett shakes his head. "I had thirty-three in training camp, and I thought it was lucky, so I kept it."

"And it is lucky because now we have three people in our family. One, two, three." He points to each of us.

"That's right, we do. Maybe that's why it was lucky."

"Do you think they are going to miss you when you free-tirement?"

"When I *re*tire? Yeah, I think so. We will all miss playing together. Goodbyes can be hard." I rest my hand on his thigh under the table. Barrett told me he wished he could play his last season with Sully by his side, and I know the upcoming season will be an adjustment for him.

After dinner, we hang out by the beach to soak up some of the late summer sun.

I didn't want to get my blouse dirty, so before leaving the house, I grabbed the first crumpled up shirt I could find, trying to get down here before Arthur jumped in the lake. When I look down, I realize I'm wearing one of Barrett's. *I SHAVED MY BALLS FOR THIS?*

Classy, Bear. Real nice...

The man himself comes up behind me and wraps his arms around from behind, and I lean into him. "Pretty girl, pretty sunset."

"Hmm." I smile.

"So we're doing it tonight, right, Dad? You're gonna ask Mom—"

"Mini Bear!" I spin around in time to see Barrett's eyes turn to saucers, and he gives him a look. "Why don't we feed the ducks, buddy?"

"Sure! What are we going to give them?"

He's looking around him as if he's hoping a bag of oatmeal will appear out of thin air. "I dunno, whatever's on the ground. Rocks or something."

"You can't feed ducks rocks!"

I raise my eyebrows at Barrett. "You're seriously suggesting Little Mister World Wildlife Federation feed rocks to the local waterfowl?"

"If you're not going to ask her, then why did we buy the ring?! I want to show it to her!"

"Holy shit, bud! I'm changing your nickname from Mini Bear to Bean Spiller."

He got a ring? Oh my god, is that why he had me get my nails done. He told me it was because he wanted to *see those pretty nails wrapped around his cock.*

No! He can't do it now! He better not ask me to marry him while I'm wearing a shirt that says BALLS in bright red letters.

"Well, first can we—"

"Yup! Yup! Yup, we can do it now."

He laughs, and I fall in love all over again with the smile he's giving Arthur. I don't care about the shirt anymore. If he's about to ask, this is exactly how I want it to go down.

Barrett stops walking and spins in a circle, staring at the ground. "Um... Yeah..." He comes back to me and holds my hand. "Yeah. Okay."

"Let's hear it."

He drops down to one knee, and Arthur mimics his movements, imitating Barrett's form. Side by side, posed the same, they've never looked more like father and son. The same half smile on both their faces, showcasing the same dimple. They are so alike, and my heart somersaults. "Yay! We're doing the disposal!"

Barrett's shoulders shake, and he groans through laughter. "Proposal."

I nearly double over at the absurdity of it all, it reminds me of our first date. From the outside, it looks like a disaster, little blunders left and right, but it's fine because we're together— and that's all we need to be happy. It doesn't matter how many hiccups we run into, from where I stand, it's flawless. I'll trade a picture-perfect aesthetically pleasing proposal for my five-year-old informant and an oversized *BALLS* shirt-wearing "disposal" any day.

He pulls a ring box from his pocket and opens to reveal the most gorgeous pale-pink sapphire ring. *The man knows me.*

"I had this whole thing planned out, but I can't even remember it anymore, so I'm gonna wing it. Um... When I saw you in that Lakes box, it was a literal dream come true. And when I saw Arthur, I knew he was mine. Laying eyes on you both was like peeking into the future. That feeling has only happened one other time—the night we first met. We found each other again because fate knew we were always meant to be. I am sorry it took me so long. If I had known we were going to lose contact, I probably would have asked you to marry me on our first date, but instead I'm asking now. Raleigh, we lost so many years, I won't lose any more...So, will you marry me?"

The laughing tears are now happy tears. I drop to my knees and do my best to wrap my arms around them, my bears.

"Yes. Always, yes."

FIFTY-SIX
Barrett

I offer to do the bedtime routine so she can take a shower. Tonight we're celebrating our one-month engagement. As I close Arthur's bedroom door, I hear the water turn off. The sound of other people living here is less and less unusual every day. It's comforting. We're together under one roof, the way it's meant to be.

I love seeing her car next to mine in the garage. I love that both sides of the bed are messy in the morning. I even love all the random toys I trip over, though I suspect that will get old before long. It's all a reminder of how fucking lucky I am.

She steps out of the steamy bathroom wrapped in a towel, and I intercept her before she can put on anything else. Water droplets bead at the tips of her hair, and I run my fingers through the wet strands, admiring the goose bumps that spread across her shoulders. Her fingers toy with the waistband on my sweatpants to let me know what she needs. Below her ear, I suck the rosy shower-fresh skin. Her soft sigh spurs me to keep going. She'll be wearing her hair down all week after the mark I leave.

She grips my arms as I walk us closer to the bed. I've wanted to get inside her all night. Based on the way she's digging her fingers into my sides, the feeling is mutual. Nothing would make me happier than to help ease some of her tension she's been taking on the last couple weeks. I'll take care of her the way she needs.

Right before the back of her knees hit the mattress, she spins us around, backing me into the bed. I rip away the towel and chuck it in the corner of the room. I'll never tire of seeing her naked. She drops to her knees, and I melt. Her nails scrape my ass as she drags down my sweats.

Taking in the view of Raleigh, naked, wet, on her knees, and licking her lips... it's almost too much.

"Damn," I hiss.

I sit on the edge of the bed and take her hand, licking it palm to fingertip. She makes a fist and pushes the head of my cock into her closed palm, then follows with the other.

"Spread your thighs."

I've recently learned I enjoy getting a view of her pussy whenever she does this. She parts her knees, and I bite my lip. The only thing that pulls me away is seeing her full lips open and her tongue swirl around the crown before popping off and repeating the move twice more. I keep my gaze locked on her face, not wanting to miss the best part. I know my patience will be rewarded, but it doesn't make waiting any easier.

Her eyes meet mine. Here it comes...

Those cinnamon-colored eyes sparkle as she takes the rest of me between her lips.

"Fuuuuuck."

That look demolishes me. She enjoys transforming me into a puddle as much as I enjoy watching her work my cock.

Each suck, lick, and deep push conquers me and I forget about everything else around us. Nobody sucks me off like Raleigh. I love that she knows exactly how I like it.

Gripping one side of her wet hair around my palm, my fingertips sift through the loose strands on the other side. She shivers as the opposing sensations flood her senses. Her eyelids flutter, and it makes me grin. I use the hold on her hair to keep her head in place while I snap my hips, fucking her mouth. Slowing only to push myself deeper into her throat. I toss my head back and groan. She steadies herself against my thighs. Seeing her take me like this is such a turn-on. I forget to breathe when the tip of her nose kisses my pelvis and the tears spill over her pink cheeks.

"Mmhmm," I approve.

I pull out and she eagerly fights back, swirling the string of saliva around the tip.

"You have a sinful tongue, love." I shove her down on my cock, loving her sounds. "So fucking sinful."

It would be so easy to grip her head again and finish down her throat, but I can't. Nothing beats seeing my cum leak out of her pussy. Pushing it back inside and making her keep it. I growl, using every bit of self-control I have to pull her off me. Leaning down to kiss her, I taste myself on her tongue. She's so goddamn generous with her mouth.

"Done with me already?" She teases.

"Not even close." I pull her into my lap, sliding two fingers inside her drenched pussy. "This for me?"

"You know how wet I get."

"Yeah, I do. But I want to see it." I slide her off me and bend her over the bed. "You know what I need. Show me your sweet cunt, Raleigh." She goes up on her toes, and I spread her cheeks. Her glistening bare pussy gets me harder than when her lips were around me. *Fuck.*

She trembles at my touch.

"That's it." My fingers glide through her folds; she's drenched. "Ask me nicely."

"Please, Bear."

"Please what?"

She groans in response.

"Please, *what*?"

"Please come inside me. I want you to fill me up. I need it."

Fisting my cock, I massage it over her clit, making her sob and clench her legs together. My hand travels up her smooth tanned back until I reach her neck, I wrap my fingers around as I slap the crown where she's most sensitive. The sharp sting causes her to fall forward, planting her cheek into the mattress, but she stays on her tiptoes, wanting relief above all else. I chuckle at her desperation, as she holds perfectly still while waiting.

Like an asshole, I take my time sweeping a hand over her back, thighs, and ass. After letting the anticipation build, I thrust inside. Tight, warm, and *so wet*. Her immediate gulp of air makes my balls seize.

"Oh, god," she mumbles.

I hold her firm while striking her ass and sliding myself in and out of the sensual death-grip she has on my cock. She grasps the sheets in front of her, not far from her climax. I can feel it. Her head is turned to the side, and with each push, her eyes seem to roll back.

"Who owns your pussy, Raleigh?"

"You."

"That's right, love."

My free hand works over her hips and ass. I can't get enough. She's on the edge of exploding. She's so pretty like this. I let go to hook my arms under her thighs and lift her up, driving hard. Her erotic moans fill the space while I ravage her pussy. Thank God for soundproof walls. She says something about how good it feels, but I don't make out all the garbled sentences. It's such an ego stroke to scramble her thoughts like that.

"Are you going to come for me already?"

I hammer harder until her whimpers turn to wails. The

way her arms stretch in front of her and that back arches . . . *goddamn.* It makes me feral. I knead each of her ass cheeks before slapping one of them and making her cry out.

"Bear!"

"That's better."

I flip her on her back and scoot her farther back on the mattress so I can climb over her. With a hand braced on each of her knees, I spread her open to watch the pulsations of her recent orgasm. My thumb brushes overtop, and her overstimulated clit jerks at the touch. My lips cover her peaked nipples, and she arches into my mouth.

When I plunge inside again, she constricts around me.

"God, I wish you weren't on birth control."

"You want more babies, Conway?"

My eyes snap to hers. When she talks like that, it turns me into an animal. I grumble at her teasing. She knows I want more kids.

"You're going to be so full of my cum when I'm done with you."

"Then I should probably tell you I had my IUD removed on Tuesday."

Narrowing my eyes, I tilt my head away, waiting for her to say she's kidding. But we stare at each other in silence. A soft smile forms on her face.

I roll us so she's on top.

"Are you being serious? Don't fuck with me, Raleigh."

She nods. "I love you so much, Bear. I want to get married and have children and spend the rest of our days living happily ever after." Her hips roll and she does that thing I like, grinding against me in figure eights.

"Swear to God, woman. If you make me cry, I'm gonna lose this hard-on." Actually, the thought of her round belly filled with our baby makes me harder than ever.

Ral's eyes swell, and I see how truly happy she is. *This is our normal.*

Even with tears she's the most gorgeous thing I've ever seen. "Are you gonna ride my cock with those tears running down your cheeks?"

"Yeah, I am." She smiles through the sniveling.

"Mmm, I love that." Reaching up, my thumb brushes under her eye and clears one side away. She's the most beautiful woman I've ever seen, and that she's up for adding to our family makes her even sexier. I want her pregnant yesterday.

She's so snug, but vaults up and down my cock, gripping and leaking more with each pass. Her lips curve into a smile against mine and it's like she can read my mind. "You're going to put so many babies in me." I groan. *Glad we're on the same page.*

"I'm ready to get started when you are."

She shakes her head and giggles. "Wait!"

I roll my eyes. "What now?"

"We can't have another kid before we get married!"

I grip her round ass and dig my fingers in until she squeals. "Come on, love. That's not our style. You know that." She slaps my chest, and I pull her down on my cock hard enough to get one of those cute gasps out of her. Her eyes are filled with love and adoration.

Our journey has been rocky. It's not the one I would have chosen for us—I hate that we lost years together—but I'd do it three times over if I had to. We found our way back to each other and made this messy life ours. *This is our normal.*

EPILOGUE
Barrett

"We can see the head, you're almost there!" Heather says, smiling at Raleigh. She's been talking about having Heather at her labor for the last three months, her shift already ended, but she's stayed on for Raleigh. It's a testament to how loved she is by everyone she meets.

She grits her teeth and squeezes my hand harder, her whole body shaking. Holy fuck, she's got some serious strength in that grip. I don't say a word, she can scream and curse and crush the living fuck out of my hand as much as she needs.

"You're doing so good, baby!"

"I'm so tired!" she sobs.

"I know, you've been giving it your all. I'm so proud of you."

I want to watch, but she's insisted I stay by her side. The doctor maneuvers his hands in a different way.

"The head is out Raleigh, one more big push! Last one!"

She bears down and digs deep. I've played numerous rounds of overtime before, testing my stamina like nothing I thought possible, but I swear to God, there's not one player out there who could endure what Raleigh has tonight.

Her last groan is more like a war cry as she crouches forward, pushing against the stirrups and then she falls back and gasps as the doctor cheers. "It's a girl!"

She bursts into tears along with me, and I pull her into my arms to kiss her face. They put the baby on her chest, and we lie in awe of our new daughter.

"She's so beautiful," Raleigh whispers, and she's absolutely right. She's the most beautiful baby girl I've ever seen, I can't believe we made her. I've felt her kick for almost five months now, and that couldn't have prepared me for hearing her first cry or cupping her tiny head in my hand. As soon as the warm blanket covers her back, she begins to settle, and within five minutes, she's peacefully resting.

I push the damp strands sticking to Raleigh's face aside and tuck them up into the messy bun on top of her head. The view of my two girls together makes me suck in a breath.

Fuck, how did I get so lucky?

"I love you so much, Raleigh. You did so well, I'm so proud of you."

She gives me a soft smile and leans her head into mine. "I love you too."

I keep my arm protectively wrapped over them as we snuggle the newest member of our family.

"Do you want to name her?"

Raleigh said she wanted to wait until we saw the baby to decide. "You want me to choose her name?"

"I chose Arthur's, I think you should choose hers." *I know exactly what I want to name her.*

"Darby."

"Darby?"

"You named Arthur because it meant Bear. Darby means deer park, pretty close to deer meadow. I want her named after you."

394

She raises her eyebrows and pouts out her lip with a smile. "Darby...I like it. How about Darby Sue? After your mom."

I smile. Raleigh and my mother have a special relationship. She's always wanted that maternal connection she never had. My mom has loved Raleigh since the day she met her and adores filling that void for her. I'm thankful my mom's over-the-top affection has never scared her away, and if anything, I think it brought them closer together.

Raleigh's mother will not be bothering us anytime soon after she was found to have stolen twenty-two other identities over the years. She used them to do everything from stealing social security checks to blackmail—similar to the way she came after Raleigh and me. She's currently being held at a facility in Indiana. Raleigh has chosen to end all contact, and I support her decision wholeheartedly.

"Oh God, she's gonna flip."

Darby wraps her tiny fist around my finger, and I run my thumb over the soft dimpled knuckles on her tiny pudgy hand.

"It's perfect," Raleigh says. "Darby Sue Conway."

Introducing Arthur to Darby was... *interesting*.

"Can she do any tricks?"

I laugh. "Do you count sleeping, crying, and pooping as tricks?"

Arthur follows me into the nursery while we wait for Raleigh to prepare a bottle. A small lamp illuminates the cream walls in a warm light, and Darby pecks at my shoulder as I bounce her in my arms.

"No. I can do all those things already." He rolls his eyes. Six-year-olds have attitudes.

The recliner is my new favorite seat in the house. It sits under framed, matted illustrations of baby bears that Raleigh created. Now that she's moved out of her admin role and is one of the creative leads at Method Marketing, she's recently discovered her new talent for drawing and sketching. Next to her artwork is Arthur's. His space penises have improved dramatically, thanks to her.

"Can you do them at the same time like she does?"

"I hope not!" Raleigh hollers from the other room.

I chuckle. I swear motherhood has made her hearing superhuman. "She might not be able to do much now, but that's why your job as a big brother is so important. You're going to have to help teach her all the cool things you know how to do."

"Like blowing bubbles with my butt in the bathtub?" he whispers.

I snort. "No, she's already got that one covered. Like crawling and walking and talking. Then later you can teach her more fun things like how to catch a ball, or ride on a scooter, or play hide and seek—playing hockey!"

He smiles at that. Last winter, I shoveled off a portion of the lake and flooded a small section for him to get some practice to see how he liked it. When I saw his face light up with excitement, I knew he had the same hockey bug I had when I was younger. My chest thumps thinking of all the playing we'll do as he grows. Maybe Darby will be the same.

"We can all teach her hockey!" he exclaims.

I love that we can play hockey as a family. Ral's still got it. I'm starting to think there's nothing she can't do. "Darby'll be a duster for a few more years before she can get in the game, but we'll get her off the bench and in skates before you know it."

Raleigh returns with a bottle and hands it to me.

Her phone dings, and she pulls it out of her pocket.

"Better not be Rob." Now that she's managing her own team of creatives, Method is more desperate than ever to get her back. This time she's taking her full sixteen weeks.

She shakes her head and gives a light smack to my arm. "The girls want to get together for drinks on Wednesday." *That reminds me, I need to text Sully.*

> You hear about Banksy?

"WAG Wednesdays?"

"Yeah, Birdie and I are always the slackers, life is so busy with Arthur in school and activities, work, and Darby. Thank god I have this hot trophy husband..." she mutters. *She's more than earned me.*

SULLY

> Yeah. Fucking wild.

I chuckle as I tuck my phone back in my pocket and hold out the bottle to Arthur. "Do you want to feed her?"

He cocks his head to the side, unsure, but eventually nods. It doesn't take long to situate him on the chair. I tuck a pillow under his arm while Ral shows him how to hold the bottle. As soon as she starts to suck, his eyes light up. "She's doing it! You're doing it, Darby! Good job!"

Pretty sure we both melted into a pool of joy as he cheered her on during the feeding. They stared at each other the whole time. We stood in awe, watching them observe one another. I wrap my arms around Raleigh from behind and press a kiss to her head, she strokes my arm while we look on.

This is the happily ever after we've created. The four of us. *Together.*

THE END

.

OTHER BOOKS BY SLOANE ST. JAMES

ACKNOWLEDGMENTS

Where do I begin? This book was a journey and a half. I want to start by thanking my readers—I love you all. You have impacted my life in the very best way and I'm forever grateful for your kind messages and recommending my books to your friends.

Next, my husband. The sacrifices you make to help me chase this dream does not go unnoticed. Thank you so much for the long hours you put in with the kids when I'm holed up in the bedroom writing and editing all day. You believe in me even when I don't. I love you and our kids so much.

The true heroes of this story are my alpha*/beta readers: Catie, Emma*, Jenna*, Jess, Kailey, Leia, Lorelei, Megan, Nicole, Rachel, Sarah, Shannon*, and Tricia. Yes, it's a lot of readers. Yes, I need all of them. Thank you so much for your time, dedication, criticisms, and support. If it weren't for your input, In The Game would not be what it is today—*not by a long shot.* I put you all through hell with this book but I've witnessed the most beautiful friendship come from this experience. Was it a trauma bond? Possibly. More details about that at the end.

Shannon, my PA, I love you. You are just as chaotic as me, but somehow you know how to keep my shit in line and are always two steps ahead of me. I'd be lost without you. You've been with me from the get-go and I appreciate all you do. Thank you for setting me straight when I get too deep into my thoughts.

My incredible ARC readers—I'm so grateful for the time

and energy you put into writing reviews for Barrett and Raleigh. Your words are so valuable to me and vital to my success as a writer. After months of hard work, lost sleep, and numerous mental breakdowns, release day is the absolute best part—and I love sharing it with you! When this book goes live, it's the ARC readers who bring the fucking party. Thank you for being my launch team!

My line editor, Dee Houpt (Dee's Notes), you've been with me on this journey three times now and I gave you a doozy with this one, but as usual, you made it shine. I appreciate your dedication to your craft as well as your friendship. Can't wait to give you the next one in the series!

My developmental editor, Victoria Ellis (Cruel Ink)— thank you so much for all of your detailed notes and helping me make Barrett even better!

My formatter, CC, for making my book more realistic with text messages and emojis. You are such an artist!

My hype squad. Damn. You all show up and show out every day and I'll never find the words to express how much your support means to me. I'm sure I'm missing some people, but thank you for consistently sharing my books and interacting with my posts! Amy, Tahnika, Leia, Christina, Sarina, Katrina, Kenadhe, Leesha, Katie, Julie, J.R., Nadia, Dani, Kristen, along with all of my alpha and beta readers.

To my friends Megan, Katie, Katie, Jenn, and all of my loves in Ohana—Mandi, Matt, Casey, Maddie, Tristan, Erik, Kelly, and Nicole. Thank you for filling my cup and always being supportive. I love you all dearly.

The Wet Spot Pod (@thewetspotpod). Please, for the love of god, if you enjoy reading smut, you must check out this podcast. These women are wildly funny and inappropriate, you'll laugh your ass off and get tons of awesome book recs while you're at it.

The original story for this book was nothing like the end result and my beta readers can attest to that. There will be a special episode on The Wet Spot Pod that details the making of this book and the cruel social experiment that the beta readers unknowingly participated in, mostly for my own twisted enjoyment.

Just for fun, I'd like to share some of my favorite quotes from the beta group chat after they finished reading the *original* version of this book:

- *"NO."*
- *"I hate you"*
- *"FUCK YOUR FEELINGS FOR REAL 😂"*
- *"I'm not saying people would come for you... I'm just saying Michigan isn't that far away... I've driven to Minnesota before."*
- *"I AM PISSED WITH A CAPITAL FUCK YOU ALSO"*
- *"I need my anxiety medication."*
- *"GIVE ME THE DAD RIGHT NOW, respectfully."*
- *"MY TITS ARE SWEATING IM SO MAD"*

I couldn't say thank you without mentioning these awesome content creators! Thank you so much for sharing my work with your followers, I have found so many amazing readers through you. Readers, grab your phone and follow each of these Booktokers and Bookstagrammers to find your next great read!

TikTok:
Mackenzie @readingwithkenzz
Ashley @ashleybooksandbarbells
Jamie @nerdthatreads
Chanelle @chanellehelle

Haily @hailyreads
Ashley @ashleyanreads
Nina @author.nina.wolf.reads
Chelsey @chelseyjeannee
Jenna @confessionsofasmutslut
Kassi @kassinicole.reads
Truly.the.Antihero @truly.the.antihero
Instagram:
Christina @christinareadsbooks
Sarina @booktrovert_rina
Jamie @reading.with.jamie
Ashley @ashleyanreads
Catie @catiesshelfofsmut
Ash & Jess @bestiebookshelf_
Nicole @nicoleleannemreads
Sarah @what_sarahs_read

If you enjoyed reading this book, please help spread the word
by leaving a review on Amazon, Goodreads, Bookbub,
Facebook Reader Groups, Booktok, Bookstagram, or
wherever you talk smut.

And now I'm going to shamelessly beg:
Please, tell your friends and followers. Recommend this book
and share the hell out of it.
If you already have, you have my endless gratitude. I hope you
sleep well knowing that you are making some woman's mid-
life crisis dreams come true!

I love to connect with my readers!
SloaneStJamesWrites@gmail.com

Want to join my ARC team?
SloaneStJames.com

Facebook Reader Group:
Sloane's Good Girl Book Club

Made in the USA
Coppell, TX
11 September 2024

37053877R00246